A GUIDE
TO CRAFT
BREWING

A GUIDE TO CRAFT BREWING

John Alexander

THE CROWOOD PRESS

First published in 2006 by
The Crowood Press Ltd
Ramsbury, Marlborough
Wiltshire SN8 2HR

www.crowood.com

© John Alexander 2006

British Library Cataloguing-in-Publication Data
A catalogue record for this book is available from the British
Library.

ISBN 1 86126 899 8
EAN 978 1 86126 899 0

DEDICATION

To Kelly

ACKNOWLEDGEMENTS

I am indebted to the following, who have made a contribution to the
success of this book: Gilbert Dallas, MBE BSc; John Peacock and
Andy Janes of Muntons; Simpson's Malt; Bairds Malt; Brulab Ltd,
County Durham; Charles McMaster, MA, Scottish brewing historian;
Dr Stuart Rivers; George Howell, Head Brewer, Belhaven Brewery,
Dunbar; Cooper, Dave Thorton; Dr Iain Bruinvis, Amsterdam; Colin
Johnson, BAcc CA; James Mackrill, Botanix (formally English Hops)
Paddock Wood, Kent; National Hop Association of England;
Dr Rosemary Douglass, San Francisco; Dr Keith Alexander, Oregon,
USA; Keith Robson, BA; Neil Kerr, Frank Wallace; Dave Martin of
Edina Home Brew, Edinburgh; Forfar Home Brew; Robert Burton,
BSc PhD MBA, Production Director; Caledonian Brewery,
Edinburgh; Dr Les. Howarth; Bill Cooper; Ian McInally; Derek
Blackie; Stevenson & Reeves (Hydrometers) Edinburgh; Harris
Filters; Ritchie Products Ltd; Young's Home Brew; Clive Donald of
Brupaks; Kelly Filmer BSc MRSC and David Johnstone BSc. F. I.
Brew, for kindly reading my first draft and his help and suggestions.
However, despite such input from such a notable forum, any *faux
pas* herein are my responsibility.

Typeset by S R Nova Pvt Ltd, Bangalore, India

Printed and bound in Spain by GraphyCems

CONTENTS

INTRODUCTION

Home brewing is as old as man himself. It is thought to have originated in Mesopotamia, 'the land between the rivers', the Tigris and Euphrates, at least 7,000 years ago. In the first great civilization, Sumeria, maltsters and brewers were held in high esteem. Their beer was made from mashed bread that was strained and left to ferment by the inoculation of wild yeast. The resultant brew was flavoured with spices and dates, and sweetened with wild honey; it was considered to have had medicinal properties. The brewers had their own guild, and had certain obligations to the temples and the Gods.

With each subsequent civilization, the craft of brewing eventually spread throughout the Middle East and Europe. The British, too, have always been home brewers, and were fermenting beverages from barley in the first century AD. The monasteries were largely responsible for the continuation of brewing in Britain, and strangers were welcomed in for the night with ale and bread, the staple diet of the day. It is recorded that the monks of St Paul's Cathedral brewed 60,000 gallons (272,000ltr) per year (that's 480,000 pints!), and that the Canons had a weekly allowance of 34 pints per day!

Many noted brewing centres today owe their origins to the early monastic establishments, and many breweries still draw their liquor from wells sunk by monks centuries ago. Eventually we brewed in the home, on the farm, in alehouses, taverns, inns and colleges, and by the nineteenth century on a gigantic commercial scale. Queen Victoria summed it all up thus: 'Give my people plenty of beer, good beer, cheap beer, and you will have no revolution amongst them!'

As the brewing industry grew, many styles of beer evolved and Scotch ales, Burton ales, bitters, India pale ales, pale ales, porters, stouts, light ales, amber ales, brown ales, mild ales and, eventually, Pilsner-style lagers satisfied the thirst of every social class. Although the craft of home brewing waxed and waned over the years, it never died out in Britain. Until 1963, home brewers were obliged to pay tax on their brews, but how successful the Inland Revenue was in collecting it, one can only guess.

Today, the craft of home brewing is ever gaining in popularity, with a professional back-up that underpins the aspirations of the budding artisan brewer. The home brew industry has spared no effort in its desire to ensure that high quality ingredients and equipment are obtainable. The local home brew shop, too, is the bedrock of the craft, and what they don't stock, they will get for you.

There is also great interest in researching and brewing the beers of the nineteenth and early twentieth centuries. Today, craft brewers can produce any style of beer with fairly modest equipment, and yet turn out a product with the highest degree of excellence!

CHAPTER 1

BRITISH BEER STYLES

Traditional beer styles vary throughout the country with local and regional variations, and it is this great diversity that makes British beers so appealing.

TRADITIONAL BRITISH BEER STYLES

Burton Ale

This ale is the English equivalent of Scotch ale, and in nineteenth-century London it was offered as an alternative to Scotch ale, although many pubs sold both beers. The characteristics of Burton ale are its high gravity, OG 1070–1110, a very red colour, full dry-hopped flavour and an enticing aroma. Old Burton (barley wine) was a much stronger brew, with an OG of up to 1145!

Bitter

The term historically evolved as a colloquialism in order to distinguish between highly hopped mature 'bitter' beers and the 'mildness' of less hopped beer. The quality of palate in today's bitters is more associated with hop character and aroma than actual bitterness, and such spicy floral fruitiness gives them their pleasing charm. Their typical profile is a straw to amber colour of 15–25 EBC°; an ABV of 3.5–4.4 per cent; and bitterness, 20–35 IBUs.

Best Bitters

When brewed to full gravity, this is one of England's finest beers. The colour may be straw to amber, the palate malty, well balanced with hop bitterness and, perhaps, a touch fruity, with a slight bitter edge. ABV 4.5–5.5 per cent; IBUs 28–55; EBC° 15–30.

Light Ales

These ales are refreshing, low gravity, bottled bitter beers. They were sometimes sold as 'family' or 'dinner' ales, are usually pale amber in colour, with a dry hoppy finish, lively condition and good head retention. Sadly, 'light' is rarely brewed today. Colour is 8–20 EBC°, ABV 2.9–3.4, IBUs 10–15.

Pale Ales

Traditionally in England, pale ales were the bottled equivalent of draught bitter. The character varies on locality due to the water, brewing tradition and local taste. The colour may be straw to rich amber, and the flavour medium malt with good hop character and aroma. Top fermenting practices might influence some estery notes in the finish. The condition should be lively with a fast-rising bead, producing good head formation and retention. Colour is 10–30 EBC°, ABV 4.5–5.5 per cent; bitterness 20–40 IBUs.

India Pale Ale (IPA)

This is the illustrious colonial beer of the nineteenth century. Due to the Trent

Navigation Act, Burton brewers successfully exported porter and ales to Russia and the Baltic. The strength of such beers, plus the cold northern sea routes, meant that they arrived in sound condition. After Napoleon's Berlin Degree in 1806 designed to disrupt British commerce, the German and Baltic ports were no longer an option and British brewers were forced to look elsewhere.

The answer came from an unlikely source: India. To produce ale that would survive the long, hot, tortuous sea journey – half way round the world, crossing the equator twice – and arrive in good condition was no mean task. But as luck would have it, George Hodgson's stock pale ale was ideal: it was brewed high in alcohol and was very highly hopped, providing plenty of antiseptics. Crates of bottles and casks were stored well below the waterline, acting as ballast; this also kept the beer cool and sound as it matured during the voyage.

Here is a description of this ale, entitled 'That Tender Froth', from the *Cornhill Magazine,* March 1891:

> The drinking of a glass of Bass's pale ale, iced in India, in the hot weather; how it diffuses itself through you! It would produce a soul under the ribs of death. The clean, hoppy perfume. What bouquet of wine ever equalled it? And as you hold the glass lovingly up before you, what ruby or purple of what wine ever equalled that amber tint? The beaded bubbles winking at the brim of a glass of champagne, what are they compared to that tender froth?

IPA may be straw to vivid amber in colour with good malt flavour, balanced by a clean hop bitterness and a seductive floral bouquet. Modern strengths vary from 4.5 to 5.5 per cent ABV, with hopping rates of 40–60 IBUs; colour typically 8–15 EBC°.

Mild Ale

Mild ale is the only English beer with an unbroken antiquity stretching back to the Middle Ages. By the eighteenth century it developed into a strong, immature, lightly hopped beer, often brewed at quick notice during the summer months as a stopgap brew to augment diminishing stocks of October beers. It was often blended to freshen up the remaining stocks of ailing winter brews. By the middle of the twentieth century, the gravity and price had fallen, largely making mild a working class beverage, rejuvenating the thirst and energy of low paid, manual workers. Mild ale today is usually dark, sometimes deep amber, and rarely pale; it is low in alcohol, mildly hopped and sweet, particularly from caramel priming sugars. ABV 2.8–3.5 per cent; IBUs 10–25; EBC° 20–55. **Strong mild**: OG 1055; IBUs 20–35; EBC° 30–55.

Brown Ale

This ale is the bottled equivalent of mild, but it is usually fuller bodied and stronger. It, too, varies according to locality and was sometimes referred to as 'home brewed'. London browns are sweet and malty, low in hops and with a deep brown garnet colour; traditionally they were referred to as ale, sometimes mild or simply beer. 3–3.5 per cent ABV, 15–20 IBUs. The northern example, such as Newcastle brown ale, first brewed in 1927, is less sweet, amber in colour, and with a bitter character. ABV 4–4.4 per cent, IBUs 15–25; London EBC° 30–40; Northern EBC° 20–25.

Old Ales

The appellation 'old ales' refers to strong, dark beers that are well matured; they are sometimes called Burton. The original gravity might be as high as 1065, producing about 6 per cent ABV. IBUs 25–30.

Barley Wines

Barley wines are extra strong ales with original gravities of 1075–1100, producing some 7–9 per cent ABV. The colour may be rich amber to tawny, the palate rounded but vinous, the aroma rich and fruity. Due to the high alcoholic content, head retention is usually light and short-lived. Hopping varies, but should be about 40–60 IBUs. EBC° 28–45.

Porter

Porter is the weaker progenitor of stout that evolved in London during the reign of King George I. It was an immediate success, and the great London brewers all made their fortunes due to its popularity. Many attempts have been made to identify the source of the name 'porter', the most accepted version being that it was popular with working-class Londoners, many of whom were porters.

Alternatively, the name might actually derive from the strong wine known as 'port': we know that porter was acidified during storage by Brettanomyces and other microflora, and acquired a piquant flavour. Alfred Barnard, the Victorian brewery historian, referred to porter as being vinous, and various writers have claimed that high gravity stouts acquired a port-like quality with age. In 1820, Accum referred to porter brewed with pale malts as 'Old Hock', and visitors to Britain sampling porter initially thought it was wine; so perhaps this vinous, port-like drink acquired the colloquialism 'porter'. The colour of porter may be deep garnet to black, hopping at 20–40 IBUs; ABV 4–6 per cent; EBC° 40–60.

Stout

Stout was originally called 'stout-porter', due to its greater strength and robust character. The colour is liquorice, with a creamy oatmeal head, strength about 4–6 per cent ABV, and a woody, or iron-like palate. IBUs 30–60; EBC° 80–90.

Scotch Ales

These ales are robust beers with OGs of 1070–1130, and they were brewed to several gravities numbered from 1 to 6. The mashing heats were high, typically at 70°C, influencing high permanent gravities, about one third of the OG, producing an ABV of some 6–12 per cent. The hopping rates were only sufficient to check the residual sweetness, creating a full, malty, rich palate. Fermentation temperatures were low, usually 10–15°C, keeping esters and diacetyl low. Brews with the suffix 'L' were destined for the London market and might be less strong, but more highly hopped for the English palate.

Scottish pale malt at this time was kilned to a higher degree than English pale malt at 7–9 EBC°, and due to the huge amounts used, the colour of the brew would be quite dark. This is born out in *The Younger Centuries* by David Keir, where there is a reference to Oxford boat crews being allowed beer during training. The brew was Younger's Scotch ale, and it is described as nut-brown ale. Today the colour of Scottish beers ranges from mellow gold through rich amber to dark brown.

Historically they were classified by what became known as the 'shilling terminology' (shillings =/-). The shilling terminology related to the invoice price per barrel, the real price being determined by taking into account duty and the discounts offered by the brewers. The discounts could be substantial, and some publicans might negotiate a discount of 50 per cent per barrel! Hence the invoice price was only an indication of the type of beer. Consequently, publicans were very secretive about what they paid for their beer in order to steal a march on their competitors.

In the late nineteenth century, mild ales retailed at 40/-, 42/-, 60/- and 70/- strong mild, and pale ales from 48/-, 56/- and 80/-, all of which referred to the price per barrel (36 gallons). Beer delivered in a hogshead (54 gallons) was usually for bottling by the publican and underwent a change in designation; thus 42/- mild retailed as 3 Guinea ale, 56/- ale became 4 Guinea ale, 60/- mild became 90/- ale, 70/- strong mild became 5 Guinea ale, and 80/- pale ale became 120/- ale. Strong ales also sold as 10, 12 and 15 Guinea ales.

Over time, the terms became meaningless, although they remained in force as a trade means of identifying a type of beer. Due to economic circumstances after 1945, the beer market underwent rationalization, and with less beer being produced, the terminology gave way to 'light', 'heavy' and 'export', although the shillings' rating was resurrected with the 'real ale' crusade in the 1970s. Today, all the descriptions are used indiscriminately and do not always reflect the strength or character of the traditional beer styles.

60/- Ale

This ale is a light beer of OG 1033-35, ABV 3–3.5 per cent. The colour may be mellow gold to dark amber in colour at 25–40 EBC°. It has a light, malty, sometimes estery palate balanced by low hop bitterness, about 10–20 IBUs, and a light malt aroma. It is rarely brewed these days.

70/- Ale

70/- ale now retails as 'heavy', but might also be described as 'light' in some localities. The OG is about 1035–40, ABV 3.5–3.8 per cent. The colour might be pale, amber or dark brown at 25–75 EBC°. Medium maltiness, balanced with a light hop character

with 15–20 IBUs. A good session beer; however, production is in decline.

Export, or 80/- Ale

Export retails as 80/- Ale, but might also be referred to as 'heavy'; it is the most popular style with a full, malty palate, tempered with a degree of soft bitterness at 15–25 IBUs. The colour varies from pale to amber to antique copper at 25–75 EBC°. The OG 1040–55, with ABV 3.8–5.4.

MIXTURES OF BEER

Beer mixing used to be a very common practice, as the drinker could liven up a flat pint with sparkling bottled ale. Also, mixing two types of beer produced another quality, and the sweetness, or bitterness, could be altered to taste. Here are some old favourites:

Across the Taps Equal amounts of best bitter and ordinary bitter.

Black and Tan A half pint of draught bitter, or pale ale, perked up with a bottle of sweet or dry stout.

Black Velvet A bottle of sweet, or dry, stout topped up with an equal amount of cider, or champagne.

Port and Guinness A pint of Guinness and a tot of port added.

Dublin Depth Charge A pint of Guinness and a measure of rum.

Boilermaker (Brown and Mild) Half a pint of mild ale, livened up with a half-pint bottle of brown ale.

B & B Equal amounts of bitter and Burton.

Half and a Half Half a pint of mild and bitter.

Half and a Half In eighteenth-century London, a half of ale and porter.

Half and a Half In Scotland, a nip of whisky and a half pint of beer as a chaser.

Happy Day Half a pint of bitter, or pale ale, plus a bottle of barley wine.

Light and Bitter (Light Split) Half a pint of bitter and a small bottle of light ale.

Horse's Neck A pint of beer, plus a nip of whisky.

Light and Mild Half a pint of mild, perked up with a bottle of pale ale.

Mild and Bitter (M & B) Equal amounts of mild and bitter.

Mother-in-Law (Old and Bitter) Half a pint of old ale (or Burton) and bitter.

Stout and Bitter (Also **Mother-in-Law**) Use equal quantities of each.

A Granny (Old and Mild) Half a pint of old ale and half a pint of mild.

Stout and Mild Half a pint of mild and a bottle of sweet stout.

Dog's Nose A pint of beer and measure of gin.

Lager and Lime A pint of lager and a dash of lime juice cordial.

Lager and Blackcurrant A pint of lager and a dash of blackcurrant cordial.

Tops Almost a full pint with a dash of lemonade.

Shandy Equal measures of beer and lemonade.

Shandy Gaff Half a pint of mild and a small bottle of ginger ale.

Scotch Shandy Gaff Half a pint of Scotch ale and a small bottle of ginger beer, plus a nip of whisky or brandy.

Dragon's Blood A bottle of barley wine and a tot of rum.

Moscow Mule A pint of lager plus a large measure of Vodka added.

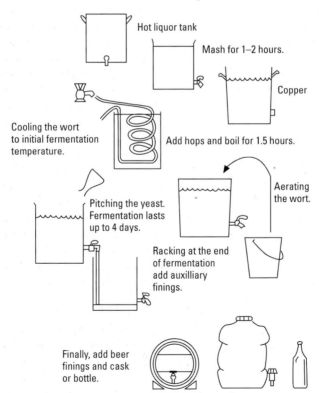

Hot liquor tank

Mash for 1–2 hours.

Copper

Cooling the wort to initial fermentation temperature.

Add hops and boil for 1.5 hours.

Aerating the wort.

Pitching the yeast. Fermentation lasts up to 4 days.

Racking at the end of fermentation add auxilliary finings.

Finally, add beer finings and cask or bottle.

The craft-brewing process. Commercial practices are closely followed.

CHAPTER 2

BUILDING A BREWERY

Over many years, the home brew industry has progressively raised the standard of brewing equipment and ingredients to meet the exacting standards of craft brewers. Many brewers, however, prefer the enjoyment of making their own plant, and that is all part of the fun of the hobby. Such enthusiasm has led to a range of interesting inventions over the years, and many of these have been adopted by the industry. The following list is not meant to be exhaustive, or a retailer's catalogue, but it lays out the general scheme of things. A trip to your local retailer and a little imagination should do the rest!

BREWING EQUIPMENT

Hot Liquor Tank (HLT)

Ideally we require a vessel that will hold the total mashing and sparging volume: a catering boiler is excellent. Remove the original tap and replace it with a 22mm right-angled tank connector, pointing upwards. Reduce to 15mm, and attach to this a length of clear, heat-resistant plastic hose, or glass tube, to act as a sight glass. Graduate the boiler in gallons or ltr.

My own set-up uses a 15mm tank connector as a single drain outlet from the bottom of the HLT connected to a 'T', which is also connected to two straight washing-machine 'on/off' taps. Plastic domestic water hose connects the HLT to the sparger and spray attachment. The tap on the HLT controls the flow to the sparger. The sparger requires at least 200mm head pressure to produce a good jet reaction. Both the HLT and hose should be insulated. You can also utilize a strong plastic bucket fitted with a heating element as an HLT.

Mash Tuns

The Bruheat/Electrim bins have been around now for about 30 years, and so they are clearly popular and efficient vessels. They are dual purpose, and also act as coppers. To mash successfully, a mash screen or strainer is necessary, which sits just above the tap. The mashing volume should be calculated after the mash screen is just covered with liquor. Both vessels are fitted with a sensitive *simmerstat*, which helps control the mashing temperature and can simmer, or boil, the wort.

Brupaks produce a 29ltr enamelled steel mash tun/boiler with an 1,800-watt element, plus a mash screen and tap. Combined mash tun/boilers are fine, but they cannot be used for both purposes at the same time! Therefore when sparging, the wort has to be collected in a separate vessel and then transferred to the boiler, or a separate mash tun is necessary, the latter being preferable. Also, when mashing with such vessels, the large volume above the mash continually draws heat away from the goods, which makes heat control difficult; the answer is to insulate the void with a plug of polystyrene.

Many retailers also sell insulated picnic coolers that have been converted to mash tuns. They are fitted with a straining device and a tap and, depending on the volume of grist you intend to mash, might hold 7–10kg of grain. Plug the void as before.

My present mashing system consists of an old catering boiler that has been adapted. It is fitted with an Electrim Bin simmerstat for temperature control, and two 15mm tank connectors are plumbed to right-angled washing-machine taps. The higher outlet acts as a hydrostatic head, and this ensures that the goods always float just above the mash screen. The lower tap is used occasionally to balance the flow, or drain the tun.

A catering boiler can also be adapted so that the mash heat is thermostatically controlled by a water jacket.

Mash Screens

These are designed to strain out the wort from the goods after mashing. A mash screen may be made from expanded aluminium/stainless steel supplied by the

Brupaks mash tun.

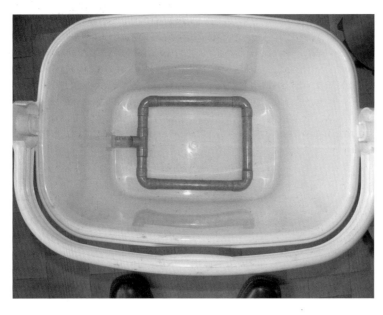

A bird's eye view of copper straining pipes inside a picnic cooler.

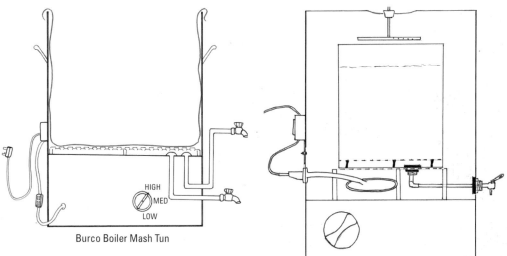

Burco Boiler Mash Tun

The Burco mash tun.

The Aqua mash tun.

Expanded Metal Company, Hartlepool. The Type ES3100 has an open area of 21 per cent, making it admirably suited for the mash tun. Where this is not available, the next best size is Type ES3500 with 50 per cent open area, and this should be clamped in half register to provide a tight strainer.

The screen is secured on three legs just above the draw-off pipe/tap. Expanded metal can also be used as a hop back in the copper. In this case the percentage opening should be 50 per cent, to allow the strong ebullition currents of the boiling wort to flow free, otherwise it will flip it over.

Another idea is to use 22mm copper pipe shaped to the circumference of the boiler and secured to the tap outlet by a bend and T-shaped couplings. To strain the wort, the pipes are partially cut through with a hacksaw, about 4–5mm apart. The easiest way to do this is to lay the pipe between two pieces of wood, just thick enough to come up half way, then gently saw down to the wood.

Grain bags are also excellent, and they do not interfere with extract recovery. If you employ a mash tun/boiler, then the mash can be lifted and transferred into a suitable bucket with its base riddled with holes for sparging. Heat loss, however, is inevitable.

My 'mash mixer' consists of a food mixer head secured in a short length of 8mm copper pipe. The other end was heated and an old twist drill jammed inside; when cooled, it is secured in a vice-like grip. If used manually, the mixer is very efficient. I also attach it to a cordless drill with variable speed, which makes short work of any doughed starch! As the speed can be controlled and the head of the mixer kept below the surface of the goods, the minimum of heat loss and oxygenation occurs.

Phil's Rotating Sparging Arms
These are available through your local home brew shop, and are discussed in the chapter on sweet wort (p. 73).

Coppers
Apart from the custom-made products previously mentioned, a number of stainless steel tanks and catering pans will

A simple hop strainer inside my copper.

suffice; these can be fired with propane gas, or by an electric element. A propane gas system will be more expensive, and they require a number of fittings plus a spare cylinder in case one runs out during a weekend brewing session! Some types are suitable for indoor use, such as a garage/brewery, but for safety reasons, not in the home. Whilst they are undoubtedly efficient, the convenience, cleanliness and cheapness of electricity is preferable.

Many brewers are fitting two elements to their boilers to speed up the initial coppering, which will rapidly stabilize the sugar ratio by halting any further enzyme activity. All HLTs, mash tuns and coppers should be insulated to retain heat.

Brewing Tidy

A tower to hold HLT, mash tun and copper can be made from 50mm × 50mm timber. Four 2m high uprights are secured to four crossbeams at the top, and three at the middle and bottom. The HLT sits on a stout shelf on top, and the mash tun sits on the middle shelf, which is secured between two strong runners so that it can be drawn out to mash, and pushed back when not in use. The copper sits on a trolley on the floor, and the whole operation is neat and tidy.

Cooling and Gauging Vessel

Take a strong 30ltr plastic container, and secure to each side at the top a 15mm tank connector with the compression fitting on the inside. Solder a 75mm length of 15mm copper pipe into the openings on the flat side, which will become the cold water inlet and outlet. Garden hose may be attached to these by jubilee clips or brass hose fittings. The 15mm copper cooling coil should be fashioned with a plumber's bending tool as it is not possible to do by hand. This is now secured to the tank connectors by the compression fitting. The vessel can now be calibrated to your own requirements. If circumstances permit, the cooler can also act as

A view inside my mash tun.

an FV, and the fermentation temperature controlled by running through cold/hot water as required.

Before use, immersion cooling coils should be scrubbed clean with wire wool and soapy water and rinsed with clean water. After use, a wash with soapy water is sufficient.

Wort Aeration

Traditionally home brewers have successfully splashed the cooled wort from one vessel to another to aerate it. An aquarium air pump and air stone (a plastic or artificial porous stone that creates masses of microbubbles as the air passes through it) is also popular, and these can deliver 2–3ltr of air per minute.

Fermentation Vessels

There is a variety of polypropylene vessels available, with volumes ranging from 30 to 210ltr, so there is a size to meet everyone's thirst! Brupaks also distribute a range of stainless-steel fermenters of 50–100ltr;

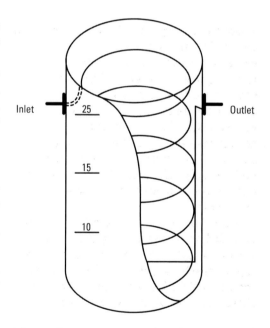

Inlet 25 Outlet

15

10

The cooling and gauging vessel.

these come with lid and tap and can be adopted as mash tuns, boilers or fermenters – it all depends on your ambitions! Stainless-steel restaurant boiling

17

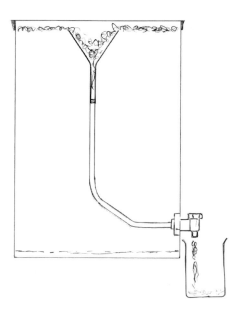

The fermentation parachute.

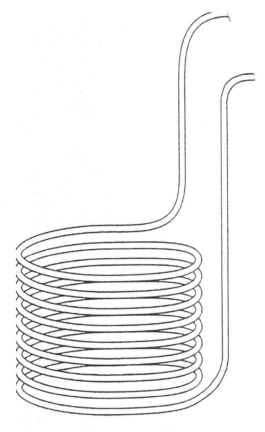

Immersion wort chiller

The cooling coil.

pans will also make good fermenters, and can also be adopted as mash tuns and boilers. Cubitainers make excellent secondary fermenters as they fit inside a fridge easily. The 20ltr size is fine, but unfortunately the 25ltr size is no longer available.

The system illustrated is a simple method of closed fermentation. As the yeast head builds up, the evolving CO_2 forces the yeast head down the 'parachute' into the collection vessel.

Draught Systems

The ubiquitous plastic pressure barrel has been on the scene for almost forty years,

and so has stood the test of time! They are available in various sizes and qualities, which reflects on their price. They might have a narrow neck, or a wide neck for ease of cleaning, and the cap accepts a CO_2 injector system and a pressure relief valve. Stainless-steel Cornelius kegs are also very popular.

A variety of CO_2 injector systems is available for all the above containers. Soda kegs can either use a flexy-hose tap, or a free-flow keg font. A hand pump (beer engine) is required for true English-style draught beer. The barrel should initially be vented, and after a session flushed out with CO_2. Thereafter, bring the cask to slight pressure with CO_2 until required again.

Grain Mill

There is a variety of grain mills available that will give a satisfactory crush to malt. However, this is not something to rush out and buy initially, and it is possible to make do with the convenience of ready-crushed malt. Nevertheless, once you become more experienced or ambitious, you might like to consider one. Prices vary from reasonable to expensive.

Refrigeration

If your circumstances permit, a refrigerator is essential! By using a 24-hour segment timer the desired fermentation temperature can be maintained during warm weather. The glass shelf should be replaced with 75mm plywood, and if necessary the door shelves might require trimming to accept some types of fermenter.

A fridge can also double up as a fermentation cabinet during cold weather. Fit an electric bulb holder with a 60w bulb to the bottom rear of the cabinet. Wire this up to a domestic heating room thermostat positioned at the top front, but far enough back so as not to snag the door. The shelf should be cut out just above the bulb to allow the heat to flow around the cabinet. By utilizing a fridge in this way, we can brew all year round. We can also adjust the height of the shelf, and warm and cold condition bottled beer. Draught beer, too, can be kept at a cellar temperature of 12–14°C for pale ales and 8–10°C for lagers.

Rinsemaster Mk 11

My bottle rinser is an update of Ken Shale's Rinsemaster. Whilst he used 8mm copper pipe and soldered the joints, these are very prone to snapping off with the slightest knock. To overcome this, 15mm copper pipe can be used for the base, with 15–8mm running 'T' reducers, to secure the spraying upstands. The running 'T's secure the upstands very securely, and they do not get accidentally knocked off. The ends of the upstands should simply be pinched to obtain a good spray rinse. With a bit of ingenuity you should be able to fit the rinser inside a plastic bottle crate.

My stainless steel FV in the fridge.

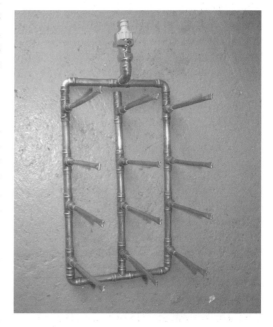

My Rinsemaster.

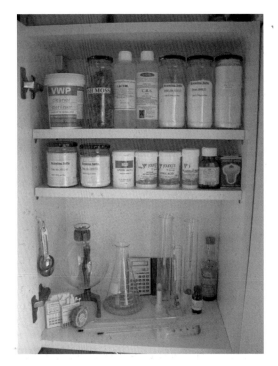

The home brewer's laboratory!

Insulation

A camping matt covered with radiator foil is a popular choice to insulate the HLT. A piece of foam-backed carpet will also make good insulation. The mash tun requires more efficient insulation, and I have found that two layers of domestic hot tank insulation secured with parcel tape around the mash tun is excellent. Alternatively use Superquilt, or similar trade material. Such insulation consists of layers of aluminium foil, polythene and fibreglass. This material is only about 25mm thick, but has the same thermal value as 100mm of high-density polystyrene foam.

THE HOME BREWER'S LABORATORY

One of the most important items in your laboratory will be the saccharometer. This

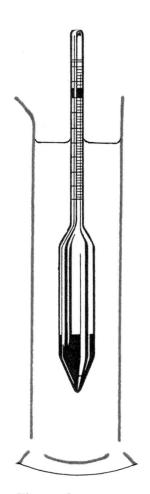

The saccharometer.

is used to record the original gravity (OG), and also to work out the efficiency of mashing and extract recovery. The progress of the fermentation can also be followed, although with experience, we should be able to tell the stage of fermentation by the appearance of the yeast head. The PG is recorded too, and this is important to ensure that we bottle at a stable gravity.

The strength of the brew is also calculated from the OG and the PG: for example, $OG - PG \times 0.1275 = $ alcohol by volume (ABV), or by $0.102 = $ alcohol by weight (ABW). Traditionally, saccharometers were made of brass, but glass has long been the favoured material, and flat plastic types were in vogue for a while. Thermosaccharometers might eventually come to the home-brew scene, when temperature and gravity can be taken at the same time.

Historically, the saccharometer was gauged to the weight of 100 Imperial gallons of distilled water. 100gal × 10lb per gallon became 1,000lb which became 1000°, the gravity of pure water. When the saccharometer is placed in distilled water, it will sink until it reaches equilibrium, displacing a quantity of water equal to its own mass. The point of intersection at 20°C will be 1000°. Other gravities were specifically related to 1000°, and the reading termed the specific gravity. Today specific gravity is referred to as just 'gravity'.

The saccharometer is not, however, 100 per cent accurate as it does not take into account non-sugar solutes and alcohol, and it is only accurate at the temperature at which it was designed to form an equilibrium at 1000°. It has a permitted error up to one degree. Since 1979 saccharometers have been designed to be read at 20°C, rather than 60°F/15.5°C. Should the wort temperature be higher than 20°C then it will be thinner due to its expansion and so the instrument will sink a little lower into the wort. Should it be lower than 20°C, the wort density will be greater due to its contraction, and so the saccharometer will rise a little higher. This results in a false reading. Surface films and finger marks can also produce a false reading, so the instrument should always be cleaned prior to use.

As fermentation temperatures are out with 20°C, there is always going to be a discrepancy with the readings. As the gravities from brewing ingredients are calculated in LDK at 20°C, it is essential that gravities taken with a 60°F saccharometer be corrected to 20°C to obtain the true reading. Experienced brewers know that to obtain a true reading, the instrument should initially be spun in the medium to dislodge any bubbles that might be clinging to it, thereby aiding its buoyancy and creating an inaccuracy. Also, once the saccharometer settles in the wort, it forms a meniscus that obscures the true reading. Such capillary action is caused by surface tension, and it is more evident on round-stemmed saccharometers than flat ones. The discrepancy between the true reading and the top of the meniscus is about one degree; as the saccharometer bobs up and down, keep an eye on the meniscus, and if it appears to drag out of shape, this indicates that the instrument is not clean.

A reading should be taken at eye level, and a degree of judgement is made to adjust for the meniscus: a small magnifying glass is useful in this respect. With pale ales and lagers it is possible to obtain a very accurate reading by looking underneath the wort surface, as the intersection is more easily seen.

A trial jar is necessary to float the saccharometer, and a graduated type is very useful for measuring various fluids; they are available in glass or plastic. The third item needed is the thermometer. A coloured alcohol type is very easy to read and is much safer than a mercury one should it break. Adhesive thermometer strips are useful on fermentation vessels, as the temperature can be seen at a glance.

A conical 500ml (or larger) flask is useful for rehydrating yeast, and also for preparing starter mediums. In some

Taking a saccharometer reading.

regular calibration in a buffer solution. A small bottle of iodine is required for starch tests. A white eggcup will make a good receptacle in which to test a sample of wort and keep the iodine bottle tidy.

Water-treatment salts should be kept dry in screw-topped jars; calcium chloride is very hygroscopic and will quickly absorb moisture and turn solid. A label should identify the type of beer, and the salt and its quantities, including the amount to add per litre.

A gram scale is useful for weighing small quantities of ingredients. For those who own a balance scale and require various weights, then currency coins are ideal.

circumstances an air lock might be required. pH papers 4.5–10 are recommended for those who have to indulge in treating bicarbonate water with sulphuric acid or lime. pH papers 4–6 are necessary for all water treatments, plus checking mash, wort and beer acidity. A digital pH meter is also an option, and requires

CARE AND MAINTENANCE

Always use the appropriate cleaner for the material, and follow the manufacturers' instructions. Glass and plastic will benefit from a lengthy soak in a cleaning fluid to ensure surface films are removed. Dishwasher powder is excellent for glass, plastic and stainless steel, and a good soak in tepid water leaves such items spotlessly clean. My beer bottles are soaked at 75°C for about one hour, and then thoroughly rinsed with the Rinsemaster Mk 11. Dishwasher powder, however, contains *sodium*

Table 1 A gram scale using currency coins as weights

British		Euro		USA		
£2	11.9553g	2	8.4225g	½ dollar	50c	11.2786g
£1	9.3863	1	7.4635	quarter	25c	5.5349
50p	7.9686	50c	7.8214	dime	10c	2.2700
20p	5.0001	20c	5.6955	nickel	5c	4.9655
10p	6.4428	10c	4.0937	penny	1c	2.4983
5p	3.2623	5c	3.9042			
2p	7.0658	1c	2.2711			
1p	3.5310					

disilicate that will irritate eyes and skin, so wear rubber gloves and avoid splashing. Also, read the product safety instructions before use.

Draught beer containers, too, will benefit from the occasional good soak in a cleaning fluid to ensure that the surface film of fine matter that clings and builds up primarily to the lower half of the vessel, is removed. The tap and any auxiliary fittings will also benefit from being stripped down and given a good soak. Also check that the cap and washers are sound.

All electrical apparatus should be checked regularly to ensure that they are in good condition without any loose wires or fraying cables. The heating element of mash tuns and boilers should be scoured with steel wool after every brew, to ensure that calcium carbonate silt and burnt sugar deposits are removed. The accumulation of burnt sugar on the heating element will eventually affect the flavour of the brew.

After scrubbing out mash tuns and boilers, it is also a good idea to boil a litre or so of water in them for a few minutes to steam out the cleansing odours and leave the vessel fresh. Run the hot water out through the tap, as this will help remove any saccharine matter that might be lurking there, which might otherwise cause the tap to weld solid. Always store plastic containers away from damaging sunlight.

Table 2 Corrections to be applied to a 60°F saccharometer to give gravity of worts at 20°C

Gravity	Temperature in degrees centigrade															
	10	11	12	13	14	15	16	17	18	19	20	21	22	23	24	25
1000								0.1	0.3	0.6	0.8	1	1.3	1.5	1.7	2
1005	−0.8	−0.7	−0.6	−0.5	−0.4	−0.3	−0.1	0.1	0.3	0.6	0.8	1	1.3	1.5	1.7	2
1010	−0.8	−0.7	−0.6	−0.5	−0.4	−0.3	−0.1	0.1	0.3	0.6	0.8	1	1.3	1.5	1.8	2
1015	−0.9	−0.8	−0.7	−0.6	−0.4	−0.3	−0.2	0.1	0.3	0.6	0.8	1	1.3	1.5	1.8	2
1020	−0.9	−0.8	−0.7	−0.6	−0.5	−0.3	−0.2	0.1	0.3	0.6	0.8	1	1.3	1.5	1.8	2
1025	−1	−0.9	−0.7	−0.6	−0.5	−0.4	−0.2	0.1	0.3	0.5	0.8	1	1.3	1.5	1.8	2
1030	−1	−0.9	−0.8	−0.6	−0.5	−0.4	−0.2	0.1	0.3	0.5	0.8	1	1.3	1.5	1.8	2.1
1035	1.1	−0.9	−0.8	−0.7	−0.5	−0.4	−0.2	0	0.3	0.5	0.8	1	1.3	1.6	1.8	2.1
1040	−1.1	−1	−0.8	−0.7	−0.6	−0.4	−0.2	0	0.3	0.5	0.8	1	1.3	1.6	1.8	2.1
1045	−1.2	−1	−0.9	−0.7	−0.6	−0.4	−0.2	0	0.3	0.5	0.8	1	1.3	1.6	1.8	2.1
1050	−1.2	−1.1	−0.9	−0.8	−0.6	−0.4	−0.2	0	0.3	0.5	0.8	1	1.3	1.6	1.8	2.1
1055	−1.3	−1.1	−1	−0.8	−0.6	−0.4	−0.2	0	0.3	0.5	0.8	1	1.3	1.6	1.9	2.1
1060	−1.3	−1.2	−1	−0.8	−0.6	−0.5	−0.2	0	0.3	0.5	0.8	1	1.3	1.6	1.9	2.2
1065	−1.4	−1.2	−1	−0.8	−0.7	−0.5	−0.3	0	0.3	0.5	0.8	1	1.3	1.6	1.9	2.2
1070	−1.4	−1.2	1.1	−0.9	−0.7	−0.5	−0.3	0	0.3	0.5	0.8	1	1.3	1.6	1.9	2.2
1075	−1.5	−1.3	−1.1	−0.9	−0.7	−0.5	−0.3	0	0.2	0.5	0.8	1.1	1.3	1.6	1.9	2.2
1080	−1.5	−1.3	−1.1	−0.9	−0.7	−0.5	−0.3	0	0.2	0.5	0.8	1.1	1.3	1.6	1.9	2.2
1085	−1.6	−1.4	−1.2	−1	−0.8	−0.5	−0.3	0	0.2	0.5	0.8	1.1	1.3	1.6	1.9	2.2
1090	−1.6	−1.4	−1.2	−1	−0.8	−0.6	−0.3	−0.1	0.2	0.5	0.8	1.1	1.3	1.6	1.9	2.3
1095	−1.7	−1.4	−1.2	−1	−0.8	−0.6	−0.3	−0.1	0.2	0.5	0.8	1.1	1.3	1.7	2	2.3
1100	−1.7	−1.5	−1.3	−1.1	−0.9	−0.6	−0.3	−0.1	0.2	0.5	0.8	1.1	1.4	1.7	2	2.3

Table 3   *Corrections to be applied to a 20°C saccharometer to give gravity of worts at 20°C*

Gravity	Temperature in degrees centigrade															
	10	11	12	13	14	15	16	17	18	19	20	21	22	23	24	25
1000											0	0.3	0.6	0.8	1	1.3
1005	−1.5	−1.4	−1.3	−1.2	−1.1	−1	−0.8	−0.6	−0.4	−0.1	0	0.3	0.6	0.8	1	1.3
1010	−1.5	−1.4	−1.3	−1.2	−1.1	−1	−0.8	−0.6	−0.4	−0.1	0	0.3	0.6	0.8	1.1	1.3
1015	−1.6	−1.5	−1.4	−1.3	−1.1	−1	−0.9	−0.6	−0.4	−0.1	0	0.3	0.6	0.8	1.1	1.3
1020	−1.6	−1.5	−1.4	−1.3	−1.2	−1	−0.9	−0.6	−0.4	−0.1	0	0.3	0.6	0.8	1.1	1.3
1025	−1.7	−1.6	−1.4	−1.3	−1.2	−1.1	−0.9	−0.6	−0.4	−0.2	0	0.3	0.6	0.8	1.1	1.3
1030	−1.7	−1.6	−1.5	−1.4	−1.2	−1.1	−0.9	−0.7	−0.4	−0.2	0	0.3	0.6	0.8	1.1	1.3
1035	−1.8	−1.6	−1.5	−1.4	−1.2	−1.1	−0.9	−0.7	−0.4	−0.2	0	0.3	0.6	0.8	1.1	1.4
1040	−1.8	−1.7	−1.6	−1.4	−1.3	−1.1	−0.9	−0.7	−0.4	−0.2	0	0.3	0.6	0.9	1.1	1.4
1045	−1.9	−1.7	−1.6	−1.5	−1.3	−1.1	−0.9	−0.7	−0.4	−0.2	0	0.3	0.6	0.9	1.1	1.4
1050	−1.9	−1.8	−1.6	−1.5	−1.3	−1.2	−1	−0.7	−0.5	−0.2	0	0.3	0.6	0.9	1.1	1.4
1055	−2	−1.8	−1.7	−1.5	−1.3	−1.2	−1	−0.7	−0.5	−0.2	0	0.3	0.6	0.9	1.1	1.4
1060	−2	−1.9	−1.7	−1.5	−1.4	−1.2	−1	−0.7	−0.5	−0.2	0	0.3	0.6	0.9	1.1	1.4
1065	−2.1	−1.9	−1.8	−1.6	−1.4	−1.2	−1	−0.7	−0.5	−0.2	0	0.3	0.6	0.9	1.1	1.4
1070	−2.1	−2	−1.8	−1.6	−1.4	−1.2	−1	−0.8	−0.5	−0.2	0	0.3	0.6	0.9	1.2	1.4
1075	−2.2	−2	−1.8	−1.6	−1.4	−1.2	−1	−0.8	−0.5	−0.2	0	0.3	0.6	0.9	1.2	1.5
1080	−2.2	−2.1	−1.9	−1.7	−1.5	−1.3	−1	−0.8	−0.5	−0.2	0	0.3	0.6	0.9	1.2	1.5
1085	−2.3	−2.1	−1.9	−1.7	−1.5	−1.3	−1	−0.8	−0.5	−0.3	0	0.3	0.6	0.9	1.2	1.5
1090	−2.3	−2.2	−2	−1.7	−1.5	−1.3	−1.1	−0.8	−0.5	−0.3	0	0.3	0.6	0.9	1.2	1.5
1095	−2.4	−2.2	−2	−1.8	−1.6	−1.3	−1.1	−0.8	−0.5	−0.3	0	0.3	0.6	0.9	1.2	1.5
1100	−2.5	−2.2	−2.1	−1.8	−1.6	−1.3	−1.1	−0.8	−0.6	−0.3	0	0.3	0.6	0.9	1.2	1.5

CHAPTER 3

BARLEY, MALTING AND MALTS

BARLEY

Barley is an ancient cereal that has been cultivated in Mesopotamia, the breadbasket of the ancient world, since at least 6,000 years BC. It may have found its way to Britain with the Phoenicians, who made their way to our shores in the eighth century and traded grain for Cornish tin. As a brewing cereal, barley is unique, as the husk remains securely attached to the kernel after threshing and this ensures good filtration when sparging the goods. It also has a good yield of extract-bearing starch and nitrogenous materials for yeast growth. When malted, its Horlicks-like flavour and aroma is incomparable with other grains in balancing the bitterness and flavour of the hop.

Barley belongs to the family of cultivatable grasses known as *Graminea*. The commonest strain used in brewing is *Hordeum sativum*, which may be further sub-classified depending upon the different characteristics of the particular strain used. It is the ear of barley that gives it its individual character; as it grows, a series of spikelets develops in alternating groups of three on adjacent sides of the ear. Each spikelet contains the flowering components, and when all of these become fertile after pollination, six rows of kernels are produced. As the kernels of six-rowed barleys are tightly packed together, they become elongated and slim, and usually have a thick husk. Because of this, nineteenth-century brewers usually included a portion of six-rowed malts in the mash tun, as the extra husk material greatly assisted sparging.

European barleys are two-rowed, as only the middle spikelets become fertile, and this allows them to develop into plump, well rounded ears producing a good yield of starch. As the plant grows, its short fibrous roots take up water, nitrates and other minerals from the soil. Nitrates are a useful source of nitrogen, which is an essential component of amino acids and hence proteins. The major source of nitrogen for protein synthesis, however, is through the uptake of gaseous N_2 from the atmosphere. This process is reliant on symbiotic nitrogen-fixing bacteria occurring in nodules on the root system.

These bacteria are capable of converting gaseous nitrogen into ammonia (NH_3), which in turn is converted into dinitrogen oxide, then nitrate, and eventually nitrate NO_3. The plant uses the nitrates to build up amino acids, which in turn will be used to build up protein. The site where the amino acids are joined together is called a peptide bond, and the formation of long chains of amino acids is achieved by a joining of the amino group of one a-acid and the carboxyl group of another.

In this reaction a molecule of water is eliminated, and this is known as a condensation reaction. Two amino acids joined in this way are termed a dipeptide, three a tripeptide, and so on. Longer chains can be referred to as peptones (usually applied to the breakdown products of even larger chains) and polypeptides. These can all be called proteins, though this term is usually applied to the large complete poly-amino chains.

Nitrogen is present in barley proteins in the range 14–18 per cent, and it is normal practice for maltsters and brewers to refer to nitrogen as a measure of crude protein. This is because the amount of nitrogen present in barley can be readily determined by chemical means. Once this has been established, the amount of protein can be calculated by multiplying the nitrogen content by 6.25. This assumes an average nitrogen content of 16 per cent:

i.e. $\dfrac{\text{Nitrogen content}}{\text{Protein content}} = 16\% = \dfrac{16}{100}$

Therefore,

$\dfrac{\text{Protein content}}{\text{Nitrogen content}} = \dfrac{100}{16} = 6.25\%$

This calculation can be adjusted according to the actual levels, where these are known.

Brewers prefer malts with low levels of nitrogen because for every 1 per cent increase in nitrogen there is a decrease of 2 per cent extract-bearing starch, and consequently, more malt is required to achieve the desired original gravity. Also, during coppering, the increase in nitrogenous matter can lead to colour-control problems with pale ales: this is due to an increase in reactions between amino acids and wort carbohydrates (Maillard reactions), which produce colour pigments called elanoidins. During fermentation there is also likely to be an unwelcome rise in wort temperature due to the excess heat given off by the yeast as it metabolizes the increased nitrogenous matter in an energetic frenzy. Too high a temperature will produce racing fermentations and a disproportionate ratio of by-products, mostly esters and fusel oils, resulting in deleterious flavours.

Although much of the nitrogenous element is precipitated during coppering and cooling, plus the amount consumed by yeast during fermentation, sufficient can remain to eventually produce haze and off-flavours during storage. To avoid this, ale brewers seek malts with nitrogen levels in the range 1.4 to 1.55 per cent.

As a general rule, high nitrogen malts are best for low gravity ales as the low grist weight does not contribute too much haze potential, but at the same time provides adequate yeast nutrition. Low nitrogen malts are a necessity for high gravity ales, particularly bottled-conditioned beers, as the grist materials will provide ample yeast nutrition without causing any undue problems with clarity.

The Major Barley Proteins
Albumen
Albumen makes up as little as 4 per cent of the total protein, but it is of profound importance in brewing. It is soluble in water and dilute salt solutions. It is not affected by proteolysis during malting, and survives intact until the mashing stage where it is partially hydrolyzed into peptones and polypeptides that contribute to palate fullness and head retention.

Globulins

Globulins contribute some 31 per cent of the protein: they are insoluble in water, but soluble in salt solutions – beta globulin in particular remains largely intact after malting and mashing, and its main interest to the brewer is its tendency to form haze. It is vitally important, therefore, that the bulk of it is denatured and precipitated during coppering.

Hordein and glutelin contribute 36 per cent and 29 per cent respectively of the total nitrogen of barley. They are insoluble in water and dilute salt solutions, and are hydrolyzed into peptones, polypeptides and amino acids during malting. They survive mashing and coppering, and so remain in the wort as a source of nitrogenous nutrition for yeast growth. Proteins also act as buffers and restrict changes in pH; this has important consequences during mashing.

Proteins are also amphoteric in that they can possess a positive or negative charge, depending on the pH of their immediate environment. At their optimum pH they attain an overall neutral charge and are then said to have reached their iso-electric point. At this stage their solubility is at a minimum, and turbidity and coagulation at a maximum so that precipitation occurs most readily. This is an extremely important phenomenon that greatly influences the quality of wort and beer.

Enzymes

Enzymes are proteins that have a biological catalytic activity, and they function as highly specific catalysts that dramatically speed up the rate at which an organic reaction takes place. Despite their complexity, enzymes are capable of building up, by condensation reactions, and reducing, by hydrolytic reactions, long chains of polypeptides and starch virtually without error.

In 1884, Emil Fischer discovered the ability of enzymes to distinguish individual glycosidic links in starch, and from this he formulated his 'lock and key theory' for enzyme specificity. What this means is that the enzyme is the key, and the substrate (bonds and links) the lock. As every key will only open one lock, so each enzyme will only act on a particular bond or link, and this allows the plant to build up or reduce the materials in its foodstore in an orderly and controlled fashion.

The speed at which enzyme-controlled reactions take place depends on a number of factors such as temperature, acidity, the concentrations of the reactions substrate (s) and product (s), and the presence of activator, or inhibitor, molecules. Enzymes are typically characterized according to the type of reaction they catalyse and usually have the suffix-'ase'; the disaccharide maltose, for example, is broken down into its glucose monomers by the enzyme maltase. The brewer controls, as best he can, the above factors to produce balanced wort and a sound brew.

Carbohydrates

As the leaf structure of the plant develops, it starts to produce the green pigment chlorophyll, which it uses to gather light energy from sunlight. This energy is then used to produce glucose molecules via a complicated series of reactions starting from carbon dioxide and water (photosynthesis). The newly formed molecules are highly soluble, and if allowed to accumulate would present the plant cells with distinct problems in maintaining their normal metabolic processes and osmotic balance, by causing an influx of water into the cell. As such, the molecules are transported from the cells to the endosperm (the foodstore), where they are joined together to form long sugar chains

The structure of amylopectin.

by a series of condensation reactions. Two molecules of glucose joined in this way form maltose, add another and maltotriose is formed, then maltotetraose, and so on. When many molecules are joined like this, they form starch that is insoluble in cold water and so does not interfere with cellular processes. Starch makes up about 65 per cent of the materials in the foodstore, and when mixed with hot water the granules swell up and produce a colloidal suspension from which two forms are identified.

Amylose makes up 20–25 per cent of the starch, and consists of upwards of 1,000 glucose units joined by the first carbon atom of one molecule to the fourth carbon atom of another: these are typically referred to as the 1–4 alpha-glycosidic bonds. *Amylopectin* has a more complex branched structure and consists of about 75–80 per cent of the starch. The straight chains of glucose units are joined by the 1–4 linkages, but the branches are joined to these by the first carbon atom of the molecule and the sixth carbon atom of another to form, 1–6 alpha-glycosidic bonds.

Physiology

The barley kernel consists of the embryo and its foodstore, and these are contained within several layers of cell material covered by the husk.

The Embryo

The embryo is the undeveloped germ of the kernel, and contains all the genetic information for the development of the plant. It is directly attached to the inside of the outer wall, and is separated from the foodstore by a mass of material known as the scutellum and a layer of epithelial cells.

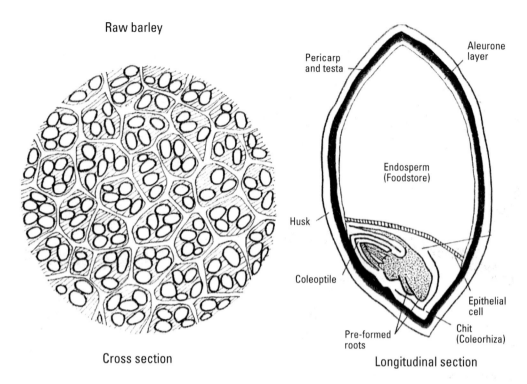

Raw barley

Cross section

Longitudinal section

A cross-section of barley.

Within the embryo are the coleorhiza that will eventually form the rootlets, plus the coleoptile (acrospire) that will develop into the first blade of grass.

The *endosperm* is the embryo's food-store and is comprised of starch granules tightly bound within a protein and cellulose structure. The *husk* consists of the embryo's outer skin, but for simplicity we shall include the several layers of organic material that encase the embryo and its foodstore.

The *aleurone* is the first layer surrounding the embryo and consists of proteinaceous material, plus some carbohydrate (sucrose and raffinose), phosphates (phytin) and the enzymes, β-amylase. The aleurone itself is contained within a protective waterproof skin called the *testa* (or seedcoat) that contains waxy molecules, cellulose and lipids.

Finally, we come to the *pericarp* and husk proper, which is largely made up of cellulose. Some hemicellulose is also present: this is another carbohydrate similar to cellulose, but containing complex polysaccharides called *pentosans* and the viscous β-*glucan*. The husk is also rich in *silica*, which is highly abrasive, and *phenols* (tannins) that are astringent.

MALTING

In nature, the ripe kernels eventually fall to the ground; they remain dormant during the cold winter months. When the wet and warm conditions of spring arrive, growth of the seedling is triggered off,

29

fuelled by the energy contained in the foodstore until such time as the developing shoot and root systems are capable of sustaining the plant.

In order to trick the embryo into germinating, the maltster creates spring-like conditions by steeping the grain in water at about 20°C for two to three days. The embryo now starts to respire, taking oxygen from the water and releasing carbon dioxide. The grain is drained periodically to rest the embryo and prevent it from drowning. Re-steeping introduces a fresh charge of oxygen that promotes growth, and during this period the kernel will have softened and swollen to almost double in size.

After steeping, the maltster now controls the growth of the seedling so that sufficient growth takes place to develop the enzymes necessary to modify the materials in the foodstore, without depleting the reserve store of starch. He can achieve this either by the traditional hand-turned 'floor' method, or by modern automatic mechanical plant: in both cases the aim is the same. By continually turning the 'piece' (the bed of barley) the grain is aerated and the embryo respires freely. Moisture and carbon dioxide are dissipated so that the embryo does not suffocate in its own by-products. Turning the piece also helps control its temperature to about 20°C and prevents the rootlets from becoming entangled.

As germination proceeds, a great many sophisticated biochemical changes take place within the kernel. Vital enzymatic activity takes place in the scutellum so that its protein and carbohydrate are solubilized to feed the growing shoots. Initially, the embryo will rapidly deplete the reserves in the scutellum, and then it has to utilize the starch in the foodstore. It does this by secreting gibberelins that migrate into the protein-rich aleurone to produce gibberalic acid, a plant hormone that accelerates the synthesis of a host of enzymes, which will reinforce those already active in the scutellum and aleurone. They in turn slowly distribute themselves into the foodstore and start to break down the starch and protein. This activity is called *hydrolysis*, as the enzymes are inserting a molecule of water into the system that is the opposite of condensation reactions that the plant used to build up its foodstore. Hydrolysis converts the insoluble materials in the foodstore into a more friable state, so they can slowly diffuse back into the scutellum to nourish the growing shoots.

The enzymes are synthesized in a methodical manner so that hydrolysis takes place in an orderly fashion. Thus cytase breaks down cellulose into cellibiose, a two-molecule sugar similar to maltose, but only slowly fermentable by brewery yeast. The hemicellulases attack β-glucan in the aleurone and in the cell walls, reducing them into less viscous products. Similarly the polysaccharide, pentosan, is degraded into less gluey sugars, arabinose and xylose, and these will eventually contribute to palate fullness and head retention. Had these materials not been broken down, their viscosity might cause slow sparging problems.

The proteases assault Hordein and glutelin (but have little effect on albumen or globulin), and reduce them into proteoses and peptones. These in turn are further simplified by a range of peptidases into polypeptides, peptides and amino acids. As the simplification of protein takes place, the enzyme β-amylase is released from its protein matrix in the aleurone and the enzyme, α-amylase, is synthesized. Phytase, too, becomes active and is busy reducing phytate into the vitamin, inositol, which is beneficial for the embryo's growth, and also yeast growth during fermentation. Phytase also produces a range of inorganic phosphates that act as buffers that greatly influence the regulation of pH during mashing, coppering and fermentation.

When sufficient demolition of proteinaceous structure of the foodstore has taken place, its carbohydrates are more open to attack by the de-branching enzymes, α-glucosidase (maltase) and dextrinase. These enzymes hydrolyze the 1–6 glycosidic linkages of amylopectin and reduce them into shorter chain lengths of amylose. This activity is vital if α-amylase and β-amylase are to eventually co-operate successfully and reduce amylose and amylopectin into the range of sugars required by the brewer during mashing.

Malting is considered to be complete when the rootlets are about 1cm long and the acrospire has grown about three-quarters the length of the grain. At this stage the malt is fully modified. Shorter acrospire growth produces under-modified malt and longer lengths, and is undesirable, resulting in an excessive depletion of starch.

The maltster now has to dry and cure the malt before it can be passed on to the brewer.

Kilning

Kilning gives malt its character by inducing a great many complex reactions that influence colour, flavour, acidity and aroma. This changes *green* malt into true malt with a friable interior. The temperature profile has important consequences for the type of malt being produced. At first a low temperature with plenty of draught ensures that the malt dries rapidly and arrests, but does not destroy, enzyme activity. Initially the proteases and amylases are stimulated

in this warm moist environment, but this is soon halted and so no further starch/sugar conversion takes place. This also ensures that the *Maillard reactions*, that produce colouring pigments, are also halted and so the colour of the malt remains pale.

Coloured malts are made from high nitrogen barleys and may be made from green malt or cured malt. In both cases their moisture levels are always increased to produce plenty of moisture in the roasting drums to ensure a greater degree of hydrolysis and, therefore, an ample supply of amino acids and sugars that are necessary for colour and flavour formation.

The *reducing sugars* glucose and fructose (often as invert sugar) and maltose have the power to reduce copper salts to cuprous oxide when mixed with an alkaline solution, which will be deposited in solid form (Tollens' or Benedict's reagents). Such sugars combine with amino acids by condensation reactions to form complex solutions with high viscosity. Further polymerization and intricate reactions produce colour pigments with rich, caramel-like flavours, and these are called *melanoidins*. These materials are named after Professor Louis Maillard (1878–1936), who discovered them. The importance of reducing sugars is that they react favourably as described above during kilning and to a limited degree during mashing, but more importantly during coppering where they will influence the character of the brew.

Diastatic Power

'Diastase' is the original name given to the group of enzymes that act upon starch during malting and mashing. Diastatic power is often referred to as degrees Lintner, (°L), named after Professor C. J. Lintner, (1855–1923), the German scientist who first analysed and tabled this activity.

'Turning the piece'.

Diastatic levels in malt roughly correlate to the levels of protein so that malts with varying levels of nitrogen will have various levels of diastase. The higher the diastatic level in malt, the greater is its ability to convert added starch materials in the mash tun. The nitrogen content of some American six-rowed malts can be as high as 2 to 2.2 per cent, with Lintner degrees as high as 200. Because of this, American brewers can employ some 40 per cent of adjuncts in their mash tuns. British two-row malts are very low in nitrogen by comparison, say on average about 1.5 per cent, with Lintner degrees of about 35. Consequently, mash tun adjuncts rarely exceed 15 per cent.

MALT

'The soul of the beer', C. J. Lintner.

Lager Malt

British lager malts are produced from two-rowed barleys and are usually slightly undermodified, although the exact degree of modification is controlled to suit the needs of individual brewers. Nitrogen levels are typically in the range 1.65 per cent to 1.75 per cent. Such malts are initially dried at 50°C, with final curing at 80°–85°C to ensure the colour remains very pale at 2 to 2.5 EBC. The low temperatures ensure that the thermolabile proteases survive and will be activated at various temperature rests during decoctions.

During malting, a sulphur-related amino acid, s-methyl-methionine (SMM), is produced during proteolysis and it is broken down during mashing into dymethyl sulphide (DMS). DMS has a potent sweet-corn-like flavour that will strongly influence the palate of any lager in which it is present. DMS in British lager malt varies from brewery to brewery. Some brewers do not like it at all, whilst others seek levels up to 100ppb.

Pale Ale Malt

Ideally, only the best pale ale malts should be used in high gravity all-malt pale ales, particularly if the beer is to be bottled and is to maintain lasting brilliance and stability in storage. Such malts should be fully modified with a nitrogen content of 1.4 per cent to 1.5 per cent, and at least 35–45°L. The initial drying heat on the kiln is 55°–65°C, which ensures that the amylases survive. The final curing at 103°C destroys the proteases and produces a slightly darker colour than lager malt at 5.0 EBC°. Also, curing at 103°C prevents the formation of the DMS precursor from s-methyl-methionine, and so DMS is not found in pale ale malts.

Popular varieties are winter-sown Pearl, Regina and Fanfare, plus spring-sown

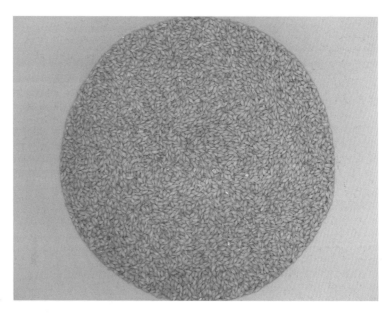

Malt, nature's bounty.

Optic and Cellar. Typical extracts are 304–6 LDK; colour is 5 EBC°.

Scottish Pale Malt

This malt is usually kilned to a slightly darker hue at 5–7 EBC°, with diastatic levels of 60°L. Spring-sown Optic, Chalice and Decanter, however, are the dominant varieties, with extracts of 305–308 LDK.

Mild Ale Malt

This malt can have a nitrogen level of 1.65 per cent and need not be as fully modified as pale malt. The slightly higher nitrogen content means that up to 25 per cent of adjuncts can be used without adversely diluting the essential FAN required for yeast growth. Its diastatic power ranges from 35–48°L and so mild malt can tolerate up to 15 per cent of mash tun adjuncts. Mild malt is cured to 6–7 EBC°.

Wheat Malt

On account of its thin husk, wheat malt provides some 8 per cent more starch than pale malt. Its nitrogen can be as high as 2.5 per cent, providing ample glycopolypeptides and pentosans, which provide fullness of palate and improved head retention. Wheat malt is also thought to extract more fatty acids from the wort due to the greater precipitates of trub produced during the hot and cold breaks and, consequently, head retention is enhanced. Wheat malt is a good adjunct for any beer, but is most beneficial in low gravity beers as it provides yeast nutrition, plus bodybuilding and head-retaining products. It has a diastatic power of about 70°L. The variety *Atlantis* is very popular due to its resistance to fungal attack, particularly Fusaria with its tendency to promote gushing.

Oat Malt

This malt is popular in stouts. Its husk content is 26 per cent and so it will provide extra mash tun roughage and good running of worts. Its lipid content is about 5.5 per cent, and this might have a deleterious effect on head retention, although it is likely to be swamped to a degree by the acidity of the roast malt and barley.

Vienna Malt

This malt is produced from well modified lager malt that is toasted to 5–10 EBC°. It is used primarily in Vienna beers but can be used to impart character nuances in other beer styles.

Munich Malt

This malt is made from modified lager malt, but the acrospire is allowed to continue growing during the kilning cycle. The final curing takes place at 105°–120°C, producing a full malty flavour and a colour of about 20 EBC°. It is primarily used in dark Munich-style lagers, but its fullness and malty aroma can be useful in other beer styles. The diastase power is usually not less than 40°L.

Acid Malt

Such malt is made by steeping green malt in biologically prepared lactic acid. It is useful as part of a water-treatment programme in carbonate-rich water localities, for increasing the acidification of the mash. It can also be used in soft water to acidify lager worts without needing to use gypsum or to prepare a lactic-acid mash. This keeps the liquor soft, with the beneficial influence on hop character. Typical amounts to add are between 1 per cent and 5 per cent. Acid malt can also be used to introduce subtle 'tart' nuances into porters and stouts.

COLOURED MALTS

Coloured malts were perfected in 1817 with the introduction of Wheeler's cylindrical drum roasting machine, and the Roasted Maltsters Act was introduced in 1842 to protect the conditions of maltsters. In Britain, winter barleys are preferred in the production of coloured malts.

Caramalt

Also known as carapils, caristan or dextrin malt, Caramalt is produced from moist germinating grain that is mashed in a roasting drum at 65°C for up to one hour. During this time, the starch and proteins are hydrolyzed before the heat is boosted to 150°C to secure the essential Maillard reactions. The final curing crystallizes the interior and the flavour becomes a luscious caramel, or toffee-like. Three grades are produced, and Caramalt finds most use in lager brewing as it provides smoothness of flavour without adding too much colour.

Crystal Malt

Also known as caramel malt, crystal malt is made in much the same way as Caramalt, although the roasting regime is at a higher temperature and for a longer period. Crystal malt has a delicious, sweet caramel flavour that intensifies with the roasting regime and colour formation. All recipes in this book are based on 140 EBC°. Higher grades are usually reserved for dark beers and malt liquors.

Amber Malt

This malt was traditionally made from mild ale malts with about 4 per cent moisture, but lager malt is now preferred. It is kilned from 90°C to 149°C to achieve a pale amber colour of 35–100 EBC°. Amber malt has a nutty, fruity flavour, and is available in diastatic and non-diastatic forms.

Brown Malt

This malt is made from mild malt, but is roasted from 50–170°C to produce colours ranging up to 400 EBC°. It has a nutty, caramel flavour and is used to provide

Table 4   Pale malts

Pale Malts	EBC°	Lab. LDK	HB°= 90%	Characteristics and nuances
Pilsner	2–25	305	274	Clean crisp malt flavour
British lager	2–5.3	306	275	Light malt flavour and aroma
Carapils	3.5	284	255	Full-bodied malt with malty aroma
English ale	5.0	306	275	Medium malt flavour. Horlicks-like aroma
Scottish ale	5–6	307	276	Full malt flavour and aroma
Belgium pale	7.0	306	275	Rich malt flavour and colour
Wheat	4.6	315	283	Clean flavour, good head retention
Oat malt	5.7	260	234	Soft chewy mouth-feel
Rye malt	3–5	315	283	Bready malty flavour and aroma
Mild ale	6.7	300	270	Full malt flavour
Vienna	5–10	300	270	Good for colour, flavour and aroma
Golden oats	10–20	275	247	Huskless oat crystal malt. Nutty flavour
Munich	18–22	296	266	Full malt flavour with rich aroma

HB° = Home Brew Degrees

nuances in some bitter and mild beers, and in some special bottled ones.

Chocolate Malt

As the name suggests, chocolate malt is a medium-brown chocolate colour of 900–1100 EBC°. It is produced from malt with about 1.7 per cent nitrogen and 5 per cent moisture. It is initially dried at 50°C, but the final curing is omitted. Roasting starts off at around 75°C, rising to 145°C during the first hour, then to 175°C, before peaking at 230°C for the last 15min of a 2¼hr cycle. This malt is good for milds and stouts, influencing a mocha nuance. Amounts greater than 10 per cent will produce a cloying, chewy palate.

Roast Malt

This product is well known to home brewers as black malt. It has a rich, dark, coffee-bean colour of 1100 EBC°. It undergoes a similar roasting regime as chocolate malt, but final heats can be as high as 250°C. Roast malt has a sweetish mocha flavour, and is used primarily in milds, porters and stouts.

Roasted Barley

This is an unmalted grain and, therefore, technically an adjunct. It is kilned much the same as black malt but about 5–10°C lower in the initial phase. Final heats are between 230–250°C, producing a colour of 1100–1400 EBC°. It has a dryish, burnt coffee bean-like flavour ideally suited to dry stouts.

Melanoidin Malt

This malt is rich in nitrogen-hetrocyclic materials that are produced by increasing the nitrogen (amino acids) content of the malt, the reducing sugars and the moisture content of the malt. The temperature and time of the kilning cycle gives rise to a product with 70 EBC° of colour and sweet caramel-like flavour formation. Materials such as glycine, plus maltose, produce very dark pigments with malty aromas. Valine and fructose, proline and maltose also promote the malt flavour, and alanine plus glucose give us warm, biscuity flavours.

Table 5   Coloured malts

Coloured malts	EBC°	Lab. LDK	HB° 90%	Characteristics and nuances
Carahelle	25–35	280	252	Malt sweetness. Delicate amber hue
Caramalt	25–30	275	247	Caramel flavour with a touch burnt notes
(Carastan)	35–45	275	247	Sweet caramel/toffee flavour increasing
	50–70	275	247	with the intensity of the colour
Imperial malt	50	300	270	Increases colour, flavour and aroma
Aromatic malt	50–70	290	261	An interesting hint of raisins
Amber malt	35–100	275	247	Nutty and fruity flavour
Crystal malt	100–120	275	247	Sweet malt with a light amber colour
	140–160	275	247	Luscious malty sweet. Fullness of palate
	180–210	275	247	Intense caramel and burnt notes
Brown malt	400	275	247	Nutty with caramel notes
Rye crystal	220–400	278	250	Sweet, malty. Warm bread crust flavour
Special B	300–350	278	250	Sweet caramel notes
Choc. wheat	220–400	278	250	Soft mellow coffee
Chocolate	900–1100	260	234	Sweet roast coffee bean character
Roast malt	1100–1300	260	234	Sweet and roasty mocha mouth-feel
Roast barley*	1100–1400	250	225	Dry, smoky roast coffee-bean character
Roast wheat*	200–400	300	270	Smooth burnt toast/roasted coffee flavour

* Technically adjuncts

STORING MALTS

As warm air contains more moisture than cold air, malt, whether it is whole or crushed, should be stored under *cool dry conditions*, ideally at 10–15°C and no higher than 18°C. This should keep it relatively free from moisture uptake. Avoid the airing cupboard!

The moisture level should be about 3–4 per cent, and when it rises above this figure, the malt is said to have become slack. The main problem with slack malt is that it absorbs more heat than dry malt, which results in the initial mash heat falling below that, which is desired. This is not so important in decoction mashing due to the initial low temperature rests employed, and six-rowed lager malts can tolerate moisture levels of 5–6 per cent.

As slack malt has a higher moisture content it will weigh more than dry malt, and so on a weight-for-weight basis it will produce a lower yield of extract. Such losses on our scale are small, but nonetheless there are ways in which this can be overcome. First of all, we can anticipate the loss of extract to be about 2–4 per cent, and can adjust the grist weight accordingly. Just before mashing we can dry the grain in the oven and bring its temperature closer to the desired initial heat in the mash tun. This also reduces the 'thermal trauma' of the scalding strike liquor on the malt enzymes.

High moisture malts and other cereals deteriorate in storage due to moulds and musty flavours, and so it is important for the home brewer to calculate his needs so that the ingredients are used up within a reasonable time. Malt is supplied to us in various quantities, either whole or crushed, with the smaller volumes sealed in polythene bags so that their moisture content remains constant until opened. Bulk purchases are an attractive buy for the enthusiast, and 20–25kg are supplied in a strong polythene bag, secured in a tough outer polypropylene sacking. A good idea for bulk purchases is to break them down into recipe volumes: identify each recipe, and seal the bag.

Crushed Malt

Ready-crushed malt is prepared to the same high standards as for commercial brewers, which ensures a good yield, efficient sparging and freedom from a set mash. Maltsters and brewers typically set their gristmills and sieves to obtain the following percentages of grist factions:

	Infusion	Decoction
The course faction, or husk	20%	15%
Coarse grits	0%	23%
The intermediate faction, or fine grits	70%	30%
The fine faction, or flour	10%	32%

Poorly crushed or over-crushed malt will not achieve the above ideals. The latter will also result in excessive extraction of undesirable polyphenols and silica from the husk during mashing and sparging, plus poor extract recovery and beer clarity. A number of malt mills are available for home brewers, and you should carefully weigh up the cost, plus the time and trouble of milling, against the convenience of ready-crushed malts.

Veteran home brewer, Bill Cooper, crushing his malt.

CHAPTER 4

ADJUNCTS: 'THE CONTROVERSY OF BEER'

Historically, the use of adjuncts in brewing has been a contentious issue for a number of reasons. Some states, such as Bavaria, banned adjuncts in brewing for agricultural reasons, to regulate the supply of barley and wheat for beer and bread, the staple diet of the day. This denied foreign grain imports and supported their farming communities. In Britain, they were banned for reasons of economy. Beer was first taxed in 1660, and the additional Malt Tax was introduced in 1697: should non-taxable adjuncts be employed there would be a loss of revenue for the Exchequer. To avoid this, a law was passed in 1802 stating that only malt and hops should be employed in brewing.

In the *Art of Brewing*, published in 1823, Hayman described how up to 20 per cent of adjuncts could replace malt in the mash tun. In the 1850s, smooth roller mills were introduced, as they would satisfactorily crush crisp friable malts; but they would not crush unmalted grain. Therefore, if raw barley were used, this would result in low extracts, poor flavours and haze, and would be uneconomical. Cheats, too, would be easily caught.

When brewers accepted the saccharometer, Gladstone repealed the Malt Tax in 1880 and levied a tax on wort gravity and volume. Brewers were now free to prepare worts from materials of their choice. But despite this freedom, there was no widespread abuse of adjuncts, and by 1899, the 'glorious year of the maltster', the average brewers' grist consisted of 85 per cent malt, 5 per cent mash tun adjuncts and 10 per cent copper sugars.

The quality of wort is important, and the use of adjuncts in brewing has to be balanced against many factors, such as the nitrogen content of the malt, clarity, flavour, head retention, the anticipated period of storage, and the stability of the brew.

NITROGEN CONTROL

The primary role of adjuncts is to dilute the nitrogen levels in wort. This is an advantage in terms of colloidal stability and, with the exception of barley adjuncts, insignificant amounts of polyphenols (tannins). Large amounts of tannins are undesirable as they contribute to a harshness of palate. They form non-biological haze complexes in conjunction with protein, and should they become oxidized, they increase the colour of wort by forming colouring pigments during coppering, traditionally called phlobanthenes.

In a typical fermentation, yeast requires about 150mg/ltr of free amino nitrogen (FAN). However, all-malt wort will have substantially higher amounts than this, and the excess not metabolized by the yeast will end up in the beer. As bacteria also have an affinity for FAN there is a risk of unpasteurized beer becoming infected during storage. Consequently, it is safer to dilute malts containing 1.7–1.8 per cent nitrogen with up to 20 per cent carbohydrate.

By diluting wort nitrogen, particularly with high gravity beers, not only do we secure the above benefits, but we avoid racing fermentations with accompanying high temperatures and an excess of fusel alcohols by reducing the amount of FAN for yeast metabolism. The dilution of FAN also limits the formation of melanoidins and consequently limits colour formation during coppering. A small amount of wort-extender added to the copper can be useful in limiting colour that is important for pale beers.

Most malts on offer today have about 1.45 per cent to 1.55 per cent nitrogen, which suits the higher range of low gravity brews in vogue commercially. Such malts are suitable for all-malt craft brews with gravities up to around 1,045 or so, without incurring any serious technical difficulties. A small percentage of a nitrogen-diluting cereal might secure a sharper focus of clarity at the higher gravity range. To employ such malts in high gravity brews (1055–75) might require 10–15 per cent of nitrogen-diluting flakes to secure the essential brilliance and stability of flavour.

Should you be fortunate enough to acquire malt with about 1.4–1.5 per cent nitrogen and intend to brew low gravity beers, do not use any nitrogen-diluting grain otherwise the brew will lack body and head retention. It is also advisable to employ a protein-rich cereal such as wheat, to enrich the yeast nutrient properties, and this is particularly important if you are re-using the same yeast. Yeast that is continually pitched into low gravity worts quickly loses its vitality. Obviously, this is not so important with sachets of dried yeast, but don't overlook the benefits of wheat adjuncts.

The use of nitrogen-diluting cereals will not alter the carbohydrate composition to any significant degree, as their starches are acted upon in the same way as malt starch by the amylases. The flavour of the brew will, however, be altered somewhat, but to what degree will depend on the type and quantity of the cereal. In most cases, adjuncts only influence a very subtle nuance into the brew, but the shelf life is increased due to the dilution of astringent and haze-forming polyphenols, and foam-destroying lipids.

Excessive amounts of nitrogen-diluting adjuncts should be avoided as they curtail the buffering power of worts so that during fermentation the pH of the wort might remain higher than expected, with the consequential effect on flavour and the increased risk of bacterial infections.

MASH TUN ADJUNCTS

The preparation of starch-rich cereals is important for beer quality. Cereal oil, for example, has a strong flavour and smell, and rapidly becomes rancid when exposed to air as would happen during milling. It is essential, therefore, to remove as much starch as possible from cereals prior to brewing so that the flavour and head retention does not suffer. Dilution of the lipid content is also important as it destroys head retention, and should they oxidize during storage, staling aldehydes are formed.

Nitrogen-Diluting Cereals

The most popular adjuncts used in the isothermal mash tun are maize and rice flakes, and these products can be prepared in two ways.

Maize

Traditionally, maize was called 'maize malt', and it has formed part of the grist of traditional ales for well over a century. Its gelatinization temperature range is from 62°–74°C, but it needs prolonged treatment to ensure its solubility. It is not, therefore, added direct to the mash tun in its raw state, as the starches will not be adequately solubilized at 65°C, during a 1½hr mash. Likewise, should the mash temperature be boosted to 74°–78°C to achieve gelatinization, the malt enzymes will perish.

To prepare maize for mashing, the grain is rough milled to remove its husk and oil-rich embryo, which immediately reduces the lipid content from about 4.8 per cent to 1.8 per cent. Next, the moisture content of the grain is boosted to about 19 per cent, and this is followed by steaming under gentle pressure to weaken the endosperm structure and partially gelatinize the starch. Finally, the grain is passed through flaking mills at 85°C to produce corn flakes, and dried to about 9 per cent moisture. Thereafter, the grain is slightly crushed to reduce its bulk density.

The alternative to steaming and flaking is to micronize and flake. This concept uses gas-produced infra-red rays as the source of energy. Initially the cereal is moistened to about 16 per cent, and then fed into the micronizer on a vibrating wire-mesh conveyor belt.

The continual vibration of the grain ensures that the kernels are being turned constantly to ensure even cooking. The gas burners heat up the ceramic tiles immediately above the grain, and emit infra-red rays. As the moist grain absorbs the rays, they cause the interior molecules to vibrate at 60,000 to 150,000 megacycles per second. The ensuing friction causes a rapid increase of internal temperature to about 140°C, and this in turn increases the internal vapour pressure of the grain; as a result the grain softens and becomes swollen, and quickly ruptures. Finally, the grain is flaked without drying and retains some 8 per cent moisture. Flaked maize adds fullness to a beer, and as long as amounts are kept below 15 per cent, its corn nuance is unobtrusive.

Rice Flakes

This product is the alternative to maize, and it is considered to be superior as its oil is tasteless and odourless and does not oxidize on milling. Its gelatinization temperature is 61°–76°C, but it requires the same pre-brewing treatment as maize. Flaked rice is a particularly good nitrogen dilutant, but it is rarely used commercially because of its cost.

Barley and Wheat

These can be steamed or micronized before flaking. Barley starch readily gelatinizes at 60°–62°C, and so it can be added directly to the mash tun. Raw barley is deficient in proteinase, β-glucanase and α-amylase, but otherwise has a similar composition to malt. Care must be taken when steaming barley as excessive processing can lead to elevated levels of viscous β-glucan being extracted. Whilst these materials are beneficial in moderate amounts, excessive quantities can give rise to highly viscous worts and gelatinous precipitates in the brew. Micronized barley is to be preferred, as the process reduces the extraction of β-glucan. Barley flakes add a grainy nuance in beer, and are an essential requirement for the character and head retention in dry stouts.

If barley and wheat are not to be flaked, they are left in their 'popped' state and should be crushed prior to mashing. Over the years, torrified barley has given way to torrified wheat, which provided greater extract for the same price.

Flaked Wheat
This cereal is rich in viscous pentosans and is particularly valuable for promoting head retention. Wheat starch gelatinizes at 54°–62°C, and like raw barley it can be added direct to the mash tun. Wheat flour can also be added direct to the mash tun, and as it is rich in pentosans and other polysaccharides, but low in polyphenols and lipids, it promotes head retention and a longer shelf life. Its nitrogen content is

about 1 per cent, but amounts added to the mash tun are best kept below 10 per cent otherwise viscosity problems might arise during sparging. Care should be taken when mixing wheat flour, as it has a tendency to dough. It is also available as pellets.

Oatmeal
Oatmeal is produced by removing the oat husk and sieving the grain to remove it and other debris. It is now kilned to reduce the moisture level and stabilize enzyme activity. Finally, the kernels are milled to produce pinhead oatmeal. Flaked oats are produced by gently steaming the oatmeal and flaking it between heated rollers.

Copper Adjuncts
Copper adjuncts refer to any carbohydrate added to the wort during boiling. Depending on their characteristics and the manner in which they influence the character of the brew, they can be divided into wort extenders and wort replacement.

Table 6 Mash tun adjuncts

Cereal	Lab. LDK	HB° 90%	Characteristics and nuances
Flaked rice	325	292	Dry flavour, dilutes protein and phenols
Flaked maize	315	283	Adds fullness of palate, subtle corn nuance
Flaked barley	255	229	Grainy flavour. Aids head retention
Flaked wheat	280	252	Adds crispness and aids head retention
Flaked oats	260	234	Smooth, creamy finish
Flaked rye	280	252	Crisp grainy flavour. Assists head retention
Rice grits	330	297	Not commonly used by home brewers
Maize grits	281	252	Rice and maize grits are nitrogen dilutents
Brewing flour	302	271	Fullness of body and gravity
Wheat flour	305	274	Precipitates lipids, aids head retention
Wheat pellets	305	274	As above
Torrified barley	253	227	Nutty/chewy mouth-feel
Torrified wheat	275	247	Low in β-glucan, aids head retention
Pinhead oats	260	234	Smooth, creamy finish

Wort Replacement Syrups

Wort replacement syrups are employed either to replace a portion of wort, or to add to it to increase gravity and volume.

Malt Extract

Malt extract is an all-malt syrup produced from malted barley with nitrogen levels of 1.7–2 per cent. After an initial protein rest at 50°C, it is mashed at 65°C to secure the range and balance of wort sugars necessary for a balanced brew. As soon as this is achieved, diastatic extracts are concentrated to syrup containing 80 per cent solids at 40°C at one bar pressure in a batch evaporator. Non-diastatic syrups are concentrated in a multi-stage evaporator where it is initially vaporized at 80°C. The next stage takes place at 40°C, and the extract is finally condensed to 70–80 per cent solids at one bar pressure.

The Customs and Excise first approved diastatic extracts as a mash tun adjunct in 1906, as it was necessary to augment the poor quality malts available at this time. This practice should not be necessary today as malts on offer are of a sound and regular quality. Special malt extracts containing lactic acid to increase acidity in the mash tun, or elevated levels of FAN for enhanced fermentation, are also available. Non-diastatic extract is used in the copper to increase volume when mash tuns cannot cope when demand for beer is high. British malt extracts are second to none, and when used intelligently without abuses – such as an excess of sugar adjuncts – will produce excellent beers.

Theoretically, malt extract can replace malt kilogram for kilogram, but quantities should be reduced to take account of the differences between kitchen brewhouse extraction rates from malt and that of extracts. Also, as malt extract has a fuller flavour, it can tolerate a flavour dilution with 10 per cent sugar. A few trials, of course, will determine one's preference.

One difficulty facing the home brewer is accurately measuring the viscous syrup: in all probability most simply employ it by the full tinful. Spraymalts are useful for adjusting gravities and making starters. Leftovers can be sealed and stored in the freezer where they will remain dry almost indefinitely.

Barley Syrup

Barley syrup can be produced from a lower grade of barley than is required for malt extract. During manufacture, hydrolysis is carried out by a range of fungi, plus plant and industrial enzymes, and the process follows the same pathway as for malt extract. Barley syrup has roughly the same carbohydrate and nitrogenous content as malt extract and malt wort, and can be used as a replacement for these in the copper. Barley syrup will not add any maltiness to the brew. Wheat and maize syrups are also made in the same way.

Wort Extenders

These consist of any forms of carbohydrate that will increase the gravity of a brew, but do not contribute nitrogenous materials for yeast growth. Consequently they are also nitrogen dilutents, and by altering the carbohydrate/nitrogen ratio, they affect beer flavour.

Cane Sugar Products

These products have been legalized in brewing since 1847, and were taxable from 1850 to 1880; they are the traditional copper adjuncts historically imported from our colonies. Sugars influence a subtle molasses nuance in the beer. *Granulated sugars* consist of pure sucrose and are 95–100 per cent fermentable. Large amounts of cane sugar are to be avoided as the FAN will become severely diluted, upsetting the yeast's metabolism resulting in an imbalance of by-products and deleterious tangy flavours. Also, yeast collected from such brews will not be suitable for re-pitching.

Demerara sugar, traditionally called 'yellow crystals', is an unrefined sugar made by crystallizing raw cane juice. Demerara sugar will impart a light raw sugar nuance, and the darker *Barbados and Muscovado sugars* introduce stronger flavours due to the higher quantity of molasses they contain. The latter are probably best restricted for dark brews.

Invert sugars are not much used commercially today, as products derived from maize have ousted them. *Lyall's Golden Syrup* is a first-class copper sugar for all styles of beer: it consists of 48 per cent invert sugar, 32 per cent sucrose, 1.5 per cent minerals, 2 per cent organic matter and 16.5 per cent water. Useful sizes are 680g (1.5lb) and 454g (1lb).

Glucose Products (Dextrose)
These products have long ousted cane sugars in commercial brewing, and are available to the amateur in several forms. Confectioner's glucose is made by breaking down refined maize starch with dilute hydrochloric acid. The slurry is then neutralized with soda ash and filtered through carbon to remove impurities before being dried in a vacuum band drier. The product contains glucose, maltose, maltotriose and dextrins, and is 30–50 per cent fermentable. *Glucose chips* are not so popular these days; they are produced in much the same way but contain mostly glucose, and their fermentability is about 80–90 per cent. Some types of 'chip' sugars have sucrose blended in to enhance flavour.

Glucose Syrup
This syrup was first made in 1811, the product being produced by a full acid conversion. Today it is made by a two-stage process whereby the initial hydrolysis is by acid, followed by a further breakdown by selected enzymes. The resultant syrup has a range of glucose, maltose, maltotriose and dextrins, with a fermentability of 75–95 per cent. This product is sometimes sold as 'maize syrup' and usually has sucrose added for flavour.

Glucose and fructose, plus sucrose that will be inverted into glucose and fructose by the yeast, should not contribute more than 15 per cent of the total wort carbohydrate, as this can lead to a fermentation disorder called the Crabtree effect (glucose effect or catabolic repression). When glucose is in abundance, the yeast will preferentially metabolize it, and does not synthesize the maltose permease enzymes. The consequences of this is that when all the glucose is consumed, the fermentation will slow down severely, or perhaps stop altogether, until the yeast goes through another 'lag phase' in order to build up sufficient maltose permease enzymes necessary to continue consuming the maltose. Abnormally high levels of glucose also distort flavour as high levels of esters and higher alcohols are produced.

Caramels
Caramels are produced from glucose syrup, or invert sugar, by conversion in ammonia at 140°C. This induces the Maillard reactions, and the character of the product can be controlled to suit the needs of individual brewers and might be mildly sweet, sweet, or acrid. The product may be electronegative or electropositive, but only the latter is used in brewing, as it does not clash with electronegative finings.

43

Table 7   Brewing sugars

(Compiled from various sources)

Copper adjuncts	LDK	% ferm.	Characteristics and nuances
Malt extract, liquid	303	65–75	Full malt flavour. Sugar ratio is fixed
Malt extract, dried	375	65–75	Full malt flavour. Very hygroscopic
Barley syrup	297	60–75	Fullness of palate without maltiness
Wheat syrup	297	60–75	Dry flavour. Influences head retention
Maize syrup	315	70–80	Subtle corn nuance. Fullness of palate
Golden syrup	320	75–80	Sucrose 32%, invert sugar 48%
Glucose syrup	321	75–95	Dry-flavours the brew
Malto-dextrin	300	25–35	Adds body and residual sweetness
Solid maize sugar	315	85–90	Unobtrusive corn flavour
Cane sugar syrup	260	95–100	Dilutes nitrogen. Alter beer character
Sucrose crystals	385	95–100	As above
Sucrose solid	384	95–100	As above
Coloured sugar	365	95–100	Subtle coloured tints. Raw cane nuance
Confectioner's glucose	320	30–50	Less sweet over a range of gravities
Dextrose monohydrate	320	75–80	As above
Lactose	275	nil	Sweet and cloying. Unfermentable!
Caramel	265	nil	Colour. 36,000 to 48,000 EBC°

Cross & Blackwell recommend their 'Browning' for home brew, advising 1tsp to 1tbsp per 3gal (13.6ltr); 'Browning' contains colouring, E150c, water, salt and glucose syrup. The salt is present in a minuscule amount and should not upset the brewing liquor. Browning is excellent for colour adjustment without interfering with the beer flavour.

Lactose
This is a milk sugar consisting of glucose units linked to galactose units. As brewers' yeast does not secrete the enzyme 'lactase', this sugar remains in the wort as a sweetener. In pre-pasteurization days, lactose was popular for sweetening 'milk stouts', but it is little used these days as it can be bettered by maize products. Lactose is, however, still available to the home brewer, and quantities to use are typically 8–12 per cent of the total extract. Lactose has an extract roughly on a par with cane sugar, but its sweetening power is only 55 per cent of sucrose. Lactose is unfermentable, so don't forget that the PG of the brew will be higher than otherwise anticipated.

CHAPTER 5

HOPS: 'THE HEART OF A GOOD PINT'

The hop that swings so lightly, the hop that shines so brightly, Shall still be cherished rightly, by all good men and true! (Old song)

The hop is a herb native to Eurasia and the Americas, of the genus *Humulus* belonging to the family Cannabinaceae (hemp). The Romans called it *lupa salictarious*, and first brought it to Britain for culinary and medicinal purposes. French monks are accredited with perfecting the use of hops in brewing in the thirteenth century, and some time before the Reformation, Dutch traders acquainted Kentish folk with their merits in brewing. The Dutch influence remains with us to this day, with oast-houses and cask names such as 'hogshead', a derivative of *Okshooft*, plus 'kilderkin' (*Kindeken*) and firkin (*Vierdeken*), meaning a 'half' and a 'quarter' respectively. Long before commercial hop agriculture began, hops were grown by the gentry, farmers and innkeepers to flavour and preserve their home-brewed beer.

The hop, *Humulus lupulus*, is a perennial climbing vine with a long hollow stalk, three to five lobed leaves, and small declinious apetalous flowers with a one-celled ovary. It grows, twining clockwise, as high as 6 metres, but many new hops are dwarf varieties that only grow to 2 metres in height, which makes them easier to harvest. The male flowers have short stems and are borne on many-branched clusters, but they are not considered for brewing: it is the female flowers that contain the essential bittering and aromatic properties.

When the female plant flowers it is said to have come into 'burr', and after pollination by wind-borne pollen released by the male plant, it comes into 'brush'. From this stage, the female comes into 'hop' as it starts to form the catkin-like fruit clusters, or 'strobil'. The strobil has a central stem known as the 'strig', which is bent at obtuse, alternating angles along its length. Four short branches radiate from each angle, and each branch consists of a seed contained in a 'bracteole', below which two 'stipular bracts' (resembling small green leaves) are attached to the main stem. The successive rows of bracts overlap one another, producing the cone-like shape. It is the bracteoles that are of brewing importance, as they contain the lupulin gland and seeds at their base. The seeds themselves are of no brewing value, but the lupulin gland contains the resins and aromatic oils; these materials are unique to the hop and impart the characteristic spicy flavour and enticing aroma.

Historically, all British hops were fertilized, with the seeds making up some 25 per cent of the weight of the cone. Traditional varieties, such as Goldings and Fuggles, remain so today and do not yield bountiful crops when grown seedless. In order to compete with the continental 'seedless' market, and to meet demand from modern brewing plant that is not designed to cope with seeded hops, many new varieties are grown seedless.

After harvesting in the autumn, the hops are dried under controlled conditions in an oast house to reduce their moisture level to 8 to 10 per cent. The low moisture level prevents moulds developing during storage, and refrigeration restricts the deterioration of the resins.

HOP CHEMISTRY

Hop chemistry is highly complex, but we can separate its constituents into useful and non-useful parts, as shown in the table below.

The Resins
The resins are divided into hard and soft, depending on their solubility in organic solvents: hard resin is insoluble and does not contribute to the quality of the beer. It is the soft resins that are extremely important for flavour, aroma, and the ability to restrict the growth of various strains of bacteria.

α-acid
α-acid is the main bittering ingredient in hops, and it consists of three compounds: humulone, cohumulone and adhumulone. In their natural state these materials are neither soluble nor bitter, and it requires the application of heat to make them so. During coppering at over 100°C, the molecular structure of the α-acid undergoes isomerization as certain bonds in its structure are broken and rejoined at another site, resulting in the formation of a slightly altered, though very similar structure. The new molecules are called iso-α-acids (viz. isohumulone, isocohulone and isoadhumulone), and these compounds are soluble and bitter in wort.

It takes a full 90min boiling to achieve maximum isomerization, but total utilization is only between 15 and 30 per cent. Utilization is affected by the gravity of the wort, and the higher the gravity, the less isomerization. Also, the higher the hopping rate, the poorer the isomerization. Iso-α-acids are also lost into the yeast head during fermentation and deposited with trub during the hot and cold breaks. More iso-α-acids are lost with highly

Table 8   An analysis of hops

Brewing value	%	Non-useful matter	%
A-acid (humulone) soft resin	7.0	Cellulose	37.0
B-acid (lupulone) " "	9.5	Lipids and wax	3.0
Aromatic oils	0.5	Ash	8.0
Fructose and sucrose	2.0	Pectin	2.0
Tannin	4.0	Moisture	9.0
Protein	15.0	Hard resins	3.0
Total	38.0	Total	62.0

flocculating top-fermenting yeast than bottom-fermenting yeast. Isomerization is greater in carbonate liquors due to the higher pH, but the flavour can be somewhat harsh. Liquors rich in gypsum, with a low pH, restrict isomerization and achieve a cleaner, hoppy palate.

β-acids

β-acids consist of lupulone, colupulone and adlupulone, which in their fresh state do not contribute to bitterness of the beer. During storage, however, oxygenation effects a chemical change that makes them bitter; and during coppering, β-acids can contribute some 5 per cent of the bitterness of the brew. This partially offsets the deterioration of the α-acids during storage, although the flavour is not as exciting as that of fresh hops.

Preservative Value

The soft resins provide the preservative quality of hops. α-acid (iso-humulone) is more important than β-acid (Lupulone) in this respect, since it inhibits the growth of thermophilic lactic-acid bacteria that can infect the goods and sweet wort. The iso-humulone continues to repress lactic and acetic bacteria during fermentation and storage, and their growth rate is very slow. Although the β-acids are present in larger amounts, most of it is precipitated during coppering and fermentation. In old, stale hops, however, the preservative value of β-acids increases. Lambic brewers make use of old hops that have lost their flavour and aroma, but have retained their preservative qualities.

Aromatic Oils

The aromatic oils have a greater influence on aroma than other grist materials, and impart the familiar hoppy 'nose', or aroma. Such 'essential oils' are made up of various hydrocarbons, and several types are found in hop oil. The composition of the oil depends on the variety, and whether the hop is grown with, or without, seeds. The maturity of the hop is also important, as the quantity of the hop oil increases as the hop matures. Initially, the sesquiterpene hydrocarbons are synthesized, followed by a rapid build-up of monoterpene hydrocarbon as the hop approaches maturity.

By selecting the harvesting period, the grower can select hops with little or no monoterpene hydrocarbon, but substantial amounts of sesquiterpine hydrocarbons. The hop analyst only measures the major hydrocarbons such as myrcene (a monoterpene), plus caryophylene, humulene and selinene (sesquiterpenes). These can contribute up to 60 per cent.

The complexity of hop oil is demonstrated in the table, and the Fuggles data

Table 9   Percentage of aromatic oils
(Wye College, Kent)

Hops 1985	Myrcene	Humulene	Caryophylene	Farnecene	Selinene
Goldings	18.4	52.0	15.8	0.0	2.0
Challenger	24.7	35.2	11.6	1.2	12.9
Northdown	18.5	50.8	16.4	1.0	1.8
Saaz	41.8	41.8	10.9	23.4	2.5
Fuggles 1.	1.4	45.1	11.4	4.0	2.2
2.	10.4	43.1	12.2	5.4	1.6
3.	27.8	39.4	12.0	6.2	0.9

further demonstrates how this complexity is compounded within the same year's crop. Myrcene is the least wanted fraction of the hydrocarbons due to its solvent-like taste and aroma. Its presence varies considerably from variety to variety, and it is usually more evident in high α-acid hops. Brewer's Gold, for example, can have myrcene levels of up to 63 per cent, and the overall effect is astringent. Consequently, such hops are only added to the copper to bitter the brew, and the pungent volatile aromas are evaporated.

Humulene and caryophylene have rather more pleasant spruce-like aromas, resembling freshly sawn cedarwood, and they and their converted products such as geranoil and linalool produce the seductive floral perfume that pervades the aroma of the brew.

Tannins

The tannins in beer come from the malt and hops, and are basically a class of chemicals called polyphenols. The hop tannins are extracted from the strig and petals during coppering, and they set up various reactions, some of which are desirable and others that are not. The main benefit derived from the tannins is their ability to react with wort proteins to form insoluble colloids that precipitate as trub during coppering and cooling.

HOP VARIETIES

English hops have a long and proud history, and they are exported all over the world. Hop research is carried out at the world-renowned Wye College, at Wye, Ashford, in Kent. It is quite fitting, of course, that the research college should be by Ashford, as this was where the first hop gardens were grown in 1520. Many new enticing varieties have been propagated at Wye College, and such is the esteem of English hops that at least 30 per cent of the world's crop has English hops in their ancestry. In 1659, Samuel Hartklib wrote: 'It is now known that Hopps of England are the best in the world.' After nearly 350 years that statement still holds good today!

Admiral

A new 'alpha' variety with high bittering potential to rival Target.

Brambling Cross

A hop that was crossbred from a Golding hop at Brambling, just outside Canterbury, in 1885. It is an early ripening hop with good flavour and aroma characteristics that blends well with other hops in the copper. A good aroma hop for the copper and cask.

Challenger

First introduced in 1971, this hop can fill many roles. Its rich but agreeable resin makes it a good all-round hop for ales and lagers. Its fragrant oils make it a good choice for late or dry hopping.

First Gold

A dual-purpose hop imparting a spicy fruity flavour in the copper. Its excellent aromatic qualities are ideal for late copper hopping and dry hopping in the cask.

The Fuggle

It was by pure chance that the Fuggle was introduced into brewing. Legend has it that the seed was thought to have been discarded with the crumbs from a hop picker's piece bag, and this simple act of hygiene was eventually responsible for a variety of hops that would dominate the market for the next 70 years or so. The hop was spotted growing wild by Richard

Fuggle in 1875, and he cultivated it so successfully that, at its peak, the Fuggle accounted for some 80 per cent of the total crop. Sadly, in the 1950s the acreage allocated to this fine hop declined due to the devastating effects of wilt and mildew and the introduction of new disease-resistant varieties.

Although in declining use, the Fuggle is still grown in England and the USA. Lord Aberdeen introduced the Fuggle into North America in the mid-nineteenth century, and although declining, it still commands a good acreage and has clearly faired well in the Pacific North West. The Fuggle has also been bred into Czech and Slovakian hops.

The Golding

The aristocrat, the Golding has stood the test of time. A Mr Golding cultivated the original variety in 1780, from a cutting he took from a Canterbury hop garden. There are many crossbreeds within the Golding family, and as these ripen at various times, picking can be staggered to suit the grower. Goldings posses a most elegant flavour and bouquet ideally suited for high class pale ales. Goldings also blend well with Fuggles in the copper, and despite being slowly ousted by new disease-resistant varieties, it is still in demand by brewers of traditional ales. Home brewers, too, should continue to make much use of this excellent hop.

Herald

A high alpha hop possessing good all-round flavour and bittering potential.

PHOENIX

An alpha copper hop with a very acceptable flavour and bitterness.

PIONEER

A good copper hop with a well balanced bitterness and typical British aroma.

Northdown

This hop was introduced in 1971, propagated from a seedling of Northern Brewer, a high resin disease-resistant copper hop that was first introduced in 1944. Northern Brewer was named to honour Younger's of Edinburgh, who conducted trials with the hop during World War II. It is no longer grown in Britain, but continues to be grown in Germany, Belgium and the United States. Its excellent characteristics have been bred into record hops and Yugoslavian super alphas. With this impressive heritage, it is no wonder that Northdown is an excellent all-round hop for pale ales, stouts and lagers. It keeps well in the deep freeze, and is a popular choice for hop extracts.

Progress

This hop was introduced in 1964, alongside a now-forgotten hop, Alliance, as a Fuggle replacement; it is related to Whitbread's Golding Variety. It is an excellent dual-purpose hop possessing a pleasing bitterness in the copper, and an enticing aroma.

Target

Since its introduction in 1975, Target quickly established itself as a grower's and accountant's favourite due to its consistently high resin content and pleasing aroma. It is resistant to wilt and powdery mildew, and it became the saviour to hop growers in the Weald and mid-Kent, who were badly hit with these diseases. Its all-round attributes make it suitable for ales, stouts and lagers.

Robert Burton proudly shows off his flower hops at the Caledonian Brewery, Edinburgh.

Whitbread's Golding Variety

Originally cultivated by E. A. White early in the nineteenth century, White's Golding never made an impression on the hop industry until the 1930s, when it was noted that it was more able to withstand the devastating effect of wilt than other hops. Abbreviated to WGV, its anti-wilt characteristics were bred into Progress hops and are well suited for traditional ales.

HOP MATERIALS

Although hop materials have been researched over the past 160 years, it is only in the last 35 years or so that they have come into regular use. Traditionally,

only leaf hops were used in the copper and cask, to impart that essential hoppy, nettle-like tang on the palate and the irresistible aroma. The decline in the use of leaf hops worldwide has come about as a result of demand from modern brewing plant, which is not designed to utilize whole hops. Also, hop products are not so bulky as leaf hops, and so take up less space during transportation, shipping and storage, and are cheaper to manage. Hop products are more economical as they do not deteriorate to the same degree during storage, and are more fully utilized during brewing. In the UK today, only about 15 per cent of leaf hops are used, the rest being processed into 70 per cent pellets, and 15 per cent extracts. The amounts of leaf hops, however, might well be on the rise due to the number of micro-breweries employing them, and the ever-increasing band of craft brewers who seem to prefer them.

Leaf Hops

Leaf hops are well known to the home brewer and are the main product used by the kitchen brewer. High quality leaf hops should have a good spring in their feel, and have a fresh, lustrous sheen. A degree of stickiness from the resins should also be evident, and the aroma should be spicy and fresh. Old hops, or badly stored hops, look lifeless, and the tacky feel of the resins is absent. The aroma might have a sweaty or cheesy odour, and this is caused by oxidation reactions with lipids.

The α-acids, too, are not stable in storage, and can deteriorate dramatically within a short space of time. Temperature and oxygen are the culprits and cause an irreversible conversion of the soft resin into the worthless hard resin. It is very important that we store our hops in the freezer or the refrigerator; under no circumstances should hops be stored at ambient temperatures. Even frozen, hops will still slowly deteriorate, and it is usually the high alpha acid varieties that are most susceptible. The home brewer should anticipate his brewing schedule and storage capacity, and only purchase enough hops to satisfy these criteria.

Leaf hops are excellent in assisting wort agitation, and benefit the disassociation of protein materials from the wort as trub, or break. They also provide a good filter bed and strain out the unwanted trub, which might otherwise cause clarity defects in the brew.

Pelleted Hops
Pelleted hops are produced from hop cones that have been re-dried to 6–7 per cent moisture, and deep frozen to reduce the viscosity of the resins, which prevents the glogging up of the mechanisms of the hammer mills that will pulverize them into a powder. The powder is now compressed through an extruder into 6mm cylindrical pellets, resembling rabbit droppings! These are now sealed in foil sachets, or multi-laminated polythene bags flushed out with CO_2 or nitrogen and vacuum packed to prevent oxygenation. Pellets may be a single hop variety, or a blend of varieties.

The practice of identifying pellets by a number originated in Germany. Type 90 is the most common product, and these should be added at the beginning of coppering to obtain the maximum utilization, which is about 10 per cent better than whole hops. Type 100 are similar, but re-drying is omitted before processing. Bentonite, or negatively charged clay, may be mixed into the pelletization process as a powder; this increases the surface area for isomerization, obtaining 20 per cent more utilization in the copper than leaf hops.

Enriched hop pellets are available in three forms. Type 33 is the most highly enriched type, and is made by pulverizing and sieving hops at −35°C to collect the resin-rich portions. This results in a highly concentrated product with double the α-acids and half the weight of whole hops. Type 45 is slightly less concentrated, and Type 75 is reduced a little more, but these are still superior to whole hops and standard pellets.

Stabilized pellets are prepared by adding about 2 per cent of calcium or magnesium hydroxide to the hop powder; this bonds with the α-acids and makes them more durable against oxidation. If the calcium or magnesium hydroxide and the α-acids are in the right molar ratio, they readily go into solution and isomerization occurs very efficiently.

Isomerized pellets are produced by heating stabilized pellets at 80°C for two hours to achieve the necessary molecular rearrangements of the α-acids. Isomerized pellets give greatly improved utilization of about 50 per cent over leaf hops or Type 90 pellets. They may be added at any time during coppering, and afford the brewer greater control of bitterness.

Hop Plugs
These are leaf hops compressed into blocks 100mm × 50mm × 25mm thick, weighing 113g. They are sealed in foil, and have excellent keeping properties.

Hop Extracts
Hop extracts were originally obtained by leaching out the resins with a variety of solvents. Initially they did not prove too popular with brewers, as the latter were not convinced that they conferred the true character of fresh hops. Brewers were also concerned about the possibility of having solvent residues in their beer. Today, ethyl

alcohol, steam distillation and liquefied CO_2 are the main materials used to leach out the extract.

The Russians were the first to successfully employ liquefied CO_2 in 1965. This is a highly efficient process, and shredded hops are saturated with the gas under high pressure at 70°C. The extracts produced are rich in alpha and beta acids, plus aromatic oil, and are virtually free from unwanted hard resin and foreign trace elements. Tannin-free extracts also enhance head retention. Such extracts are useful for home brewers with a copper of only limited capacity, where the extract can replace, or partially replace, cone hops. An isomerized extract is also produced, and these are added to the wort after coppering; they are excellent for post-fermentative treatments.

Hop Oils

These oils are extracted by modifying the process for extract production by applying the same pressure, but the temperature is raised to 20°C, when the oils are more readily leached out of the soft resins. Used with some care, hop oils are a good replacement for dry hops. Some extracts are available as

Robert Burton measures up to a hopsack.

named varieties. Hop oils and extracts are supplied with a recommended dosage, and this should be initially followed with further adjustments as required.

Table 10   Classification of British hops

Variety	α-acid %	β-acid %	Aroma
Admiral	13.5–16.2	4.8–6.0	Doubtful
Brambling Cross	6.0–7.8	2.2–2.8	Yes
First Gold	5.6–8.7	2.3–3.6	Yes
Fuggle	3.0–5.6	2.0–2.7	Yes
Goldings	4.4–6.7	1.9–2.8	Yes
Herald	11.0–13.0	4.8–5.5	Yes
Phoenix	12.0–15.0	3.3–5.3	Doubtful
Pioneer	8.0–10.0	3.5–4.0	No
Progress	6.0–7.5	2.0–2.7	Yes
WGV	5.4–7.7	2.0–3.3	Yes
Challenger	6.5–8.5	2.5–4.3	Yes
Northdown	6.8–9.6	3.3–6.2	Doubtful
Target	9.9–12.6	4.3–5.7	Yes

Table 11   Classification of rest of the world hops

Variety	α-acid %	Origin	Aroma
Hallertauer Hersbrucker	2.5–3.5	Germany	Yes
Tettnang	3.0–4.0	"	Yes
Perle	6.0–7.0	"	No
Hallertauer Mittlefruh	5.0–6.0	"	Yes
Brewer's Gold	5.0–6.0	"	No
Northern Brewer	7.8–8.0	"	Yes
Styrian Goldings	4.5–5.5	Slovenia	Yes
Saaz	2.5–3.5	Czech Republic	Yes
Pacific Gem	14.0–15.0	New Zealand	No
Pacific Hallertauer	4.5–5.5	"	Yes
Hallertauer Aroma	8.0–9.0	"	Yes
Hallertauer Organic	8.5–9.5	"	Yes
Green Bullet	12.5–15.0	"	No
Crystal	4.0–5.0	American	Yes
Liberty	3.5–4.5	"	Yes
Mount Hood	4.0–5.0	"	Yes
Willamette	4.5–5.5	"	Yes
Cascade	5.5–6.5	"	Yes
Galena	13.0–14.0	"	No

Depending on their characteristics, hops are classified as either 'alpha' hops or 'aroma' hops. Alpha hops are the high α-acid varieties that are usually, but not always, added to the copper solely for bitterness, and they are also referred to as 'copper' hops. Many types have a pleasing aroma and can, with caution, be employed throughout the brew as 'dual purpose' hops; Target hops, for example, are used as a single variety in Scottish pale ale, English bitter and lagers. Aroma hops are the low α-acid varieties, which can be used in the copper for bitterness, or late copper aroma hopping, or dry hopping in the cask.

CHAPTER 6

BREWING LIQUOR

Water districts.

THE SIGNIFICANCE OF WATER PROPERTIES

Water covers 70 per cent of the earth's surface, and it is estimated that every minute some 15 million tonnes of water evaporate from its surface. This precipitates as rain or snow forming rivers and lakes, sometimes held back by dams. Large amounts drain through the topsoil and eventually seep into the rock formations below to become absorbed, to a greater or lesser extent, in the underlying strata. This accumulation is known as the water table, which usually exists at a considerable depth below the land surface. The water table gives rise to a variety of water features, including natural springs, artesian wells and cisterns, as well as underground streams and galleries.

Historically, brewers have sunk wells into the water table to draw upon the purer supplies that have undergone considerable filtration as they percolate down through the layers of rock. Bore holes, too, often hundreds of metres deep, are used to tap the unadulterated mineral-rich supplies. Many of these ancient sources are still in use, but many have either dried up or become polluted with modern effluents and been abandoned. A large number of breweries, therefore, rely on the local domestic supply for all their brewing needs.

The Variability of Domestic Water Supplies

Scotland Mostly from lochs and reservoirs, plus a contribution from rivers. The water is very soft in the Highlands and West Coast. Edinburgh has the hardest water, with a maximum of 116mg/ltr of permanent hardness.

Wales A soft to moderately hard water supply coming mostly from reservoirs, plus rivers and bore holes. Lake Elan supplies Birmingham with soft water.

Northern Ireland Lochs and reservoirs. Soft to moderately hard water.

Table 12   Water hardness

Type of water	Mg/ltr as calcium	Mg/ltr as calcium carbonate
Soft	0–20	0–50
Moderately soft	20–40	50–100
Slightly hard	40–60	100–150
Moderately hard	60–80	150–200
Hard	80–120	200–300
Very hard	above 120	above 300

1mg/ltr = 1 Clarke°/English°

Eire   Dublin is supplied from reservoirs in the Wicklow Mountains. The water is soft, with only 50mg/ltr of total hardness, of which 20mg/ltr is carbonate hardness. Cork is supplied with soft water from the River Lee reservoir, containing about 70mg/ltr of permanent hardness, with some 43mg/ltr of carbonate hardness.

England
Northumberland   A soft to moderately hard supply coming mainly from reservoirs.
Yorkshire   A supply that varies from very soft, soft, to moderately hard, coming from reservoirs, rivers and bore holes.
North West   A fairly soft water drawn from rivers and reservoirs.
East Anglia   Equal supplies from rivers and reservoirs. It is mostly hard, but some areas of Lincolnshire are soft. Artesian wells supply Peterborough.
Severn Trent   A variable supply of soft to hard water from rivers and reservoirs.
Thames   Very hard water drawn from the Thames supplies London, with most other supplies coming from bore holes.
Southern   Mostly hard waters drawn from bore holes, rivers and reservoirs. Portsmouth is fed by springs from the South Downs.
Wessex   Hard water drawn from bore holes.
South West   A moderately hard supply drawn from rivers, reservoirs and bore holes.

Water Hardness
Historically, the hardness of water was judged on its ability to form soap solutions. Soft water, with its low saline content, foams profusely, whilst hard waters do not, due to complex reactions that destroy soap by the development of insoluble calcium and magnesium salts from the fatty acids. Hard waters are further classified as permanently hard, or temporarily hard, due to the solubility and stability of their salts on boiling. Total hardness is a measure of all the salts contributing to the permanent and temporary hardness. The dissolved solids will concentrate with drought and dilute with flood.

Surface supplies are mainly soft, whilst the water from bore holes is highly mineralized.

Hard waters contain all manner of salts producing many characteristics, ranging from clean hoppy flavours in pale ales, to harsh clinging flavours in lagers. Depending on the ratio of the salts present, the developments of flavours are at best enhanced, and at worst disguised.

THE EVAPORATE MINERALS

The important minerals in brewing are calcium, magnesium, potassium, sulphates, chlorides, bicarbonates and nitrates; these are termed 'evaporate minerals', as they

55

Table 13   The evaporate minerals

decreasing ← solubility → increasing	Potassium chloride (KCl) and Magnesium chloride ($MgCl_2$) Halite, common salt (NaCl)
	Gypsum. Hydrated calcium sulphate ($CaSO_4\ 2H_2O$) and anhydrous calcium sulphate ($CaSO_4$)
	Calcite, limestone, Calcium carbonate ($CaCO_3$) Dolomite, Calcium magnesium carbonate ($CaMg(CO_3)_2$)

(left margin: decreasing ← solubility → increasing; right margin: first → precipitation ← later)

were formed by precipitation in ancient lakes and seas, which slowly evaporated over millions of years. The rate of precipitation depends on the solubility of the mineral, and this causes them to deposit in layers. The beds of the minerals can be hundreds of metres deep, and might lie at considerable depth below the surface. Good examples of this remarkable type of formation are the mineral beds at Burton-on-Trent and the Great Chalk Basin below London.

Calcium

Calcium is a most beneficial mineral in brewing. In the mash tun it reacts with phosphates (phytin, inositol hexaphosphate) liberated during malting by the enzyme phytase. These phosphates, plus proteins, form a balanced range of primary dihydrogen phosphate, secondary and partially soluble, monohydrogen phosphate and insoluble tertiary phosphate. When calcium is in excess the tertiary phosphate is precipitated thereby upsetting the previous equilibrium and causing a change to bring the system back to a new equilibrium. This compensatory movement to the right involves the generation of hydrogen ions as they dissociate from the phosphoric acid to form firstly, dihyrogen phosphate, then monohydrogen phosphate and finally, the phosphate anion. The increase in the number of hydrogen ions increases mash acidity, which is beneficial for the hydrolytic enzymes.

Calcium also restricts the leaching out of astringent polyphenols and abrasive silica from the malt husks during sparging, and precipitates oxalate ($C_2O_4^{2-}$) or beer stone, as insoluble micro-crystals of

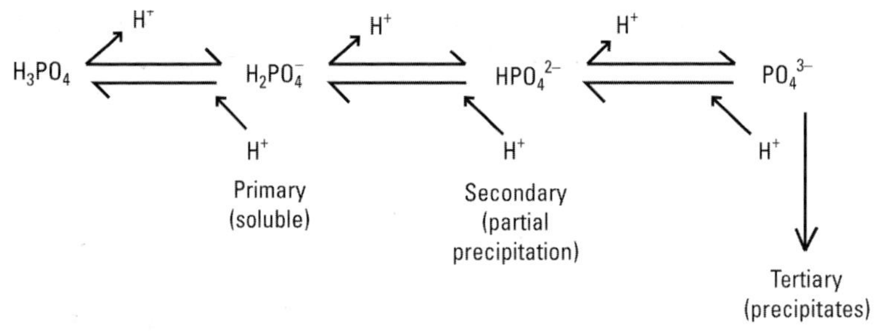

$$H_3PO_4 \underset{H^+}{\overset{H^+}{\rightleftharpoons}} H_2PO_4^- \underset{H^+}{\overset{H^+}{\rightleftharpoons}} HPO_4^{2-} \underset{H^+}{\overset{H^+}{\rightleftharpoons}} PO_4^{3-}$$

Primary (soluble)

Secondary (partial precipitation)

Tertiary (precipitates)

The mash tun phosphate reactions.

calcium oxalate, which can cause haze or gushing. The latter is caused by the micro-crystals forming nucleation sites that will spring the CO_2 causing the beer to foam or gush uncontrollably. There is little evidence, however, that gushing is a problem experienced by microbrewers or craft brewers.

During coppering, calcium continues to precipitate secondary and tertiary phosphates and so the buffering effect of the wort is reduced. Consequently, the acidity drops to about pH 5.0, which denatures β-globulin and other proteins, but only partially denatures albumin. The low pH encourages the formation of trub, which will precipitate after coppering is completed and so the beer will eventually fall bright.

The formation of melanoidins is restricted and so the colour of the beer remains pale. Calcium enhances yeast flocculation, and although it is not a requirement for yeast growth, it stimulates fermentation. Calcium restricts the isomerization of the α-acids and so an excess of bitterness is limited, allowing the use of high α-acid varieties without incurring any harshness of flavour. Comrie described gypsum-rich liquors as 'hop wasters', as more hops were required to bitter the brew.

When calcium is linked to sulphate it forms gypsum. The dual effects of this salt are the previously discussed reactions, plus the influence of the sulphate ion, with its subtle dryish bitter nuance, which influences the more-ish palate of pale ales. If calcium is linked to chloride, we still obtain the above benefits, besides which the full 'sweet' effect of the chloride ion brings out a mellow and most agreeable flavour, particularly in dark beers.

Calcium linked to bicarbonate is undesirable and should be reduced to at least 57mg/ltr for pale ales. Bicarbonates are problematic salts as they counteract all the benefits produced by calcium. In natural alkaline waters carbonate preferentially links to calcium and forms chalk (calcium carbonate), which is the least soluble. Thereafter it links to magnesium, which is partially soluble, and finally it forms sodium carbonate, which is highly soluble. Bicarbonates react as in the illustration below.

The acidity and temperature of the goods in the mash tun together drive off the carbon dioxide generated, and water vapour is lost. This alters the equilibrium and causes a compensatory shift to the left (as opposed to the right in the phosphate reactions) to restore a new equilibrium. As this shift is taking place, hydrogen ions are consumed, and hydroxyl ions are formed, and this causes a reduction in mash acidity by raising the pH: in other words, the mash becomes alkaline. Consequently, the higher pH restricts the proteolytic and amolytic enzymes, and counteracts all the benefits we would normally obtain with calcium. The brew will also have a lower-than-expected gravity.

During sparging, alkaline liquors encourage the leaching-out of harsh polyphenols and silica. During coppering, polyphenols

$$H_2O + CO_2 \rightleftharpoons H_2CO_3 \underset{H^+}{\overset{H^+}{\rightleftharpoons}} HCO_3^- \underset{H^+}{\overset{H^+}{\rightleftharpoons}} CO_3^{2-}$$

The mash tun alkaline reactions.

57

have a bad effect on beer colour, particularly lagers, by introducing rosy/amber tints. As coppering progresses, the pH of the bitter wort continues to rise, and this is counter to the ideal conditions for the denaturing of protein and the essential formation of trub. Apart from problems of clarity, the wort will contain excessive amounts of nitrogen, which encourages the growth of bacteria and will lack the necessary acidity to suppress such microbes.

Sodium carbonate is extremely soluble and does not influence the precipitation of phosphates in any way and is, therefore, a most troublesome salt. It will keep the pH high, with the consequential detrimental effects on enzyme performance. If it is present in large amounts, there are usually unwelcome ratios of sodium chloride and sodium sulphate. This type of liquor is definitely not wanted for brewing pale ales, and is only tolerated, to a degree, in stouts.

Magnesium

Magnesium is important as a trace element essential for yeast growth; it also acts as a co-factor for various enzymes, and it is considered to be more important in light gravity beers. During mashing, magnesium does not have as significant an effect as calcium in lowering the pH, as its secondary and tertiary phosphates are more soluble than calcium tertiary phosphate and so remain in solution longer. Should it be present in large amounts, it actually restricts the precipitation of calcium tertiary phosphate and so amounts should be kept low.

During coppering, however, magnesium readily precipitates, and together with calcium phosphates, lowers the pH dramatically. It also has a sour/bitter-like flavour that can be detected at 15mg/ltr. Brewing liquors, however, can tolerate twice as

much as this without ill effects, as the astringency is suppressed by calcium. When magnesium links to sulphate it forms Epsom salts, and these compliment calcium sulphate in brewing pale ales. Lager brewers do not like too much magnesium sulphate in their liquor, as it is difficult to remove due to its solubility. When magnesium joins with carbonate, the salt is much more soluble than calcium carbonate, and some 140mg/ltr can remain after boiling. To reduce this to less troublesome levels an excess of calcium is required, which will effect a double decomposition and precipitate it.

Chlorides

Chlorides are appreciated as they act as flavour enhancers; the benefits of calcium chloride have already been discussed. Sodium chloride (common salt) also adds palate fullness. It has, however, a somewhat sour/salty taste and so amounts should be kept between 75–140mg/ltr, the higher range being more acceptable in sweet stouts.

Potassium

Potassium shares chemical properties with sodium and is typically linked to chloride. It does not have the brackish taste of sodium chloride and is sometimes substituted for it. Levels in brewing liquor should be kept to below 10mg/ltr, as higher levels can adversely affect the performance of yeast.

Heavy Metals

Water supplies also contain a variety of heavy metals, such as lead and cadmium, that can be harmful to health, and water authorities keep these under strict review. Beer drinkers, however, are better protected, because such metals bind to the spent grains in the mash tun, plus trub and yeast in the FV.

WATER TREATMENTS

The aim of water treatments is to adjust the mineral composition if necessary to produce a quality of wort for individual styles of beer with the highest degree of excellence. Brewers with a soft water supply are in the best position, as treatments simply consist of making additions of salts to obtain the optimum acidic reactions and agreeable flavours. Southby set out the parameters of individual salts for different beer styles during the latter half of the nineteenth century, and these remain largely unaltered today.

The table shows what these guidelines are, and we can see that a fair degree of latitude exists within the parameters of brewing the salt recommended for each style of beer. The mid-point in brackets is a good starting point, and each salt should be accurately weighed; individual adjustments can be made, and brewers with very soft water may bias towards the higher value and those with harder water bias towards the lower value.

The table gives the weight of each salt in 32ltr. It also makes sense if we prepare the quantities for several brews because we will achieve a more regular balance from brew to brew; in this case, multiply the weights in the table by the number of brews. Now add the quantity from 'weight to add' from the table. For example, if we multiply the weights in the second column by twenty brews, we end up with a total weight of 391g, but we only add 19.5g per brew. As the parameters are fairly wide, we can round off the weights as necessary without upsetting the overall balance of the brew. For other volumes, divide by 32 × the new volume.

The Influence of Minerals on Flavour

The flavour of English pale ales is enhanced with a sulphate/chloride ratio

Table 14   The salt parameters for beer styles (mid-point in brackets)

1. Salts, mg/ltr	2. Pale ale and bitter 1,045–55	3. Pale ale and bitter 1,035–45	4. Mild and brown 1,035–55	5. Stouts and porter 1,040–55
$CaSO_4$ $2H_2O$	543 (443) 343	343 (271) 200	143 (107) 71	Nil
$MgSO_4$ $7H_2O$	114 (85) 57	114 (85) 57	57 (57) 57	57 (57) 57
$CaCl_2$	57 (42) 28	28 (28) 28	114 (85) 57	171 (142) 114
NaCl	57 (42) 28	57 (42) 28	114 (85) 57	200 (157) 114

Table 15   Weight of salts to add to 32ltr of soft water

1. Salts in grams, per 32ltr	2. Pale ale and bitter 1,045–55	3. Pale ale and bitter 1,035–45	4. Mild and brown 1,035–55	5. Stouts and porter 1,040–55
$CaSO_4$ $27H_2O$	14.176	8.672	3.424	Nil
$MgSO_4$ $7H_2O$	2.720	2.720	1.824	1.824
$CaCl_2$	1.344	0.896	2.720	4.544
NaCl	1.344	1.344	2.720	5.024
Weight to add	19.584	13.632	10.688	11.392

of 2:1, and fuller sweeter Scottish pale ales benefit from a ratio of 3:2. The mellow and luscious flavour of mild is enhanced when the ratio is about 2:3, and the fullness of stouts is secured with a ratio of 1:3.

It is important to note, however, that it is not so much the flavour of the individual salts that matters, but rather the overall balance of salts and how they enhance the quality of wort. The flavour effect of brewing salts added to plain water will be barely perceptible, but during brewing the influence on the palate of the brew can be quite noticeable. It is not so much the taste of the salts themselves that can be detected, but rather how they accentuate or suppress flavours extracted from the brewing materials by influencing good flavours, and rounding off, or masking, poorer flavours.

For example, a mild ale containing crystal or roasted malts and treated with the salts in column 4 of Table 15 (*Weight of salts to add to 32ltr*) will have a predominately smooth and mellow flavour, as the chlorides coax out the luscious flavour from such malts. In this case the flavour of the brew comes through in a most satisfying way. If the same brew were brewed with the salts in column 2 of the table, the palate is less smooth and agreeable with more hop bitterness, which dulls the overall rich and smooth flavour.

Pale ale brewed with the salts in columns 1 or 2 in Table 14 will have a predominately clean and refreshing flavour with a pleasant bitter edge from the hops. In comparison, the same beer treated with mild ale or stout salts loses its fresh, sparkling and refreshing flavour, and might taste brackish.

It is important, therefore, that a beer contains the appropriate salts for the style. A beer that contains inappropriate salts will struggle to obtain the essential degree of excellence, although it will still be a decent pint. However, if the salts are appropriate to the type of beer, and providing all other parts are equal, the quality of palate will be excellent, and will call for the comment, 'Now that really is a good pint!'

Calcium Bicarbonate Liquor

Such liquors are usually buffered to pH 7.2 to 7.5. In most cases, all that will be necessary is a slight reduction of the bicarbonates, to allow the acidifying calcium phosphate reactions to excerpt a stronger influence and lower the pH of the mash. However, it is not necessary to remove the bicarbonates completely, as residual amounts of 40–50mg/ltr are desirable for palate fullness, and for accentuating the pleasant bitter edge on the palate in pale ales. A number of methods can be used for reducing bicarbonates, and the home brewer should adopt one with which he feels competent.

Boiling

In the majority of cases, the home brewer will best secure the desirable reduction of bicarbonates by the time-honoured process of boiling. Bicarbonate starts to decompose at 70°C, and a full *one hour*'s boiling is necessary to ensure that the soluble bicarbonates (HCO_3) fully dissociate into carbonate and CO_2, which vents to the atmosphere. The carbonate then links up with any calcium or magnesium present, to form insoluble calcium/magnesium carbonates that precipitate. Once the liquor cools, the precipitate settles out and the softer liquor is carefully racked off and treated.

In most cases, the calcium bicarbonates will be reduced to about 50–60mg/ltr.

Magnesium bicarbonate is more soluble, and as much as 140mg/ltr can remain in solution. Sodium carbonate is highly soluble, and boiling has little effect on it.

A more efficient reaction takes place if there is an excess of calcium in the water, and this should be linked to sulphate for pale ales, or to chloride for dark beers and stouts. Additional calcium affects a double decomposition so that the bicarbonates remaining in solution can be as little as 35–44mg/ltr. The chemical reactions occurring can be shown using the solubility product constant (ksp). This is the equilibrium constant for the solubility of an ionic compound, which is only slightly soluble. Let us consider calcium sulphate.

[ ] = Concentration.

ksp = $[Ca^{2+}]$ $[SO_4^{2-}]$ is a fixed constant at a given temperature.

Adding more Ca^{2+} increases the concentration of calcium ions, $[Ca^{2+}]$. The solubility constant is now displaced, so $[SO_4^{2-}]$ must decrease by precipitation of calcium sulphate:

i.e. $Ca^{2+}_{(aq)} + So_4^{2-}_{(2q)} \rightarrow CaSO_{4\,(s)}$

The reduction of the sulphate ion causes the excess calcium ions to set up an equilibrium with the carbonates in the solution:

$CO_3^{2-}_{(aq)} + Ca^{2+}_{(2q)} \leftrightarrow CaCO_{3\,(s)}$

The solubility product constant is now:
ksp = $[Ca^{2+}]$ $[CO_3^{2-}]$ = constant.

Therefore, to reduce $[CO_3^{2-}]$ add a soluble calcium salt which increases $[Ca^{2+}]$, so to maintain ksp $[CO_3^{2-}]$ must decrease.

i.e. $Ca^{2+}_{(aq)} + CO_3^{2-}_{(aq)} \rightarrow CaCO_{3\,(s)}$.

The table has been composed from the principles laid down by Comrie, which states that we need to add calcium so that the quantity is at least twice the equivalent of the bicarbonates present. An hour's boiling reduces the liquor to 32ltr.

Treatments are additions of calcium sulphate and/or calcium chloride, as the case might be, to achieve the desirable pH and flavour profile, and these should be added *before* the boiling. After boiling and cooling, the liquor is racked. Ideally, we want to produce a liquor with a pH of about 7.5–7.2, and it might also be necessary to adjust to this value with some lactic acid after boiling. The heating element also makes the process more efficient by attracting the precipitating calcium bicarbonates. Should you fire up your copper with propane gas, then throw in an old spoon that will serve the same purpose.

Overall, boiling the liquor is best for most brewers. At the current competitive costs of electricity (2006), this works out at 9p per kW/hour. Thus a 3kW element boiling for 1 hour will only cost you 27p!

Boiling also removes chlorine that is present in domestic supplies to suppress bacteria. Chlorine in excess of 0.5mg/ltr can react with chemical materials from malt and hops, and possibly organic matter that has leached into the municipal supply, to produce deleterious medicinal TCP-like flavours. All the brewing liquor should be boiled for at least 15min to reduce chlorine. Such deaeration also restricts the formation of deleterious oxidative reactions with lipids, polyphenols and melanoidins in the mash.

Lime Treatment (Calcium Hydroxide, Ca(OH$_2$))

Adding lime to chalky water changes calcium bicarbonate into hydrogen carbonate, and magnesium bicarbonate into hydroxide; thereafter the insoluble carbonates precipitate. However, due to the solubility and ratio of the ions the reactions are never complete, and we can

Table 16 The reduction of calcium bi-carbonate in 34ltr volumes

(For other volumes divide by 34 × new volume)

Hardness as CaCO₃	Pale ale and bitter		Mild and brown ale		Stout and porter
Mg/ltr	CaSO₄ 2H₂O	CaCl₂	CaSO₄ 2H₂O	CaCl₂	CaCl₂
100	7.6	2.62	4.3	4.7	7.5
150	11.5	3.9	6.4	7.1	11.2
200	15.2	5.2	8.6	9.5	15.0
250	19.1	6.5	10.8	11.0	18.8
300	23.0	7.8	13.0	14.2	22.5
350	26.8	9.1	15.1	16.6	26.3
400	30.5	10.4	17.2	19.0	30.1

expect to retain 50–60mg/ltr. The amount of lime to be added will vary according to the composition of the water. In the majority of water analysis sheets – certainly in my experience – the alkalinity and temporary hardness figures are usually the same. From this we can calculate the amount of lime to be added. It is also important to prepare the full brewing volume.

It takes 0.4588mg/ltr of calcium hydroxide ($Ca(OH)_2$) to neutralize 1g/ltr of bicarbonate. We can also use the following formula:

$$\frac{mg/ltr}{CaHCO_3} \times \frac{molar\ mass}{(0.74)\ of\ Ca(OH)_2}$$
$$\frac{}{1000}$$

e.g. $\dfrac{250mg/ltr\ of\ Ca(HCO_3)_2 \times 0.74}{1000}$

= add 0.185mg/ltr of lime ($Ca(OH)_2$)

If we have added an excess of lime, there is a risk that the pH will remain too high due to the hydroxyl ions produced. To check if the exercise has been successful, a pH reading below 8 should be achieved, preferably pH 7.5. Further treatment with lactic acid might be necessary to

achieve this, and bring the mash pH closer to the optimum of 5.3.

If the water contains appreciable amounts of soluble magnesium hydrogen carbonate, then extra lime is required to react with it. Also, if the water contains sodium hydrogen carbonate, then some calcium chloride will also be necessary to precipitate it. Without knowledge of chemistry, most of us have to rely on trial and error.

The correct amount of lime is now roused into the water, and it will immediately take on a milky appearance as the chemical reactions take place. Ideally we want to leave the water alone for at least twelve to twenty-four hours to give the calcium bicarbonates time to dissociate and precipitate. All such reactions are more efficient if they have a site to react upon, and sand will provide thousands of acres for this purpose. A sand filter can be made from a small plastic bucket with its base riddled with 2mm holes and filled with sand.

The soft treated liquor is now passed through the sand filter where any uncompleted reactions will be speeded up, and traces of the flocculent precipitate carried over will also be filtered out. Just like the boiling method, the reactions are also enhanced if the water contains an excess of calcium and we can use the amounts listed in Table 16 (The reduction of calcium bi-carbonate in 34ltr volumes). To ensure a satisfactory reaction, the salt should be added *before* the lime.

The treated liquor should now be tested to judge the success of the process. If the pH is still high, say over 7.5, then it should be further treated with lactic acid to reduce it to 7.5. If the alkalinity cannot be brought down below pH 8, then it is not suitable for brewing. Add the lactic acid, drop by drop, to one litre of the liquor until the desired pH is obtained, and then multiply this figure by the number of litres to be treated. Further treatments of calcium sulphate and chloride should ensure a satisfactory mash tun acidity, sound fermentation and agreeable flavours.

Dilution

The idea of using rainwater to dilute hard water is not new, but not everyone agrees that we should use it due to the 'acid rain' theory. However, much investigation has revealed that rainwater is suitable, and many countries around the world collect it for drinking and brewing. Due to the absorption of acidic carbon dioxide, natural rainwater has an acidity of about pH 6.5 to 5.6.

By definition, 50 per cent rainwater will dilute the temporary and permanent hardness by 50 per cent, and so additions of calcium/lactic acid should be considered to achieve the correct pH. Should rainwater be used on its own, then it is advisable to use the full water treatment recommended for ales and stouts in Table 14 (Salt parameters for beer styles) on p. 59. For lager brewing, adjustments to pH are made with calcium for Dortmunder's and lactic acid for Pilsners.

Nitrates

EU health standards set upper limits of 50mg dm^{-3} nitrate (NO_3) for drinking water, although in some parts of England river supplies have contained as much as 100mg dm^{-3}; water authorities reduce this by blending with low nitrate supplies. Nitrates also increase wort colour and are reduced to toxic nitrite acid by yeast. Such self-inflicted wounds poison the cell, making it oviform, mutagenic and prone to weakness. The toxicity is also elevated in the presence of chloride ions in excess of 285mg/ltr. Weak fermentations with poor attenuation are most common, plus an increase in the formation of diacetyl, and such yeasts are not harvested for repitching. Nitrate ions can also be reduced to nitrite by the bacteria *Obesumbacteria proteus*, and these in turn can react with wort amines to form nitrosamines that are carcinogenic.

Swamping

Due to the difficulties with lime treatments, many brewers simply swamp the bicarbonates with calcium (Ca^{2+}) ions. This works extremely well with a moderate bicarbonate content as long as the amounts of other salts are also low.

0.250mg/ltr of calcium is required to neutralize 1g/ltr of calcium bicarbonate; for example, if the water analysis shows 135mg/ltr of temporary hardness as $CaCO_3$, we add $135 \times 0.250 = 33.75mg$ of Ca. The calcium may be linked to sulphate or chloride as the case might be. Alternatively, we may add the appropriate weights of calcium sulphate and chloride, as the case might be, from Table 16 on p. 62: note the effects on pH, and adjust future amounts to suit.

Should the water contain large amounts of soluble sodium carbonate this will be problematical. Should we attempt to neutralize it with calcium sulphate, we end up with sodium sulphate, which is undesirable. If we add calcium chloride, the water

Table 17   An aid to water treatments

Salt. One gram will add		Mg/ltr	Imperial gallon	American gallon
Gypsum	Ca	232mg	51mg	61mg
	SO_4	186mg	41mg	49mg
(Anhydrous salt)	Ca	294mg	64mg	77mg
	SO_4	266mg	58mg	70mg
Epsom salts	Mg	100mg	22mg	26mg
	SO_4	133mg	29mg	35mg
(Anhydrous salt)	Ca	200mg	44mg	52mg
	SO_4	266mg	58mg	70mg
Calcium chloride	Ca	272mg	60mg	71mg
	Cl_2	483mg	106mg	127mg
(Anhydrous salt)	Ca	360mg	79mg	95mg
	Cl_2	639mg	140mg	169mg
Sodium chloride	Na	393mg	86mg	103mg
	Cl	606mg	133mg	160mg
Potassium chloride	K	523mg	115mg	139mg
	CL	476mg	104mg	125mg
Calcium carbonate	Ca	400mg	88mg	105mg
	CO_3	600mg	132mg	158mg

will be brackish due to too much sodium chloride being produced. Such scenarios, however, are quite rare. Table 17 above shows the quantities that we are adding to the water.

Acidification

The practice of using acids to counterbalance the adverse effects of bicarbonates should bring the pH into the range necessary for successful hydrolysis, but it does not soften the liquor. Sulphuric acid (H_2SO_4) is very effective, but it is also very corrosive and does demand respect. It converts the bicarbonates into an equal amount of sulphates and so it finds most favour in pale ales, unless the water already supports large amounts of this ion. It does not form buffers, however, and the danger is that we might overshoot the target pH. This will result in an excess of hydrogen ions that will have a detrimental effect on hydrolysis and sparging.

It takes 6.2ml of 1 Molar of H_2SO_4 to neutralize one gram of bicarbonate, and it is best to do a trial run with a litre of the water first and then calculate for the whole brew. As the reactions are taking place the liquor will gas quite a bit due to the release of CO_2: for example, 0.250mg/l $HCO_3 \times 6.2$ = 1.55ml of H_2SO_4. Unless you feel confident about this method, it is best avoided.

Hydrochloric acid (2HCl) may also be used. It converts calcium bicarbonate into calcium chloride and so it might be better for dark beers and stouts. 12.4ml of 1 Molar of HCl will cancel out one gram of bicarbonate: for example, 250mg/ltr $HCO_3 \times 12.4$ = 3.1ml of HCl.

Phosphoric acid (H_2PO_4) is suitable because the phosphates produced are also the same as those extracted from the grist, and react favourably with calcium during mashing. It produces buffer salts and so over-acidification of the mash is unlikely. Lactic acid is also an effective treatment, and is the commonest acid used by home brewers. It converts calcium bicarbonates into calcium and magnesium lactates, which are harmless. It, too, forms buffers, and even if we should add excess, there is little risk of over-acidification. Lactic acid produces a soft palate in lightly hopped beers, and is particularly good for Czech-style lager treatments.

In Table 18, the amounts of 75 per cent phosphoric acid added to 32ltr of liquor will reduce the alkalinity in mg/ltr: for example, if the alkalinity is 212mg/ltr and we need to reduce this to 50mg/ltr, we add 9.4ml of phosphoric acid. The procedure for 80 per cent lactic acid is exactly the same. For other volumes, divide by thirty-two and multiply by the new volume.

Brupaks Carbonate Reducing Solution (CRS)

CRS is an acid blend that offers a straight-forward approach to liquor treatment, as is demonstrated in Table 19. This is exactly the same as Table 18: that is, if we require to reduce the alkalinity by 128mg/ltr, we add 0.70ml/ltr of CRS. For 31ltr add 21.7ml of CRS. The liquor should now stand for 15min to allow the release of the CO_2 produced by the acid reaction.

As can be seen in the table, the dried liquor salts (DLS) are required to adjust the calcium content, and hence the mash pH. The calcium content of the liquor can be approximated by multiplying the alkalinity by 0.4. For example, if the alkalinity level is 274mg/ltr, we have $274/0.4 = 109$mg/ltr already in the liquor. Should we decide to brew a pale ale, then the typical calcium level is about 200mg/ltr and so we require $200–109 = 91$mg/ltr of calcium. Going by the table we add 0.5g/ltr of DLS. It is important to note that DLS is a two-stage treatment:

Stage 1: The DLS are added to the *grist*, and it is apportioned as follows. The total brewing liquor is 32ltr. Mash liquor 12ltr $\times 0.5 = 6$g added to the grist.

Table 18   Using acids to reduce alkalinity

Acid	1.9	3.8	5.6	7.5	9.4	11.7	13.3	15.0	17.0	19.0
Alk.	−32	−65	−97	−130	−162	−194	−227	−259	−291	−324

75% Phosphoric acid

Acid	1.9	3.8	5.6	7.4	9.4	11.7	13.3	15.0	17.0	19.0
Alk.	−16	−31	−47	−63	−78	−94	−110	−125	−141	−156
Acid	20	35	38	41	45	47	50	53	56	59
Alk.	−172	−188	−203	−219	−237	−250	−266	−282	−297	−313

−80% Lactic acid

(Courtesy of Murphy & son, Nottingham)

Table 19   Dried liquor salts to adjust the calcium content

CRS	0.35	0.52	0.70	0.87	1.05	1.22	1.40	1.57	1.75		
Alk.	−64	−96	−128	−160	−192	−224	−256	−288	−320		

CRS

DLS	0.1	0.2	0.3	0.4	0.5	0.6	0.7	0.8	0.9	1.0	1.1
Ca	16	31	47	63	94	109	125	141	156	172	188

DLS in gm/ltr

(Courtesy of Brupaks)

Getting ready to brew.

Stage 2: Sparge liquor = 20ltr × 0.5 = 10g added to the wort in the copper at the beginning of the boil.

Table 20   Average pH readings in the brewing schedule

Untreated domestic supply	pH 6.0–8.0
After liquor treatments	pH 6.0–8.0
Initial mash acidity	pH 5.2–5.5
First sweet worts	pH 4.8–5.2
Second sweet worts	pH 5.4–5.6
Initial copper wort	pH 5.1–5.4
Post coppering	pH 4.9–5.3
Beer, post fermentation	pH 3.7–4.2

Acid malt may form part of the grist and be used either on its own, or in conjunction with other treatments. In moderately hard waters amounts should be about 5 per cent, but in water supporting large amounts of bicarbonates, this might be as high as 10 per cent. The lay brewer has to appreciate that there are no hard and fast rules when treating water for brewing, and that all treatments are empirical.

CHAPTER 7

PREPARATION OF THE GRIST

Before we move on to preparing the grist for mashing, we should understand how the ingredients are calculated to produce the laboratory values, and the values obtained in the brewhouse. This knowledge will enable us to formulate grist and calculate the gravity and volume of the brew so that the total volume of sweet wort recovered will safely occupy the capacity of the copper and cask.

THE HOT WATER EXTRACT (HWE)

This is an analysis of the carbohydrate obtained by mashing a quantity of malt under laboratory conditions. The unit of measurement used in the UK is litre degrees per kilogram (ltr°/kg, or LDK). This is calculated by the number of litres that it takes to dilute the extract from one kilogram of malt to a gravity of 1001, at 20°C.

The process of the experimental mash is quite unlike the brewhouse mash as only distilled water is used and the mash is very fluid. The grain is crushed to a specific size and the goods are held at a specific temperature for a strict period of time. During mashing, the grains are regularly agitated, and when saccharification is complete, no sparging of the goods take place. The extract from adjuncts is calculated by adding a percentage to the goods, and the known extract from the malt content is subtracted; the resultant extract remaining is determined as coming from the cereal.

Briggs *et al* (1982) report a laboratory extract for pale malt at 296 LDK, and a typical brewhouse extraction rate of 287 LDK, making the mashing efficiency 97 per cent. Today, the laboratory figures for the HWE vary, and pale malt is now quoted at 304–307 LDK. A commercial brewery mashing efficiency rate of 287 LDK against an average laboratory extract of 305 LDK works out at 94 per cent, and this falls roughly in line with the losses depicted in Table 21. A home brew extraction rate of 275 LDK/305 LDK = 90 per cent.

Mashing efficiency will vary from brewery to brewery, but the following chart shows the typical losses in a traditional brew at an OG of 1045 containing 15 per cent sugar. Craft brewers will also experience most of these losses, but such losses are usually exaggerated.

Wort losses are also inevitable in the kitchen brewhouse, and these will depend on the number of vessels used, their geometry and size, and the number of times the brew is racked. Wort losses do not affect the extract-to-volume ratio, unless water is added to make good the loss. If you are going to make up a wort loss to a given volume,

Table 21   Typical brewing losses expected in a traditional brewery

Extract loss	% of mash tun extract	% of total extract
Difference between HWE and brewhouse extract	2.5	2.1
Incomplete mash tun conversion	1.0	0.8
Extract retained by spent grains	1.3	1.1
Extract retained by hops		2.4
Adhesion of extract to brewing plant		1.0
Total loss of extract		7.4
Extract recovered by the hop sparge		1.75
Total net loss of extract		5.65

then do so with a wort replacement syrup and/or wort extender to the same ratio.

Evaporation Loss

The loss of liquor during coppering will be about 9ltr in 90min, but the rate of evaporation will vary with the gravity of the brew and the ebullition of the wort, which is dependent on the wattage of the heating element. The evaporation rate should, therefore, be based on experience.

As the wort cools the evaporation loss is about 5 per cent, resulting in a change of volume of the brew by around 4 per cent from the end of coppering to the pitching temperature of 15–16°C. This reduces the volume, but increases the gravity, and we can restore the loss with cold liquor to adjust the original volume and gravity if necessary.

THE GRIST

Let us say we decide to brew 25ltr of pale ale with an OG of 40 (1,040). This will produce 25 × 40 = a target gravity of 1,000ltr° of extract, and we calculate the *relative percentage contribution of extract* (not the weight) of the grist materials to this figure. The grist is to consist of 75 per cent pale malt; 5 per cent crystal malt; 10 per cent wheat malt, and 10 per cent sugar. The mashing efficiency is 90 per cent of the laboratory LDK, and this is equal to 'home brew degrees' (HB°). The sugar contribution is 100 per cent:

e.g. $\dfrac{\text{Target gravity in ltr}° \times \text{\% contribution of extract}}{\text{Laboratory LDK} \times \text{\% of mashing efficiency}}$

= weight of grist in HB°

Calculated weight	*Working weight*

Pale malt $= \dfrac{1000 \times 0.75}{306 \times 0.90}$ 2.730kg

$= \dfrac{750}{275*}$

$= 2.7272722\text{kg}$

Crystal malt $= \dfrac{1000 \times 0.05}{275 \times 0.90}$ 0.200kg

$= \dfrac{50}{247*}$

$= 0.2024291\text{kg}$

Wheat malt $= \dfrac{1000 \times 0.10}{315 \times 0.90}$ 0.353kg

$= \dfrac{100}{283*}$

$= 0.3533568\text{kg}$

Calculated weight

Working weight

$$\text{Demerara} = \frac{1000 \times 0.10}{365} \qquad 0.274\text{kg}$$

$$= \frac{100}{365\,*}$$

$$= 0.2739726\text{kg}$$

* 'home brew degrees'

We were expecting an OG of 40, but let us say that we only achieved an OG of 36. As the Demerara will produce 100 per cent of LDK, the losses must have occurred in the mash tun and we now have to re-evaluate in order to adjust the gravity back to 1040. In order to do this we now calculate the potential extract from the grist by multiplying its weight by HB°:

e.g.	The brew	The mash tun
Pale malt		
$= 2.730\text{kg} \times 275° = 750.750$		750.750
Crystal malt		
$= 0.202\text{kg} \times 247° = 49.400$		49.400
Wheat malt		
$= 0.353\text{kg} \times 283° = 99.899$		99.899
Demerara		
$= 0.274\text{kg} \times 365° = 100.010$		
	1000°	900°

By removing the Demerara we deplete 4° of extract, i.e. $0.274\text{g} \times 365/25\text{ltr} = 4°$. This drops the OG to 32° so that the actual mashing efficiency $= 32° \times 25\text{ltr} = 800\text{ltr}°$.

The mashing efficiency therefore:

$$= \frac{\text{actual extract}}{\text{potential extract}} \quad \frac{800°}{900°} = 88\%$$

Once we add the sugar we arrive back to an OG of 36. An OG of 36 divided by a target OG of 40 = a total extract recovery of 90 per cent. To raise the gravity to 1040 and

achieve 100 per cent, we add 4° of dried malt extract: e.g. $4° \times 25\text{ltr}/375 = 0.266\text{g}$. To maintain the gravity in the next brew we add pale malt, i.e. $4° \times 25\text{ltr}/275 = 0.363\text{kg}$.

Once we have established the mashing efficiency the original formula can be modified and we work in 'home brew' degrees (HB°):

e.g.

$$\frac{\text{Target gravity}}{\text{in ltr°}} \times \frac{\% \text{ contribution}}{\text{of extract}}$$
$$\overline{\text{home brew degrees}}$$

i.e.

$$\text{Pale malt} = \frac{1000 \times 0.75}{275 \text{ HB°}}$$

$$= 2.7232727 = 2.730\text{kg}$$

It is also safe to assume that the percentage extract obtained for pale malt will be the same for all cereals.

Volume and Gravity

Volume and gravity should also be considered, and these, along with the total grist/liquor ratios, should be within the volume of the copper. If we take it that the maximum mashing and sparging liquor recommended is 7.0–7.5ltr/kg (6.5–7brl/qrt), we can work out in advance if the copper is capable of holding the total volume of wort, which should not be more than can be evaporated within 90–120min. Also, it is desirable that the copper should have some spare capacity for ebullition safety:

Copper capacity = Volume × OG/LDK
  × 7.5ltr + ebullition factor

If we decide to brew 25ltr of pale ale with an OG of 1040, we end up with the following: $25 \times 40/275$ LDK $\times 7.5\text{ltr} = 27\text{ltr} + 2\text{ltr}$ for ebullition = 29ltr.

I use a 45ltr Burco catering boiler, which offers more scope because 25ltr brews with gravities up to 1050 (4.6kg of grist × 7.5ltr = 34ltr) can be brewed. Strong ales with gravities above 1050 present us with even greater problems with grist/liquor ratios, but these can be overcome as follows: we are going to brew 25ltr of all malt ale at OG 1075, producing a total extract of 1875ltr°. 1875ltr°/275 LDK = 6.818kg. 6.818kg × 7.5ltr = 51ltr. This would require about 4 hours coppering to reduce the volume to 25ltr.

To keep the grist/liquor ratio within the capacity of the copper, we re-evaluate to reduce the contribution from the grist to 65 per cent, and make good the loss with 35 per cent malt extract.

$$\text{Malt} = \frac{1875\text{ltr}° \times 0.65}{275} = 4.432\text{kg}$$

$$\text{Malt extract} = \frac{1875\text{ltr}° \times 0.35}{303} = 2.166\text{kg}$$

i.e. Malt   4.432 × 275   = 1218.8°
     Extract   2.166 × 303   = 656.3°
     Total extract   1875ltr°/25ltr = OG 75

We could also employ a quantity of wort extender to augment the malt and malt extract and in this case we are going to use 25 per cent malt extract and 10 per cent Golden Syrup.

$$\text{e.g. Extract} = \frac{1875\text{ltr}° \times 0.25}{303} = 1.547\text{kg}$$

$$1.547 \times 303 = 468.7\text{ltr}°$$

$$\text{Syrup} = \frac{1875\text{ltr}° \times 0.10}{320} = 0.586\text{kg}$$

$$0.586 \times 320 = 187.5\text{ltr}°$$

Total = malt   1218.80ltr°
     extract   468.70ltr°
     syrup   187.50ltr°
            1875ltr°

1875/25ltr° = 75

In general, strong beers will incur slightly more wort than is desirable, and so high gravity beers usually require a longer coppering to reduce it. In most cases the excess of wort to be evaporated will only be a few litres, and we can conduct a short 30min boiling before adding the copper hops. Due to the high surface tension of wort it is wise to add a handful of hops at the beginning to help overcome excessive foaming. The extra time of coppering is unlikely to seriously deplete the essential FAN in the high malt content.

Another approach is to increase the grist to ensure that we obtain the desired gravity, but at the same time limit the sparging so that the total wort collected is not greater than can be evaporated within a 2-hour coppering. This method is best approached on a trial and error basis, and the following example, using a 30ltr boiler, sets out the general idea.

The brew consists of 20ltr of all malt at OG 80, which equates to 1600ltr° of extract. 1600ltr°/275 LDK = 5.818kg of malt. To recover all the extract we would end up with 5.818 × 7.5 = 43ltr of wort, requiring four hours coppering to reduce it to 20ltr. Therefore, to ensure that we hit the target gravity, the quantity of malt is increased by 25 per cent (or more if necessary), to 7.272kg. This produces 2000ltr° of extract. At most, all we can expect to recover is 80 per cent of the extract, reducing the yield to 1600ltr°: 1600/20ltr° = OG 80.

In this case we mash at 2.2ltr/kg, and sparge slowly to collect at least 28ltr. Coppering for 2 hours reduces the volume to 20ltr, and we should achieve the target gravity. Failing that, some gravity adjustment with sterile water to dilute the gravity, or dried malt extract to increase it, might be necessary. Adjust the grist as necessary in the next brew.

There should also be 400ltr° of extract remaining in the goods, and this can be sparged on to one kilogram of malt extract and 255g of sugar. Dilute to 25ltr, add twenty IBUs of hops, and copper for one hour; this will produce 20ltr of beer at OG 1039, or 25ltr at 1031.

Do not forget that whilst the initial calculations on paper are fine, most important are the results obtained in the brewhouse.

Retorrification

If the temperature differential between the grist and the strike liquor is small, we will obtain the desired 'initial mash heat' without too much difficulty and will also reduce the thermal stress on the malt enzymes. If the grist is at ambient temperature, the disparity might be as high as 15°C, but if we heat the grist to around 25–30°C, it will be as little as 5°C. To do this, warm the oven to 50–100°C, add the grist to two large roasting trays, and put it in the oven. When the desired grist temperature is reached, start mashing.

CALCULATING THE INITIAL MASH HEAT

For a more accurate approach to come within a whisker of the desired initial mash heat, we may use the following formula:

$$I = \frac{(S \times Tg) + (M \times T) + Sc}{M + S}$$

I = The initial mash heat required
S = The specific heat of the grist
Tg = The temperature of the grist in °C
M = The mash thickness in hectolitres per 100kg of grist
T = The temperature of the strike heat
Sc = The slaking heat correction

Table 22   The Slaking heat correction

% Moisture	Specific heat	Slaking heat correction
0	0.38	3°C
1	0.38	2.8°C
2	0.39	2.3°C
3	0.40	1.8°C
4	0.40	1.5°C
6	0.41	1.3°C
8	0.42	1°C

Heating grist in the oven.

71

The slaking heat correction is based on the moisture level of the grist. Without the means to determine this, it has to be guessed at, and we can assume it will be about 2 per cent. For example, we are going to mash a grist with a moisture level of 2 per cent and a temperature of 30°C. The strike heat is 70°C, and the grist/liquor ratio is 2.4 hectolitres per 100kg of grist (2.4ltr/kg):

$$I = \frac{(0.39 \times 30) + (2.4 \times 70) + 2.3}{2.4 + 0.39} = 65°C$$

However, the formula does not take into account the heat loss during mixing the mash.

Charles Clinch introduced hot grist mashing in the 1890s, and the grist heat was brought up close to the initial heat. Apart from reducing the thermal trauma on the enzymes by the strike liquor, the other reputed advantages were enhanced flavour and aroma, plus vigorous amolytic activity, brilliant wort, palate fullness and improved head retention.

CHAPTER 8

THE PRODUCTION OF SWEET WORT

Sweet wort is produced in the mash tun, and the aim of mashing is to produce balanced wort containing a variety of sugars, with various degrees of fermentability, that will satisfy a range of beer styles.

THE HYDROLYSIS OF STARCH

To re-cap, the brewer receives the malt with the protein structure of the foodstore partially demolished by the proteases; β-glucan has also been reduced by β-glucanase. The debranching enzymes have begun to chop up the complex structure of amylopectin. Such thermolabile enzymes are now dead, having been destroyed during kilning. The amylases have been deactivated, but not destroyed, by the kiln heat. The brewer now creates the best environment for the reactivation of the amylases so that the starches are further reduced to produce balanced wort.

Alpha Amylase

This amylase starts to cleave the one to four glycosidic bonds of amylose and amylopectin in a random manner, and breaks of branches of ten to fourteen glucose groups, some shorter chains of five to eight groups, plus some maltose and glucose. The larger groups are the maltodextrins, and these are only 60–20 per cent fermentable, but are further reduced by the activity of β-amylase. α-amylase does not sever the terminal one to four linkages, and cannot break the one to six linkages of amylopectin. After this assault the branched faction remaining is the α-limit dextrin.

Whilst α-amylase has the rapid starch liquefying capacity necessary to yield maximum extract, it saccharifies dextrins very slowly when compared to the action of β-amylase, which has more influence in governing the fermentability of the wort.

Beta-amylase

This amylase readily attacks the one to four linkages at the reducing ends of the chains of amylose, plus the chain ends exposed by the action of α-amylase. Whilst β-amylase can reduce amylose to maltose, plus some maltotriose, it cannot sever the one to six linkages of amylopectin or the one to four linkages immediately beside them. When acting on amylopectin, β-amylase can only deal with the outermost chain ends of the branches, chopping away maltose units. In isolation, this activity would produce about 50 per cent of maltose, and the unclipped faction remaining is the β-limit dextrin.

Table 23 An analysis of wort sugars

Carbohydrate faction	Sugars	% yield
Monosaccharides	Glucose and fructose	8–10
Disaccharides	Maltose	41.1
	Sucrose	5.5
Trisaccharide	Maltotriose	14.0
Oligosaccharides	Maltotetraose	6.1
	Dextrins	22.2

β-amylase also strikes at the shorter-branched chains cleaved off by α-amylase, so that maltotetraose (four units) is cut into two groups of maltose; maltopentraose (five units) is severed into maltose and maltotriose. Maltohexose (six units) is divided into two groups of maltotriose or three groups of maltose, and so on.

When α-amylase and β-amylase are acting in concert, as they do in the mash tun, α-amylase further degrades the amylopectin and as soon as a short side chain is exposed, it is immediately attacked by β-amylase and split into maltose groups. Since α-amylase cannot break the one to six linkages, there comes a point when there are no short chain ends for β-amylase to chop into maltose. The residual faction of molecules still connected by the one to six linkages is resistant to further degradation, and since they cannot be utilized by brewer's yeast, they remain in the wort as *stable dextrins*. When this complex activity is completed in a 60–90min mash, the wort will have approximately the sugars shown in the table.

MASH CONDITIONS

A number of factors can be controlled and altered to some degree, to influence the quality of wort. These cannot be separated in the mash tun, but for elucidation we will look at each one separately; they are: grist-to-liquor ratios; the mash temperature and time; and pH.

Grist/Liquor Ratios

The proportions of grist to the volume of liquor has a noticeable effect on the balance of sugars produced during mashing. In fluid mashes, for example, the malt starches and proteins are thinned out and so the enzymes have more room to manoeuvre without being restricted by the materials present, or inhibited by the proximity of the hydrolyzed by-products of the reactions that they are catalysing. A consequence of this is that their hydrolytic activity is increased, but unfortunately, so too is their rate of thermal inactivation. The mash acidity is also reduced a little in a dilute mash, but in practice this has little effect on enzyme performance and saccharification.

Saccharification is more rapid in dilute mashes that also favour the production of maltose-rich worts and hence fermentability is enhanced, although fusel oils also tend to increase. A fluid mash also reduces the viscosity of the goods and so running of worts is faster during sparging, with less deleterious mash material being extracted during the latter stages. In general, dilute mashes are more common in decoction mashing, and this encourages proteolysis desirable in high nitrogen malts.

In a thick mash the speed of saccharification is restricted due to the by-products of hydrolysis inhibiting the mash reactions. A thick mash encourages dextrin-rich wort and also affords a degree of thermal protection for the enzymes; α-amylase, in particular, has been known to survive until coppering.

The figures in the table are representative of the values used in traditional

Table 24   Typical grist/liquor ratios
Based on 6½–7 barrels per quarter (7–7.5 LDK) (Ebullition safety 2ltr)

The brew			Mashing 275 LDK*			Sparging*		30ltr copper capacity*		
Style	Vol.	OG	Grist wgt	Volume	C°	Volume inltr	C°	Max. liquor	Max. wort	Min. cap
Light ale	25ltr	1036	3.3kg	2.4ltr/kg	64.5	5.1ltr/kg	75.5	7.5ltr/kg	24.75ltr	27ltr
Mild ale	25ltr	1038	3.5kg	2.4ltr/kg	64.0	5.1ltr/kg	75.5	7.5ltr/kg	26.25ltr/kg	28ltr
Pale ale	25ltr	1040	3.7kg	2.7ltr/kg	66.6	4.8ltr/kg	75.5	7.5ltr/kg	27.75ltr/kg	30ltr
Pale ale	21ltr	1050	3.8kg	2.2ltr/kg	67.0	5.3ltr/kg	75.5	7.5ltr/kg	28.5ltr	30ltr
Stout	23ltr	1045	3.8kg	2.4ltr/kg	63.5	5.1ltr/kg	76.6	7.5ltr/kg	28.0ltr	30ltr

brewing, based on 7–7.5ltr/kg (6.5–7 barrels/quarter). The grist and original gravities are based on 275 LDK, and these reflect the mash and sparge ratios, which also reflect on the volume of the copper required. To maintain the original target gravity with extract rates lower than 275 LDK, or with 25ltr brews above 1045, it will be necessary to increase the grists to take account of the loss of extract retained in the goods due to the limited sparging to keep the total wort within the volume of the copper.

Controlling Temperature and Time
By controlling the temperature of the mash and the time that it is allowed to stand, we are in a position to regulate, to some degree, the composition of the wort sugars and the extent of attenuation. All of this is brought about by controlling the temperature of the mash in favour of α-amylase or β-amylase.

α-amylase activity is greatest at 64–68°C, whilst the activity of β-amylase is reduced at this temperature, and so by biasing the temperature towards the higher value, a more dextrin-rich wort will be produced. β-amylase is more efficient at 60–65°C, and so by keeping the mash heat on the low side, we obtain a greater maltose-to-dextrin ratio. As maltose is more fermentable than dextrin, a degree of control can be exercised, to produce worts suitable for different styles of beer.

Table 24 shows the mash heats that traditional brewers aimed for. Initially the beginner might find these a little tricky, but with experience and accurate control of the strike liquor and grist temperatures, these can be achieved resulting in a good balance of sugars.

The higher mash temperatures are employed when brewing keeping beers of high gravity so that a larger amount of slowly fermenting maltotriose sugars are available for slow conditioning, plus the stable dextrins that add to palate fullness and character. Lower heats are employed for beers intended for regular consumption so that ample maltose is secured for quick conditioning. Low mash heats are also a requirement when mashing with mild ale malts and roast malts, as their diastatic power is not as great as ale malts, and such heats are necessary to secure equally fermentable worts.

This practice will produce a dryish beer requiring artificial sweetening to produce the characteristic sweetness and fullness expected in mild ale. However, much better results are achieved if the process is reversed. Use pale malt and mash at 68°C to acquire a more natural sweetness. Medium-strength beers are usually mashed at 66°C, to produce a ratio of stable dextrin of about 25 per cent.

The Power of Hydrogen (pH)

Acidity and alkalinity are measured on a pH scale ranging from 1, acidity, to 14, alkalinity, with 7 representing neutrality. Essentially, the scale measures the concentration of the hydrogen ion:

that is

$$[H^+] = 1 \times 10^{-1}$$

$$pH = -Log_{10} [1^1]$$

$$pH = 1$$

Buffers

Buffers are materials or substances that resist changes in pH when limited amounts of H^+ ions (acids) or OH^- hydroxide ions (alkalis) are added to the solution. In brewing, these are mainly phosphates and proteins, plus bicarbonates in the liquor. In this case the buffer acts like a reservoir, absorbing H^+ ions

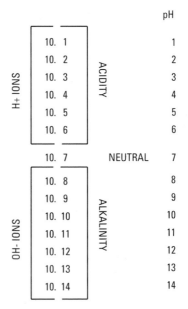

The pH scale.

from the solution when their concentration rises, and releasing them when it falls, thereby maintaining equilibrium.

For example, if we were to add acids to adjust the pH of the mash, the phosphates, proteins and carbonates, should they be present, will absorb many of the H^+ ions so that the pH will only fall slightly. Likewise, should we add calcium hydrogen carbonate, H^+ ions are released to stabilize the system and we do not experience a rapid rise in the pH. However, should we add an excess of either, the buffers are quickly exhausted and the pH of the solution will rise or fall dramatically simply because it is no longer controlled.

Throughout the brewing process, there is a continual increase in acidity from water treatment, mashing, coppering and fermentation. Of all the various criteria involved in brewing, control of the pH is the most difficult area. To attempt to regulate the pH to suit one set of reactions invariably upsets another set, and as it is not possible to satisfy them all, a compromise pH has to be found. The mash pH will alter with temperature, mash thickness and time of mashing due to the continued production of inorganic phosphates and protein degradation products. The nature of the grist will also have an influence on mash pH.

In infusion mashing, the greatest efficiency is achieved at pH 5.2 to 5.4, with the most fermentable wort being secured at pH 5.3 to 5.4. α-amylase has an infusion mash pH optima of 5.3 to 5.7, whilst β-amylase works best at 5.1 to 5.3. The compromise pH is accepted as 5.3, and this value satisfies a whole range of conditions such as good mash reactions, and efficient sparging and running of worts, without leaching out deleterious materials from the grist. Bright clear worts are obtained without any phenol bitterness, but with pleasant spiciness and floral notes. In a well balanced grist, the extract recovery for the craft brewer should be about 275 LDK (27.5Imp. gallon°/lb).

Liquor Treatments
Liquor treatments such as the dilution of bicarbonates and/or the addition of calcium should be efficient to bring the pH closer to the desirable 5.3. As previously stated, the mash pH will alter with temperature and time, and this is due to a larger dissociation of the acid buffering materials present. Such is the complexity of pH, and because 5.3 is our goal, craft brewers are advised to aim for a pH range of 5 to 5.5. This sensible parameter will be found most satisfactory and can be checked using narrow-range pH indicator papers.

It is not desirable, in my view, for craft brewers to attempt to alter the mash pH after it has been mixed. It is extremely unlikely that the acidity will be so high (low pH) as to warrant such drastic treatment as adding chalk to counteract it. In any case, do not forget that chalk is twice as effective at raising the pH as gypsum is at lowering it, and to start dabbling about with teaspoonfuls of chalk will most likely result in the pH going haywire!

Similarly, if liquor treatments have been correctly carried out, there should be no need to acidify the mash with gypsum or lactic acid, and the use of organic acids is quite likely to overcome the buffering power of the goods, with the danger that the pH will drop below 5. Should this happen, the goods will become very difficult to sparge because for every 0.1 of a unit that the pH falls below 5, the time of sparging can increase by as much as 10–20 per cent. This phenomenon is caused by the relationship between pH and viscosity, and should the pH drop to 4.7 or below, the mash will become impossible to filter.

We should also consider that the amylases are highly active during the first twenty minutes or so, and by the time we take to get it about right, the saccharification of the goods will have been completed. It is interesting to note that many brewers are not too concerned about the pH of the mash, considering it too unreliable, and prefer to adjust the pH of the wort in the copper with gypsum or lactic acid.

However, should you find that, for some reason, the pH is widely out, let's say at pH 6 (it is unlikely to be over-acidified), then you should just carry on as normal, but add 0.1mg/lg of calcium sulphate, or chloride, to the wort during coppering and this will effect an extra precipitation of the secondary and tertiary phosphates. This should bring the pH nearer to the desirable 4.2 to 3.7 after fermentation. Thereafter an investigation should be carried out to ascertain why the pH parameters were exceeded in the first place. The grist and mashing schedule, plus water treatment, should be looked at, though in most cases the fault will lie with the liquor, and alkaline waters in particular might require more treatment to ensure a greater dilution of bicarbonates.

The craft brewer's practice of adding salts to the mash tun and copper are, however, fraught with difficulty, and the reason that commercial brewers can do it simply relates to the scale of their operations. When dealing with our small plant, the difficulty of accurately weighing minuscule amounts of salts becomes problematical. That is why it is best to calculate water treatments for several brews, as the amounts are more accurately weighed and a better balance is achieved from brew to brew.

The hot liquor tank.

Preparation of the Liquor
Ideally we should treat the liquor as necessary the day before we brew to allow the salts to fully dissolve. Prior to mashing, a 15min boiling will eliminate chlorine and de-aerate the liquor sufficiently to avoid oxidizing the polyphenols, lipids and melanoidins in the mash. The liquor is now allowed to cool to the strike heat.

Infusion Mashing
Infusion mashing is designed to hydrolyze the starch of fully modified and friable malts (plus up to 20 per cent adjuncts if required) that do not require further proteolysis in the mash tun, and this is achieved with a single temperature rest. The thick, porridge-like infusion mash affords considerable thermal protection for the amylases, and α-amylase, in particular, can survive at 70°C for over two hours. Such thermal protection is also, in part, a result of keeping the temperature differential between the grist and strike liquor to a minimum, as the thermal shock on the enzymes is reduced. The mashing temperature slowly destroys the amylases, and so it is important that the desired initial temperature of the goods is maintained as closely as possible to obtain the correct sugar ratio.

Mixing the Mash
Mixing the mash should be done thoroughly and with care to avoid the grist forming dough, particularly with brewing flours, as this dough will not be acted on by the amylases, resulting in a loss of extract and possibly starch haze in the brew. Also, and equally important, the mash should not be excessively stirred because of the risk of separating fine grist particles and starch that will form sludge and clog up the underlet.

Mixing the mash with the hand-held mash-mixer.

Insulated mash tuns require to be preheated with about 10ltr of liquor at 80°C. This should be left for about 30min to warm up the vessel, or until the temperature drops to 70°C. The liquor can be taken from the total brewing volume, and should be retained to be added to the sparging liquor. As the mash tun is warming up, the mashing liquor is brought to strike heat. Next, add 2ltr to the tun and stir in, in small amounts, up to 1kg of grist. Repeat the process until all the grain is mixed, but retain a litre of liquor.

To ensure that the mash is well mixed, use either the edge of the mixing spoon and frisk it to and fro, keeping it below the surface at all times to minimize oxygenation of the goods and heat loss, or

the mash mixer attached to a cordless drill.

Mash Temperature

After all the grist is mixed, check the temperature of the goods to see if the initial heat has been achieved. If it is too low, use the reserve liquor to bring it back to the required value. Should the initial still be too low, then draw off some wort in a saucepan, bring it to 66°C and then mix it in. Do this as often as is required to achieve the correct initial.

Should the temperature be correct, add the reserve liquor when it cools closer to the initial. It is unlikely that the temperature of the goods will be so high as to require cooling, but if your calculations are widely out, then scoop-stir the mash, bringing up the hot wort from the bottom of the tun to produce rapid cooling. All of the foregoing ensures that we do not upset the grist/liquor ratios.

When employing a mash tun with a heating element *in situ*, the liquor can be brought up to strike heat in the vessel. When the correct heat is reached, stir in the grist in stages. Do this thoroughly by push-stirring the dry grist into the liquor, or use the mash mixer. When large amounts of grain are used, the grist is more difficult to mix in the latter stages due to the air trapped in the husk particles. Whilst a vigorous stirring might mix the grist well, do be careful not to lose too much heat, create oxygenation, or drive out too much air from the goods, causing it to lose its buoyancy and compact on to the mash screen.

Overall the mash heat is best adjusted by drawing off a quantity of liquor from the tap, heating it to near boiling, and mixing it into the goods. If the heating element is below the mash screen, another approach is to set the thermostat too high, and this will heat the reservoir of wort

Mixing the mash with the mash-mixer and cordless drill.

below it. By continually drawing off some wort and returning it to the goods, we can increase the temperature.

This idea can also be used to help mix in large amounts of grist. I also find a hand-held spray-sparger ideal for wetting the grist in the latter stages, which is beneficial when mixing large amounts of grist. Also, check the pH of the goods and note any changes for future use. After the grist is mixed, ensure that the temperature of the goods is maintained for the duration of the mash.

The Iodine Test

By testing a sample of wort and noting its colour reaction, we can tell how well hydrolysis is proceeding. Immediately after mixing the mash and stabilizing the initial, a sample of wort will produce an intense blue-black colour as it reacts with pure starch that still exists as long, complex, unbroken glycosidic chains. As the mash starts to liberate amylose, however, the colour becomes more of an indigo blue. Amylopectin and its immediate derivatives

Checking the mash initial.

react to produce crimson to violet colours, but this is not much in evidence initially as it is concealed by the colour produced by the amylose reactions.

As hydrolysis proceeds and amylose is reduced to less complex molecules, the colour of the wort becomes increasingly faintly crimson, until eventually it fails to react with the iodine at all. This is the *starch end point*, and it indicates that the mash has saccharified and that the starch and higher dextrins have been reduced to the desirable smaller groups.

The goods will inevitably retain residual starch in the hard ends of the kernels, plus traces of β-glucan in the husk, and this will continue to produce a positive reaction long after saccharification is complete. A wort sample will therefore give us a better indication of how well hydrolysis is proceeding – although it should not be assumed from a negative test that mashing is complete, and it should continue until the desired sugar ratio is obtained.

SPARGING THE GOODS

The first worts drawn off from the mash will contain some 40 per cent of the extract, with very high gravities of about 75°. The object of sparging is to wash out the remaining saccharine matter retained by the grains, and the manner in which this is carried out has a profound influence on the quality of the worts.

It is important immediately prior to sparging that the sweet wort is recycled until it runs relatively clear; this activity filters out trub and reduces the amount of hot break in the copper. The lipid content is also minimized, and head retention is improved.

Phil's sparging arms are available in 17.8cm (7in), 21.6cm (8.5in) and 25cm (10in). These are most efficient, with a circular mash tun, and the height should

be adjusted so that the spray just falls to the periphery of the goods. In rectangular mash tuns the water cannot spray the narrow sides of the mash tun and at the same time reach the ends of the vessel. Consequently we have an area of 'dead' mash, and poor extract recovery. Should the sparger be raised sufficiently to allow the spray to reach the ends of the vessel, then it stands to reason that much liquor will be hitting the sides of the tun and running down without washing out the extract. With rectangular mash tuns, a hand-held sparger is advised.

A closed vessel will keep the temperature of the goods at about 75°C or so, inhibiting further enzyme activity.

The Quality of the Sparging Liquor

The quality of the liquor is very important, particularly its degree of alkalinity. Too high a proportion of bicarbonates, for example, coupled to the dilution of the mash buffering materials (phosphates and nitrogenous matter), will see the mash pH rise by 0.2–0.7 units to 5.5 to 6.

The higher pH extracts more high molecular proteinaceous matter, phosphates, β-globulin, polyphenols, silicates and undigested starch: should this happen, pale beers will risk poor flavours and haze. Stout grist is more robust, as the roast grains in the grist will check to some degree the rise in pH. It is a good idea to check the pH of the wort regularly, so that should it start to rise to an unacceptable level, emergency corrective action can be taken by adding some lactic or phosphoric acids to the liquor. Many brewers acidify their sparging liquor to pH 5.7 to counteract any rise in pH. A high pH also runs the risk of poor fermentations and infection by wort-spoiling bacteria.

The viscosity of the goods can be a problem, particularly with high gravity brews

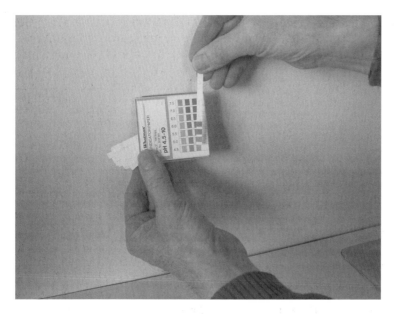

Checking the mash pH.

and stouts, or a mash pH that falls below 5, or rises above 5.5. In such circumstances, the sparging is seen to be proceeding as normal, but the runnings collected at the tap will be severely diluted in extract and colour. What is happening in this case, is that the liquor is disappearing below the surface of the goods, but it is hitting the viscous mass and is immediately directed to the side of the tun where it runs free to the copper. When brewing high gravity beers, or stouts, therefore, it is not a bad idea to check the gravity and colour of the wort periodically, so that corrective treatment can be taken. In practice, this means stirring up the goods and/or raising the temperature of the mash by a couple of degrees to dilute the viscosity. In severe cases, hot liquor might need to be added to slacken the viscosity.

The Volume of the Sparging Liquor

The volume of the sparging liquor should be just sufficient to wash out the maximum amount of sugars from the goods, thereby avoiding extracting too much of the harmful grist products. A popular home-brew practice is to employ a sparging volume equal to the volume of the brew, but this method is best avoided, as more harmful materials will be washed out in a 3kg grist than a 4.5kg grist. I always prepare 32ltr of liquor for regular 25ltr brews, but limit the total liquor to 7.5ltr/kg. Sparge until the gravity of the last runnings from the mash tun falls to 1005 for light ales and lagers, and between 1005–3 for pale ales and stouts. For brews above 1044 (4kg grist), calculate the liquor as necessary.

If the gravity of the last runnings falls to 1005 or below, and all the liquor has not been used up, then add it to the copper to increase the volume to 32ltr. If this is the case and the gravity of the brew is on target, then the sparging has been very successful. If the gravity of the last runnings is not below 1005 and all the liquor has been used up, the sparging efficiency has not been achieved. This is more usual with strong brews, or grists containing large amounts of viscous-coloured malts and/or flaked barley. In this example, make good the loss with some wort-replacement syrup, or wort extender. Wort extenders should not make up more than 15 per cent of the total extract. Now recalculate the grist for your next brew.

Overall, a thick mash will contain less liquor, and so we have more left out of our total brewing volume to successfully sparge the goods. A fluid mash uses more liquor, but as they drain very efficiently, we do not require the same sparging volume to extract the sugars.

The Temperature of the Sparging Liquor

The temperature of the liquor also has an influence on sparging, and liquor heats of 75°–77°C are typically employed. Higher temperatures should be avoided to reduce the risk of leaching out polyphenols, residual starch, dextrins and proteins retained in the hard ends of the kernels. As the proteolytic and amolytic enzymes have been severely weakened or destroyed during mashing or by the sparging temperature, they cannot act on starch and protein that might be washed out, and so they remain in the wort, causing poor flavours and haze.

An iodine test taken at the same time as the pH reading should continue to be negative with, perhaps, a hint of pink in the last runnings. A trace of blue or mauve indicates that starch and, possibly, β-glucan is present, and so the sparging temperature and the temperature of the goods should be checked and reduced if necessary.

The Time Taken

The time it takes to sparge the goods is related to the nature and weight of the grist. Light ales, for example, will filter quite rapidly and are normally completed within 30 to 40min or so. Pale ale grists containing viscous-coloured malts will take longer, but should be completed within 40 to 50min. The more viscous stout grists and high gravity brews can take up to 60min to complete the sparging. Overall, a slow sparging is more efficient.

Methods of Sparging

There are four methods of sparging adopted by craft brewers. The simplest is to wash out the sugars with jugs of hot liquor. Historically, brewers double-mashed to leach out the sweetness from the grains; in practice we drain the mash completely and immediately refill the mash tun with liquor at 80°C. Maintain this heat for about 30min, and then drain into the copper. A third mash can also be considered, as long as the total wort collected is not more than can be evaporated in 90–120min. A hand-held spray attachment taken from an electric shower attached to the HLT with 300mm of head pressure works well.

Automatic revolving sparge arms were first introduced into brewing in the nineteenth century, but the first successful type only came on the craft-brewing scene in the 1990s! Phil's Sparger (Listermann of Cincinnati, USA) is an excellent device that automatically spins due to the jet reaction as the hot liquor passes through the perforations on the sparging arms. The fine spray also makes it a superb hop sparger.

To sparge the wort, first of all check that the liquor is at the right temperature and that the tap on the copper is closed. Now partially open the tap on the mash tun, and allow the sweet wort to trickle into the copper. Wait until the wort drains just below the surface of the goods, and then start sparging. Adjust the sparger

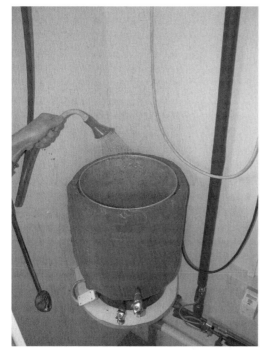

Sparging with a hand-held spray attachment.

Phil's sparger.

so that the flow just reaches the periphery of the tun. When jugging on the liquor, make sure that the whole surface area of the mash receives an equal amount (of liquor). When using a hand-held sparger, the spray should fall uniformly over the goods, and its flow should balance the flow of sweet wort leaving the tap (s); this helps keep the bed of grain buoyant and clear of, or just resting on, the false bottom of the mash tun, or other mash screens.

There are occasions during sparging when the flow of wort is greatly reduced, and this is usually caused by too much volume of fine grist particles clogging up the mash screen. This is not a problem that should be experienced very often; however, it might be caused by over-crushing the malt, or, more likely, by drawing off the first worts too quickly, sucking down

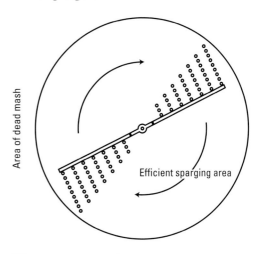

The correct sparging area.

the bed of grain on to the mash screen. Over-zealous mixing of the mash can also cause the fine matter to separate, sink to the bottom and clog up the filter. Should this occur, it could be rectified by partially flooding the mash tun to float the goods, and by gently stirring the grains to reduce its density. Now slowly open the tap and continue as before.

Should the flow of liquor exceed the running of wort, the goods will start to flood, and this is undesirable as much of the liquor will start to flow down the side of the tun. To correct this, we can either reduce the flow of liquor to match it, or should the tun be fitted with a second tap, this can be used to balance the flow. If, after the second tap is opened, the flow of wort is still too slow, with the goods still flooding, the problem lies with a set-mash situation as described above. The cure is exactly the same. Should the wort be running fast without any apparent problems, then don't worry about it, as long as the original gravity aimed for hits its target.

A problem that is often quoted in home brew literature is the cracking of the goods during sparging. Whilst this problem is discussed in the old brewing manuals, I see no reason why it should happen to small-scale craft brewers. The reason that it can happen in a traditional brewery is simply due to the sheer weight of the bed of grain floating just above the false bottom. The mash tun is also fitted with several taps, and these are opened slowly and in sequence to achieve a balanced flow; however, should one of these taps be opened more than the others, this will cause an area of low pressure, and the weight of the grain will sink at this area. This causes a crack, or fissure, across the bed of grain, and the liquor will take the least line of resistance and run down the fissure without extracting any saccharine matter. Consequently, a loss of extract occurs.

CHAPTER 9

THE PRODUCTION OF BITTER WORT

COPPERING

Sugar Ratios

It is essential that the balance of sugars established in the mash tun is stabilized and fixed as soon as possible to secure the characteristics of the brew. In the kitchen brewhouse this is achieved by switching the boiler on high as soon as the heating element is covered with wort, and at the same time adding the full quota of bittering hops. The hops will not sink into the wort until it is fully ebullient, and the bulk of them float on the surface, forming a floating lid; this conserves the heat and so the wort is brought to boiling point in the quickest possible time. A duvet will also help the copper retain its heat.

Maillard Reactions

When coppering is fully ebullient at about 102°C, the intricate amino-acid reducing sugar reactions that create the melanoidins take place. These materials are in part responsible for the increase in wort colour and brew flavour. Such products in their reduced state also act as reductones, preventing the worst of the damaging oxygen-related reactions from taking place; this helps stabilize the shelf life of the beer. Stouts in particular are rich in these materials and have, therefore, greater stability during storage. However, should these products become oxidized due to careless management before bottling or casking, they will oxidize the aromatic alcohols to aldehydes, producing stale flavours.

Trub Formation

The proteinaceous materials present in wort have advantages and disadvantages. On the one hand they are necessary for palate fullness, head retention and yeast nutrition, but on the other, they can cause cloudiness, as warm and cold haze, if concentrated too much. It is essential, then, that coppering is conducted in such a way that the nitrogenous content is reduced to prevent haze, but at the same time allows sufficient to remain to satisfy the advantage conditions. As the hydrolyzed products of hordien and glutelin are soluble, they will provide all the necessary yeast nutrition. Our main concern is the albumins and their peptones, plus β-globulin and the peptones of other globulins.

Albumin and its peptones are required for palate fullness and head retention, but β-globulin is a troublesome haze producer and so wort conditions should reflect the best environment to denature more of the β-globulins than the albumins.

Denaturation takes place when the heat of the wort causes the complex and compact structure of the protein to break its peptide links and unfold into a looser random coil. If this process were to continue, the protein would eventually be reduced to its constituent amino acids. Denatured proteins do not, however, immediately coagulate and precipitate, but remain in suspension as colloid particles until the wort conditions are right. This means that for the maximum amount of protein to be denatured and precipitated, the wort must be acidified to a pH that brings the protein to its iso-electric point and becomes electrically neutral. The iso-electric point of albumin is pH 5.9, and of β-globulin pH 4.9.

The required increase in wort acidity is provided by the continuing reactions between calcium and magnesium phosphates, which is mostly phytate. This induces the precipitation of secondary and tertiary phosphates with the consequential release of hydrogen ions into the wort, lowering the pH. By the end of coppering, the wort pH will be reduced by 0.1 to 0.2 and should be in the range of pH 4.9 to 5.3.

The pH is usually stabilized at this value due to the buffering effect of residual phosphate and carbonates, and at this range it is more advantageous for the iso-electric point of β-globulin, but much less favourable than of albumin. Consequently, more β-globulin is denatured and so the maximum amount of potential haze material is removed. The albumins and their peptones are less affected, and so remain to satisfy body and head retention.

The greater the wort acidity, the greater the degree of denaturation and eventual coagulation and precipitation. The precipitation of phosphates is greater in strong worts, and this can be checked by examining the amounts of trub deposited in the copper. The insoluble trub can also be easily seen in the wort immediately after the copper is switched off. Trub is a finely dispersed, grey-coloured flocculum up to 80 microns in diameter, and if coppering has been correctly carried out, it should rapidly co-precipitate with the hops.

It is easy to check this, and if the surface of pale ale and lager worts does not appear clean and black-looking (like a mirror) within 15min, then this might indicate incomplete removal of the carbonates that have restricted the mash reactions. This allows the pH to rise during sparging and, more importantly, delays the precipitation of phosphates in the copper. In general, lager worts will throw less trub than ale worts due to the greater digestion of protein during decoctions or a PI mash.

Trub formation is enhanced by an agitated and energetic boiling, which is met in practice within 60–90min, preferably in the presence of flower hops and copper finings. Hops contribute to beer clarity by agitating the wort, which assists the separation of protein, and contributing phenolic (tannin) material. Tannins are only partially soluble in wort, and during coppering they undergo condensation reactions that convert them into dark pigments (oxidized phenols) that contribute to the colour of wort. They also react with wort nitrogen to form insoluble protein-polyphenol complexes that sediment as trub.

Proteins are amphoteric, and in the acidic conditions of wort, they and their peptones have a net positive charge, and so readily combine with the negatively charged tannins. The resulting protein-tannin and peptone-tannin flocculum will settle out as trub.

A word of caution, however: do not forget that unhopped wort has a sufficiently high

A good rolling boil in the copper.

surface tension that can cause over-foaming, and with small boilers a dangerous boil-over might occur. In such circumstances, always add a portion of hops to reduce the surface tension. There will be more malt tannin in lager worts due to the greater extraction during decoctions, and less hop tannin as smaller amounts of hops are used. Malt tannins, however, are not as efficient as hop tannins in producing hot trub or break.

Hot trub also contains hop resin, insoluble salts and considerable amounts of fatty acids derived from the grist and hops, all of which have a bad effect on beer. Some calcium oxalate (beer stone) might also be deposited in the copper.

Copper Finings

By adding Irish moss to the copper for the last 10–15min or so of the coppering, the formation of trub (hot break) is enhanced. Such materials are derived from the seaweed, Carragheen (*Chondrus crispus* and *Gigartina stellata*) traditionally harvested off the west coast of Ireland. The extracts

from Irish moss are carrageenans and furcellarans, which are mixed with tannic acid. Irish moss consists of long chains of negatively charged galactose units (carbohydrates linked alternatively by the 1–3 and 1–4 glycosidic bonds). In boiling wort they are attracted to the positively charged proteins, forming a coagulate and precipitate. Their optimum fining action takes place at pH 5 to 5.3, and the amounts to use will vary with the gravity of the wort.

The correct amount to use is 4–8g in 100ltr, and this works out in 25ltr brews as 1g for light beers, 1½g for medium-strength beers, and 2g for beers of full gravity, (1055) or above. One gram of Irish moss roughly equates to a level half teaspoonful. Commercial brewers also use a purified extract of alginic acid linked to its sodium salt, and this is extracted from the brown algae *Phaeophyta* (*Laminaria*, *Fucus* and *Ascophyllum*).

It is important that good copper fining takes place if optimum fining with isinglass is to be obtained in the cask. Worts that are under copper-fined will contain an excess of fine particles that will remain in solution and cause haze. Such wort will also be slow to clear, and will require a hefty dose of auxiliary finings that will, inevitably, produce excess deposits of trub in the cask. Wort that is over copper-fined will retain excessive carrageenan and less than desired amounts of fine matter to coprecipitate with the isinglass. Slow fining action and poor clarity, coupled with loose fluffy trub deposits, will be inevitable, and these will flocculate with the slightest vibration. Also, the carrageenan carry-over from the copper to the FV might form gelatinous precipitates due to reactions with the continuing drop in the pH during fermentation.

CONTROLLING WORT BITTERNESS

Isomerization
In their natural state, the α-acids will not produce bitterness in the wort: to do so, they must become soluble and undergo a process known as isomerization. This is a change that takes place in the structure of the α-acid, and its molecules are separated and rejoined at another site. The new structure now becomes an iso-α-acid that is soluble and bitter.

The main difficulty is to get the α-acids into solution so that isomerization can take place, and this requires boiling temperatures for long periods. Whilst isomerization takes place within an hour, it takes at least 90min to get less than 30 per cent of the α-acids into solution, and the gravity of the wort influences this. Less solubility and isomerization takes place in strong worts, and the process is more efficient when small amounts of hops are used. Alkaline liquors enhance the isomerization, but the flavours are less favourable. Gypsum-rich liquors have a tendency to restrict the isomerization, but a finer

flavour is obtained even when high α-acid varieties are used.

A good turbulent boiling helps disperse the resins throughout the wort and so assists in marrying up the iso-α-acids with the wort constituents. The petals of flower hops have a tendency to protect the resin gland, and so it takes slightly longer to achieve full solubility and isomerization. Even so, the utilization from flower hops can be as little as 15 per cent. Pelleted hops are more efficient, as the resin gland has been ruptured during the process and this, coupled with the fact that pellets disintegrate in the copper, produces at least 10 per cent more utilization. The β-acids, too, are isomerized during coppering, but the process is much slower and so they do not influence wort bitterness to a great degree.

The time of coppering is important, and many home brewers limit the boil to 60min – but 90min is considered the optimum for full isomerization. Longer boiling times, of over 2 hours or so, are best avoided because there is a risk that the α-acids will become over-converted into non-bittering materials.

The practice of adding hops in stages will not extract the maximum bitterness, but such intermediate additions are often practised to impart character nuances into the brew. Although late hopping can rapidly distil off as much as 95 per cent of the hop oil within minutes, it is obvious that sufficient remains, particularly the monoterpene alcohols geraniol and linalool, to contribute to the floral aroma. Dry hopping is also practised to aromatize pale ales, but it takes 14 to 21 days for the essential oils to diffuse into the brew.

Hopping the Wort
Old-time brewers had to rely on experience, tradition and practice when hopping

their worts, and there was no such thing as consistent amounts added to the copper. The hop grist varied over the year as the brewer judicially balanced the less bitter old hops with the new season's crop to try and achieve a degree of consistency of bitterness and flavour. Due to the increased risk of infection in a warm spell or during the summer months, the hop rate might increase by as much as 25 per cent, to increase the antiseptic qualities.

Degrees of Bitterness

Home brewers have the choice of using international bittering units (IBUs), or IBUs per imperial or American gallon; but before investigating the merits of each, a word about α-acids. It may be a little surprising, but not all British hops are supplied stating the α-acid content on the package. However, a stated level of α-acid can only be used as a guide as to what level was present at harvesting, and it can be much lower by the time the hops are used.

When the supplier is subdividing the hop pocket into numerous small divisions there is inevitable damage to the resin gland, which results in oxidation. This continues when hops are sealed in single-laminated polythene bags that allow the ingress of oxygen. Many retailers also store their hops at ambient temperatures and in bright daylight, and so the rate of deterioration can reduce the α-acid content by as much as 50 per cent in a short space of time. Ideally hops should be refrigerated at 5°C or, better still, deep frozen.

As we also do not have the laboratory means of assessing the α-acid content in the wort, the percentage utilization can only be determined by taste. Just when we think we have got it about right, the next batch of hops suffers as above, but to another degree, and so our calculations go astray. Remember that the quality of the brewing liquor will also affect the utilization of the α-acids, as will fermentation. Greater losses of α-acids occur in top-fermenting yeast and less with bottom-fermenting yeast. If the hops are not accurately weighed, the calculation is thrown into confusion.

International Bittering Units (IBUs)

This represents one milligram of α-acid per litre. To establish the IBUs you first of all need to record the weight and α-acid content of the hops, plus the percentage utilization in the copper:

$$IBUs = \frac{\frac{\%}{utilization} \times \frac{wgt\ in}{grams} \times \frac{\%\ \alpha\text{-}}{acid} \times 1000}{Volume\ of\ the\ brew\ in\ ltr}$$

For example, a 25ltr brew estimating 20 per cent utilization using 85g of hops with 5.5 per cent α-acid produces:

$$\frac{\frac{0.20\%}{utilization} \times 85g \times 0.055\ \alpha\text{-acid} \times 100}{25ltr}$$

$$= 37.5\ IBUs$$

Let us now say that the next time we brew, the α-acid content of the hops has changed from 5.5 per cent to 6.2 per cent. To establish the weight of hops, the formula to use is as follows:

$$\frac{Grams}{of\ hops} = \frac{volume\ in\ ltr \times IBUs}{\frac{copper}{utilization} \times \frac{\%}{\alpha\text{-}acid} \times 1000}$$

e.g. $$\frac{25ltr \times 37.5\ IBUs}{\frac{0.20}{utilization} \times \frac{0.062\%}{\alpha\text{-}acid} \times 1000} = 75g$$

The above formula is also used to calculate the weight of hops in any recipes stating IBUs. Whilst IBUs are excellent for our personal use, some difficulties can arise when using other brewers' recipes.

Unless they also include the variety of hops, we can end up with a similar degree of bitterness, but with a different flavour profile. Similarly, if the hop utilization factor is not stated, or is different from yours, the formula will not work. Let us say the utilization factor is actually 25 per cent, and we use the above example, we can expect to add 60g of hops at 6.2 per cent α-acid, and so the beer will be much less bitter.

When using hop Type 90 pellets, their better 10 per cent utilization has to be considered and so we only require 90 per cent of leaf hops:

$$\text{eg} \quad \frac{25\text{ltr} \times 37.5 \text{ IBUs} \times 0.90\%}{\underset{\text{utilization}}{0.20\%} \times \underset{\alpha\text{-acid}}{0.062} \times 1000} = 68\text{g}$$

If the hop grist consists of a blend, the IBUs have to be worked out for each addition. To convert IBUs to imperial gallons, we use the following formula:

$$\text{IBUs} = \frac{\underset{\text{utilization}}{\%} \times \underset{\alpha\text{-acid}}{\%} \times \underset{\text{in oz}}{\text{wgt}} \times 6232}{\text{volume in imperial gal}}$$

$$\text{eg} = \frac{\underset{\text{utilization}}{0.20} \times \underset{\alpha\text{-acid}}{0.062\%} \times 2.6\text{oz} \times 6232}{5.5\text{gal}}$$

$$= 36.5 \text{ IBUs}$$

$$\text{oz} = \frac{\text{vol} \times \text{IBUs}}{\% \text{ utilization} \times \% \text{ } \alpha\text{-acid} \times 6232}$$

$$\text{eg} = \frac{5.5\text{gal} \times 36.5 \text{ IBUs}}{\underset{\text{utilization}}{0.20} \times \underset{\alpha\text{-acid}}{0.062\%} \times 6232} = 2.6\text{oz}$$

To convert IBUs to the smaller American gallon, use the factor 7480.

The recommended IBU parameters in the table should initially be taken as a guide and future brews adjusted, if nec-essary, so that the flavour profile suits your palate, but remains within the characteristics of the beer style. Should the beer be too bitter, then the percentage utilization must be increased (fewer hops) to maintain the IBU parameter. Likewise, if the brew lacks bitterness, the percentage utilization rating should be lowered (more hops) to compensate. Alternatively, we stick with the percentage utilization figure and adjust the IBU figure. Remember, incorrect mashing heats for the beer style, and different types of water will affect the percentage utilization and beer character.

The Hop Schedule

The timing and the amount of hops to add are where the craft brewer can learn a lot about the bitter and flavour profiles of different varieties of hop. Tasting and note-taking are essential in order to record the different results from a single hop charge added at the beginning of the boil, through to the effects of adding additional amounts at various stages throughout the copper-ing. A blend of hops can also elevate the spiciness of the brew, and so by varying this practice, a range of hop character complexity will result. Experimentation is the key to good brewing!

Aroma hopping will increase the enticing bouquet and is typically achieved by adding about 20 per cent of aroma hops 10–15min before the end of coppering. Alternatively, add the hops, replace the lid and control the heat input to provide gentle ebullition that will circulate the hops throughout the wort, liberating their aromatic qualities into the brew. After 15min, switch off and soak for another 15min to allow the hops and trub to sediment.

Copper adjuncts are added to the wort either to increase its gravity and/or volume, or to influence the character of the brew.

Table 25   International bittering units
(A guide compiled from various sources)

British beers	IBUs	Continental beers	IBUs
Strong ales	50–100	Doppel Bock	18–28
India pale ale	40–60	Bock beer	20–30
Best bitter	30–55	Bavarian dunkel	15–25
Bitter	20–40	Bavarian helles	18–25
Light ale	20–25	Vienna	22–28
Strong mild ale	20–30	Dortmunder	23–30
Mild ale	15–25	Bohemian Pilsner	35–5
Pale mild	10–24	Pilseners	30–40
Brown ale, south	15–20	Pale wheat beer	10–15
Brown ale, north	15–25	Dark wheat beer	10–15
Dublin stout	30–40	Rauchbier	20–30
Oatmeal stout	20–40	Berliner Wiese	3–6
Sweet stout	10–24	Kölsch beer	20–30
Porter	25–40	Lambic	1–23
Celtic red ale	20–30	Fruit Lambic	15–21
60/- ale	10–20		
70/- ale	12–20		
80/- alc	15–25		
Scotch ale	25–40		

The safest way to add them is to draw off a small quantity of wort, dissolve the sugar in it and return it to the copper. This ensures that the sugar is well dissolved and avoids the need for excessive rousing over a boiler of belching steam!

Evaporation

A good ebullient coppering of some 90min should evaporate about 20 per cent of wort. In practical terms, the wort is condensed to just above the desired volume required in the FV. Another idea is to control the coppering so that the volume is reduced to a level that can be made good by the hop sparge. When condensing the wort to a volume indicator on the boiler, don't forget that part of the volume is taken up with the quantity of hops, and that the volume when cooled will be less. When the wort is cooled, the volume will shrink by about 4 per cent.

With small boilers, topping up with liquor might be necessary from time to time to prevent the wort from becoming too condensed, producing too much colour in light ales and lagers. This is not so much of a problem with dark beers, as the caramelization that takes place adds to the flavoursome palate. Some liquor might also be required to adjust the racking volume.

FILTERING THE WORT

After coppering, allow the bitter wort to stand until the hop residue and wort debris have precipitated. By slowly draining the wort into the FV, or cooling vessel, the hops will act as a strainer and retain most of the hot break. The type of 'hop back' will influence the efficiency of the process. It is also important that the wort is not allowed to splash during this operation, as the oxygenation of the melanoidins

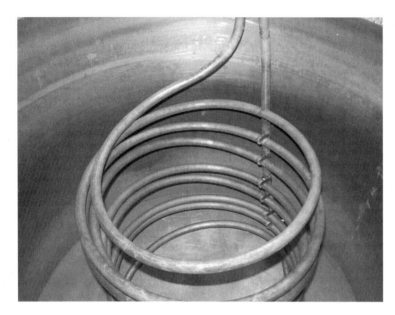

The cooling coil.

will result in staling aldehydes being produced.

Sparging Hops

As larger amounts of 'aroma' leaf hops, rather than 'alpha' leaf hops, are used to achieve the same degree of bitterness, they can retain up to 2 per cent of the extract. Should you wish to recover this, it can be achieved very efficiently with Phil's sparger, or hand spray; but regardless of the method, it is inevitable that some trub will be washed though with the runnings. To avoid this, simply collect the hop sparge in a separate bucket and then decant it into a soft drinks bottle. When this drops bright, add it to the brew.

Cooling the Wort

In practice a rapid cooling of the wort saves home brewers the many hours we would wait for it to cool naturally. Technically, a rapid cooling of bitter wort is desirable to promote and sediment the maximum amount of chill-haze protein-tannin complexes and restrict the evaporation of the aromatic oils. The optimum temperature for the removal of cold trub is when the wort cools to below 50°C, when the fine proteinaceous matter aggregates and eventually sediments. The thermophilic bacterium, *Lactobacillus delbrueckii*, can survive up to 50°C and infect wort, producing sour lactic acid. Prevention is by cleanliness and keeping the wort covered until fermentation is established. The practice of slow cooling should be avoided.

Cold trub will become insoluble when chilled, and whilst the majority will remain out of solution, a small fraction might redissolve and may cause chill haze in the future. A beer with chill haze will display a degree of opalescence. A defective hot break will result in excessive cold break, and so it is imperative that the maximum is removed during coppering.

CHAPTER 10

YEAST AND FERMENTATION

Yeasts are classified as fungi and posses a complex biological organization compared to other unicellular organisms; they are only some 8–10 microns in size. In a nutritious brewer's wort, yeast preferentially reproduces by budding (the opposite to sexual) and when this process is initiated the deoxyribonucleic acid (DNA) within the nucleus of the parent cell replicates and divides. The two copies of the genetic material then segregate, one remaining in the parent cell, the other inherited by the budding daughter cell. As a result, the daughter cell will have exactly the same genetic make-up as the parent. When budding is taking place a small bud appears on the surface of the parent cell and this steadily grows to accommodate the copy of the nuclear material coming from the parent cell.

When the transfer of DNA has taken place, the cell wall becomes fused behind the transferred material, which is then pinched off. Eventually each cell forms its own cell wall, and so we have two complete individual cells. The daughter cell might separate from the parent and continue to grow and subsequently reproduce, or it might remain attached to the parent and so with further rounds of cellular division, form a limited mycelium.

Yeast obtains the energy it requires for cellular processes from the metabolism of carbohydrates, phosphates, peptides, amino acids and lipids. Since brewer's wort contains all of these in abundance, growth and reproduction is most vigorous and healthy. The major sugar in wort is maltose, but the amount and its ratio to the other sugars will depend on the mashing conditions. A variety of other assimilable sugars, such as glucose, fructose, sucrose and maltotriose, are also utilized. The non-fermentable sugars lactose, maltotetraose and dextrins, remain in the wort, adding to palate fullness.

Yeasts can only utilize the smaller glucose and fructose molecules directly, and these are actively transported into the cell by carrier glucose permease, and metabolized. Molecules of sucrose are too large to be transported, and so the yeast secretes an enzyme called invertase (or sucrase), which hydrolyses the sucrose into its monosaccharide component parts, glucose and fructose. These can now be conveyed into the cell. Maltose and maltotriose are also conveyed into the cell by inducible parmeases, α-glucosidase (maltase) and maltotriase respectively, and hydrolysed to glucose. Since yeast does not possess lactase or amylase enzymes, lactose and the higher complex sugars are not metabolized.

THE METABOLIC PROCESS

The metabolism of glucose and fructose within the cell is highly complex, but all of this activity is designed to produce reserve stores of the energy-rich molecule called adenosine triphosphate (ATP). This molecule is the energy currency of the cell. Both aerobic and anaerobic respiratory pathways can produce ATP, though greater amounts are generated by aerobic respiration. In both cases, however, the process starts with glycolysis.

Glycolysis takes place within the cell cytoplasm and involves a series of intricate and highly complex oxidative-enzyme-sugar-phosphate reactions that ultimately produce, after a series of steps, pyruvic acid. Thereafter, respiration can continue on the aerobic route, or switch to the anaerobic fermentation pathway.

A well aerated wort is necessary for the yeast to conduct its metabolic processes. In the aerobic route the pyruvic acid is initially converted into acetyl, and thereafter the activity of respiration takes place inside specialized organelles called mitochondria. Within the mitochondria, a complex enzyme-controlled oxidative cycle involving tri-carboxylic acids (the Krebs cycle) takes place, and the acetyl is oxidized to carbon dioxide and water. The acids that are produced are citric, oxoglutaric, succinic, fumaric and malic, and these acids have an influence on wort acidity. The Krebs cycle, however, produces masses of energy-rich ATP, and yeast reproduction is most vigorous with cell division occurring every one to three hours.

The craft brewer should now appreciate why it is so important to aerate the wort before the yeast is added, so that the cells can quickly build up into a healthy colony. As the oxygen in the wort is utilized by the yeast and further aeration is restricted by the evolving carbon dioxide, plus the blanket of foamy yeast on the surface of the brew, the yeast in the wort must turn to an alternative pathway for the production of ATP. At this stage, cell growth and reproduction relies on anaerobic metabolic pathways in the process termed fermentation.

During fermentation, pyruvic acid cannot be oxidized, but it is instead converted into acetaldehyde and carbon dioxide is released by the reaction. The acetaldehyde is in turn broken down by the enzyme alcohol dehydrogenase into ethanol. This method of producing energy is very inefficient and only small amounts of ATP are produced and, consequently, reproduction only takes place every 5 to 8 hours or so.

Yeast also requires a supply of nitrogenous materials to build up its cell mass, and the preferred source is the individual constituent amino acids, but peptides are also utilized. During the course of fermentation, up to 50 per cent of the wort nitrogen available is consumed by the yeast. Lipids, vitamins and minerals are assimilated to ensure the health of the cell.

CLASSIFICATION OF YEAST

All brewing yeasts are now regarded as *Saccharomyces cerevisiae* and other types are varieties (var.), such as *S. cerevisiae var Carlsbergensis*, the lager yeast; *S. cerevisiae var Uvarum*, previously the lager yeast, is now the wine yeast.

Historically such divisions were made from observations as to whether the yeast flocculated on top of the brew, or sedimented after fermentation. The factors that influence flocculation are complex,

95

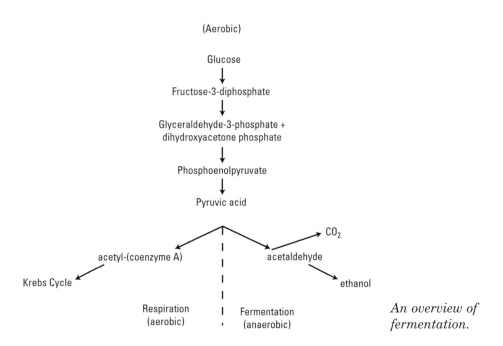

An overview of fermentation.

and this is an area that is yet to be fully elucidated. Some of the important points are as follows. In quiescent wort, all yeasts have the ability to form flocs that accumulate into clumps. This ability to flocculate is related in part to the effects of electrical charges inherent in polysaccharides on the cell surface. The degree and extent to which the charge exists on the cell surface is influenced by the pH of the surroundings. The increase in wort acidity serves to counter the negative charges on the cell surface, bringing the yeast closer to its iso-electric point, and so flocculation occurs more readily.

Wort that is rich in calcium tends to promote flocculation, and this is part of the reason why ale yeasts are more flocculent than lager yeasts. Wort nutrition also has a bearing on flocculation, and certain peptides appear to encourage it. When flocculating yeast is added to fresh wort, the maltose present actually causes

the yeast to disperse and so flocculation does not occur immediately. Glucose and fructose do not have quite the same dispersal powers as maltose, and so when fermentation is coming to an end and the inhibiting power of maltose is removed, through cellular metabolism, the yeast more readily flocculates. The surface of the cell also contains a number of small irregular mannoprotein protrusions that aids its flocculation.

The temperature of the wort will also induce flocculation, and this is much more evident in warm worts than cool worts. Temperature affects the by-products of fermentation, and high temperatures encourage unwanted levels of esters, fusel alcohols and diacetyl.

A test that is often carried out to distinguish the difference between ale and lager yeasts is one that involves examination of test-tube fermentations. Lager yeasts are capable of fermenting at a much lower temperature than ale yeasts, and they also secrete the enzyme melibiase that splits the trisaccharide raffinose into the disaccharide melibiose and the monosaccharide fructose. Ale yeasts do not secrete this enzyme, but they can split the bond between melibiose and fructose, but only ferment the latter.

Brewing yeasts are held by the National Collection of Yeast Cultures, and are regularly assessed by way of test-tube fermentations to European Brewing Convention standards. Five characteristics are looked at, and these are rated between one and five. The characteristics are:

a. The amount of yeast that accumulates on the surface during fermentation.
b. The amount of deposited yeast at the end of fermentation.
c. The degree of attenuation during fermentation.
d. The rate of fermentation.
e. The clarity of the resultant beer.

DRIED YEASTS

Dried yeasts have been the mainstay of amateurs for years. Previously baker's yeast was used, but by the 1960s good quality brewing strains became available. One problem with such yeasts was simply that they were fermented at too high a temperature, typically 25°C, with the inevitable flavour consequences. Poor storage conditions, and the lack of a 'best before' date, also meant poor flavours and performance. Such yeast, however, when used fresh and fermented between 15 and 18°C, produced a decent pint.

The problem facing the industry at this time was the limited technology to produce liquid yeast cultures with genuine brewing characteristics. During 1974–75, the Boots Company of Nottingham introduced a true brewing strain (NCYC 1245, fermentation characteristics 1:5:5:5:5) suspended in an isotonic mannitol solution; this liquid culture contained 20ml, each millilitre containing 10^5 of cells, and it was propagated prior to brewing.

By 1985, the technology for drying this type of yeast was developed, and the liquid yeast became available in dried form. Such drying techniques resulted in each gram of dried yeast containing 10^9–10^{10} of viable yeast cells, or, in other words, each sachet of 3.5g contained between 1,000 and 10,000-fold the number of viable cells compared to the yeast in suspension. As a consequence of this, it was recommended that dried yeast simply be added direct to the wort. Such technology is now used to produce many brewing strains of yeast for the craft brewer.

Dried yeasts have often been criticized as being the culprits for some of the ills that some home brewers experience, and this could well be the case if the yeast is old and/or has been badly stored. A sachet of old and/or badly stored yeast will inevitably contain masses of dead, weak and mutant cells that are quite insufficient to produce good results. However, a new sachet of dried yeast will have been propagated under the most sterile laboratory conditions to the same degree of growth, in a medium with exactly the correct amount of nutrients, and so by using a fresh sachet with each brew, very consistent results are obtained!

If for any reason, however, you are unsure as to the viability of the yeast, it can be rehydrated in hot water as follows: add 100ml of boiling water (there is no advantage in using wort) to a sterile container of at least 500ml capacity, and allow it to cool to 35°C. Stir in the yeast and the cells will immediately rehydrate and start to utilise their reserves of glycogen and trahalose, with the resulting evolution of CO_2. After 15min or so the medium should have produced copious amounts of foam – hence the need for the large container, and if this is not the case, the chances are that the yeast is not up to standard.

Dried yeast may also be built up as a 'starter medium', and in this case we use wort or malt extract to propagate the yeast. Rehydration should first of all be carried out, and then after 15min added to the well-aerated wort/extract sample. The wort, or extract, should be about 500ml with a gravity of 1040–45, acidified to pH 3 at 25°C. This will ensure a medium rich in yeast nutrients, and so the sample should quickly produce a thriving colony. Protect the starter medium with fine gauze or muslin.

The use of an air lock is best avoided, as it will prevent the natural exchange of gases between the evolving CO_2 and the ingress of oxygen. A starter medium should be roused as often as possible to force out dissolved CO_2 and to aerate the wort so that the yeast is denied fermentation and remains in the Krebs cycle mode, rapidly reproducing and building up the large colony of healthy yeast.

This sample should be ready for pitching after 24 to 48 hours, but the medium can be left for a further 24 hours or so, and in this case a further quantity of wort/extract should be added to keep the cells active and healthy. Drain off most of the wort above the yeast sediment, and replenish with one litre of fresh wort or malt extract to the original gravity.

Craft brewers should be wary of adding excessive amounts of yeast, as there is a risk of over-depleting wort nutrients as the cells compete for nourishment, resulting in low yeast growth with the risk of fermentation disorders and excessive amounts of the peardrop or solvent-like ester, *ethyl acetate*. The other point to remember is that yeast starters should be added to wort at about the same temperature, as only a few degrees below and the

Pitching a yeast starter.

cold thermal trauma retards the onset of the lag phase and hence fermentation, with the risk of infection from competing bacteria.

FERMENTATION

Fermentation marks the end of bitter wort and the beginning of beer. Whilst the primary aim is to produce ethanol, the fermentation should produce a balance of by-products ensuring a quality of wort with the desirable flavour characteristics and stability on storage.

Wort Aeration

Oxygen is vital if yeast is to successfully carry out its metabolic processes. Aeration of hot wort from the copper should be avoided to prevent oxygen/polyphenol reactions that darken the wort. Also, if the melanoidins in the wort become oxidized at this stage, they will lose their reducing power and not be available to protect the brew from oxygenation later on in the brewing process.

Aeration of cold wort, preferably at 10–15°C, greatly limits the above detrimental reactions. Cold wort also absorbs more air, particularly if it is introduced as a fine spray that creates masses of microbubbles, as these will offer a greater surface area for absorption to take place. A large surface area with plenty of agitation or stirring to form a vortex is also helpful. Some enthusiasts suggest the use of medicinal oxygen, but this should be avoided, as the amounts absorbed cannot be controlled. A wort supersaturated with pure oxygen will contain about 40mg/ltr, but this is too high and results in racing fermentations, excessive yeast growth and poor beer flavours.

Wort super-saturated with air is a safe option, as the maximum amount of oxygen absorbed is limited to 21 per cent. In this case, beers of average gravity will contain about 8.5mg/ltr of oxygen, which is satisfactory. Yeasts, however, vary in their requirements for oxygen, and the craft brewer should observe yeast performance in relation to aeration, attenuation, number of rousings and the PG of the beer. When acquiring yeast it is advisable to find out its oxygen requirements, and whether this is low, medium or high.

A yeast of low oxygen requirement might satisfactorily ferment an air-saturated wort of OG 1040–50, but might not be capable of completely fermenting a wort of 1070+, and high gravity worts usually require regular rousing to fully attenuate the brew. Excessive rousing runs the risk of oxygenating some of the wort constituents, resulting in poor beer quality.

The simplest and quickest way to super-saturate the wort with air is to run it into a sterilized bucket and return it to the FV with plenty of splashing. The yeast can be pitched at the same time, and it will be well mixed by the process. I usually do this about four to five times, and have never had any problems with picking up infections or long lag phases.

Many home brewers use an aquarium air pump and air stone, which will provide 2–3ltr of air per minute.

The Lag Phase

This refers to the time the yeast takes to acclimatize to its saccharine and nitrogenous environment and start reproducing. During the lag phase, the cells are busy utilizing their carbohydrate reserves, which will provide them with the energy required to start synthesizing the necessary enzymes that will metabolize the wort constituents necessary for healthy growth. There is little surface activity during this phase, and it is a wise precaution to protect the brew from aerial infection.

The time of the lag phase will depend on the health of the yeast, which will in most cases reflect its age and the manner in which it was stored. A healthy yeast should kick into action within 6 to 10 hours. The shorter the lag phase the better, because the more quickly that fermentation begins, the less chance there is of rival microorganisms attacking the brew.

During the first 24 hours or so, the yeast utilizes the simpler sugars such as glucose, fructose and sucrose. From about 24 to 72 hours, most of the maltose is consumed, and finally maltotriose is metabolized. If the fermentation is allowed to go to completion in the FV, practically all of the maltotriose will have been exhausted, leaving insufficient to condition the brew. This is why it is so important to control the racking gravity, so that at least 2–3° of residual and slowly fermenting maltotriose remains in the brew.

Pitching

With brewery yeasts, the pitching temperature of the wort depends on the gravity of the brew, plus the ambient temperature, and this is also reflected in the desired maximum fermenting temperature. In the past, traditional brewers pitched light beers at 16°C during the summer months, and a little higher during the winter months. The maximum fermenting temperature for light brews is about 19°C, and some sort of cooling is necessary to prevent it rising above this figure. Yeast continuously employed in light brews is progressively weakened by a lack of nourishment, and eventually becomes unsuitable for brewing.

Medium-strength brews are usually pitched at 15°C during the summer and 16°C during the winter. Such brews are normally allowed to peak at 20–21°C, and are held there until the cleansing phase.

Strong beers have a much lower warm-weather pitching temperature of 14°C, which will help counteract the excessive heat generated by the yeast in such nutritious worts. The cold-weather temperatures are slightly higher, at 15°C, as this helps the yeast perk up in the cold environment. The maximum fermenting temperature for strong beers is usually stabilized at 21–22°C, although higher gravity brews might be allowed to rise to 23°C in order to achieve the desired degree of attenuation. Such high temperatures induce autolysis, and the yeast crops are not considered for repitching.

Respiration and 'Rocky Heads'

The first sign that respiration is taking place is the appearance of small patches of froth on the surface of the wort. These patches will be more in evidence around an attemperator if in use, or the edge of the FV should it be close to a heat source such as a radiator. As the yeast slowly evolves CO_2, the gas brings the cells to the surface where they collect to form a light fluffy head. In a large vat, this head slowly builds up into a mass of 'cauliflower' heads that gradually give way to the pinnacled phenomenon of 'rocky heads'. As these occur with both top- and bottom-fermenting ale yeasts and lager yeasts, home brewers naturally think that the yeast is top fermenting. This is not the case, however.

Dried yeasts can generate enormous meringue-like top crops of 150–200mm, and these can look quite alarming, particularly if the FV is filled close to capacity. Such heads of yeast, however, dry out quickly and crumble when being skimmed.

Whilst they might look impressive, such heads contain foul-tasting oxidized resinous and nitrogenous matter, forming dirty brown patches. This should be skimmed off regularly.

The natural rise in wort temperature, possibly aided in cold weather by a gentle heat source, should be roughly 1.5–2°C in 24 hours, and this should correspond to a fall in gravity of some 6–12°. The temperature should be allowed to rise to the maximum recommended for the style of beer, and held there until the cleansing phase. Should you have difficulty in controlling this profile, then a steady, but low temperature is better than a fluctuating one, or a high one.

The Logarithmic Phase of Metabolism

During the period of 12 to 36 hours after pitching, the yeast goes through its logarithmic phase of metabolism. During this frenzied period, the ensuing evolution of gas, coupled with the yeast's natural flocculation, starts to produce a more substantial head of yeast.

After 48 hours, rousing should be conducted regularly, and this will depend on the flocculation of the yeast. Highly flocculent strains require a good rousing every 4 to 8 hours, whereas less flocculent strains might only require rousing every 6 to 12 hours or so.

During this period of accelerated yeast metabolism, a considerable amount of buffering nitrogenous materials are consumed by the yeast, and this, coupled with the formation of natural acids, increases the wort acidity. The initial drop in the pH is quite dramatic, and by the time fermentation comes to an end, the pH should be in the range 4.2 to 3.7. Yeast finds an increase in acidity beneficial for growth, but more importantly for the brewer, this natural rise in wort acidity is desirable to counteract infection by bacteria.

During the period from 48 to 72 hours, the maximum temperature is maintained, and this is the best time to harvest the crop for future brews. The earlier rocky crops are rejected as they contain unwanted resinous and albuminous matter, and in any case, they are very flocculent and do not attenuate well. Similarly, the crop that flocculates into the closed head, or seal as it is sometimes known, is not used, as the cells do not flocculate enough and attenuate rather too well! It is only the middle crops that give the desirable flocculating and attenuating characteristics, and the brewer might judge the time of harvesting to encourage, or discourage, the characteristics he requires. The best crops for continuous repitching are obtained from brews with original gravities of 1040 to 1055.

ATTENUATION

The degree of attenuation will be, in part, dependent on the flocculation properties of the yeast. Highly flocculent strains separate early in the fermentation and produce a full-bodied palate. The high-gravity beers of old were brewed with such yeasts, and they were racked when the brew had attenuated to a third of its original gravity. The slowly fermentable materials left in the brew at racking sustained it during the long storage times that were necessary to clarify and mature the brew.

Highly flocculating yeasts can usually be attenuated to the quarter gravity stage with prolonged rousing, but care should be taken not to over-oxygenate the wort. A moderately flocculating yeast is probably best for the amateur, and with proper control of the temperature and rousing, the gravity should fall to the racking gravity without too much difficulty. If the wort is well aerated prior to pitching and fermentation is rapid, rousing might not be necessary. It is, however, imperative that cooling is introduced at about 6° above the PG to slow the fermentation and effect the cleansing phase. This ensures that at the racking gravity the beer is relatively clean of yeast and nitrogenous matter, and will readily co-precipitate with the finings.

The extent of attenuation is also reflected in the style of beer, and the mashing temperature and regime determine this. Fully attenuated beers allow the hop bitterness to be more accentuated, with a sharper, bitter edge. Well attenuated beers also afford more protection against infection due to their higher alcohol content and lower nitrogenous nutrient for bacteria. The residual sweetness in less attenuated beers produces a more rounded palate that masks, to some degree, the character of the hops.

Control of Temperature
Control of the wort temperature is somewhat difficult for the amateur, but we can aim for sensible parameters and obtain good results. Light gravity brews usually present little difficulty unless ambient temperatures are high, but high gravity brews will require some degree of cooling during the summer months. The problems associated with high temperatures are the production of unacceptable levels of esters, aromatic alcohols and diacetyl. Within the range 15–21°C, these flavour molecules are subdued. Good temperature control is vital if the yeast crop is to be used to inoculate future brews.

During a cold spell sit the FV on a winemaker's heating tray, and as the temperature creeps up to 19°C or so, switch it off. Thereafter keep an eye on the temperature, and should it look as if it might creep over

the maximum, control it by having a small fan blowing on to the FV. The heating tray may be attached to a 24-hour timer, set to come on and off periodically during the night so that the wort temperature remains relatively steady and does not falter due to a sudden chill.

During warm weather a refrigerator is helpful, and the temperature can also be controlled by use of a 24-hour timer. With trial and error and a little patience, the fermentation profile can be achieved. Set the fridge thermostat to 'high', and adjust the 'on-off' settings to maintain an average temperature as required for ale brewing. For lager fermentations, turn on the thermostat so that the fridge just operates (about 8–10°C). For lagering, set the thermostat to 5°C. An external thermometer, with the probe inside the cabinet, allows us to monitor the temperature without continually opening the fridge. The brew temperature should be regularly checked, however. Alternatively, wire up the fridge with a room thermostat as discussed in Chapter 2, 'Building a Brewery'.

Rousing
Throughout the period of the fermentation, the yeast head should be cleansed and roused back into the wort. Failure to do this might mean that the fermentation cannot be controlled, the attenuation will not be regular, and due to there being so little yeast in suspension, the fermentation might come to a halt prematurely. Rousing also introduces some oxygen into the wort, and this has a tendency to hasten fermentation. Too much aeration, however, will oxygenate wort constituents, producing detrimental flavours.

Control of the Racking Gravity
We can now see that whilst a good flocculating yeast may require to be roused

regularly to ensure a steady rate of fermentation, we are also in a position to stop rousing and bring the attenuation to a halt at a pre-determined gravity. By doing so, we can also control the amount of residual fermentable matter left in the beer at racking and, consequently, the amount of CO_2 available to condition the brew. Ideally, cask-conditioned beers require an equal volume of CO_2 per volume of beer throughout its shelf life, and this is referred to as the 1–1 ratio.

In practice, the ratio will vary from around 1.3 volumes in a full cask, diminishing to about 0.8 volumes. Overall, we require about 2.5 volumes of CO_2 to satisfy a slow conditioning over the shelf life of the beer. As a drop in gravity of 1.25° produces roughly one volume of gas, we require $2.5 \times 1.25 = 3°$ of gravity.

As we are concerned with the gravity at the end of the fermentation, the residual saccharine matter will be mostly the slowly fermentable maltotriose sugar. Unfortunately, such sugars do not produce sufficient initial gas to supersaturate the beer, and so it is necessary to add priming sugars so that the beer can be served lively and refreshing as soon as it clears.

After 72 hours or so, most of the desired ethanol will have been produced and the yeast now enters its phase of restricted growth. The gravity of the wort at this stage might be a few degrees above the target to stop rousing, which is ideally 6° above the PG. As a rough guide, the PG is usually at the quarter gravity stage; for example $OG \times 0.25 = PG$. The actual PG can only be accurately determined by using the same recipe, the same mashing regime, the same yeast and the same fermentation profile. Of course, such criteria are very difficult for craft brewers, and so it is inevitable that variations will take place.

The aim of halting the rousing at 6° above the PG is to allow for the further drop of 3° that takes place during the yeast's *cleansing phase*. This ensures that when the beer is racked into the cask it will be relatively clean of yeast and nitrogenous matter and will also retain the desirable 3° of slowly fermenting products.

Regular checks should now be made on the fermentation, and the gravity should be slowly dropping by about 4° every 24 hours. By carrying out these checks we should be able to judge when the gravity to stop rousing has been reached. Let us say, for example, that a saccharometer reading of 3° is recorded above the gravity to halt rousing, and we anticipate a further drop of 4° during the next 24 hours. The time to halt rousing can be calculated as follows:

$$\frac{3°}{4°} \times 24 = \text{in 18 hours time}$$

THE CLEANSING PHASE

The cleansing phase takes place during the period of about 72 to 120 hours after pitching. After rousing is carried out for the last time, the temperature of the wort is maintained at the optimum for a further 18 to 30 hours. By doing this, the yeast will remain active and will continue to flocculate into the closed head, forming a good seal that will protect it from oxidation and help retain CO_2 in solution. During this time, the attenuation of the wort should drop by about 3°, and after 24 hours, on average, the temperature of the brew is slowly reduced to that required at racking.

The slow cooling will further encourage the flocculation of yeast into the head and the precipitation of dead and weak cells, plus proteinaceous materials.

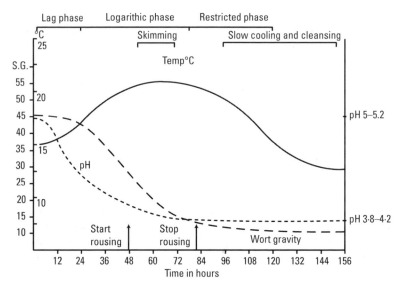

A profile of top fermentation.

Consequently, when the brew is ready to be casked, it should contain the right amount of yeast and fine nitrogenous matter to co-precipitate with the finings. The temperature of the brew at racking should ideally be about 10°–12°C, which is low enough to compensate for any rise during casking and also to allow the isinglass to work on a rising temperature to its optimum of 13–15°C.

During warm weather, I manage to lower the wort temperature to 10°C by using my wort cooling coil, which is fed by cold water coming from the hot HLT, via a commercial flash cooler set at 8°C. Alternatives to this might be fitting a copper coil inside a picnic cooler and covering it with crushed ice, plus salt, or chilling the water in a fridge.

In the illustration a single-stage fermentation (skimming system) is represented, and the end results are always satisfactory. However, a two-stage fermentation (dropping system) may also be practised, and in this case the brew is racked into another FV at a predetermined gravity. With true top yeasts it is best to do this immediately before the cleansing phase. Some aeration of the brew should be expected, but this can be kept to a minimum by running sterilized syphon tubing from the tap on the FV, and keeping the end of it on the bottom of the secondary vessel, thereby avoiding an excessive uptake of oxygen. This ensures the brew is racked off wort trub that might have a deleterious effect on the brew due to yeast autolysis with the release of fatty acids and nauseating sulphurous flavours.

Dried Yeast

Dried yeast may be added direct to the wort from the sachet, or rehydrated and pitched, or made up into a starter medium before pitching. It is always wise to pitch them at the same temperature as the wort in order to reduce the harmful consequences of thermal shock.

As the lag phase with dried yeasts is usually slightly longer than with fresh yeast, the wort should be protected until it shows positive signs that fermentation

104

is under way; this is usually after about 10 to 12 hours or so, and the surface of the wort will be covered with a light head of foam. Thereafter, we can follow the same temperature fermenting profile as for fresh yeast, or simply maintain a steady temperature of about 18°C to achieve a good balance of flavoursome by-products. We can also conduct a single- or two-stage fermentation.

Much dried yeast is of a powdery nature, and remains suspended in the wort until the end of the fermentation. Therefore after the initial skimming and rousing, there should not be any further need to carry out this practice unless the brew shows signs of becoming sluggish. This is unlikely to happen with yeast that is used well before its 'best-before' date and has been stored in the fridge.

As the fermentation slowly comes to an end, it is most unusual for dried yeasts to form a true yeast head, or seal, and it starts to break up; it is now necessary to protect the brew from aerial infection, either by replacing the lid on the FV, or by racking the brew into a closed container. The latter might be considered as part of the two-stage process, and an airlock should protect the beer.

A word of caution is due at this point. It is naturally assumed that an airlock is going to protect the brew indefinitely, and this is not the case! During very cold weather, or by using a fridge, we can expect the brew to be safe in the short term, but during the warmer months, the beer should not be left under an airlock for more than a couple of days without refrigeration: any longer than this and we run the risk of micro-organisms feeding and festering on the surface of the brew. The airspace in any container temporarily storing beer should be as small as possible to cut down the surface area on which

bacteria will grow. The airlock should be filled with a solution of sodium metabisulphite to keep the bugs at bay.

It is also a good idea to treat ales with 50mg/ltr of ascorbic acid, which acts as a reductone and helps maintain the oxidation-reduction balance of the brew. It is also safer to add a maximum of 20mg/ltr of sulphur dioxide (SO_2) for filtered beer, or 50mg/ltr for cask-conditioned beer at the same time, as this prevents the ascorbic acid reverting to an oxygen carrier, as it can do in the presence of metallic ions, causing oxidation. SO_2 should not be added to lager beer, as there is a risk of introducing unwanted sulphurous notes.

RACKING AND RESTING

As it is not easy to control the racking gravity with dried yeast, one practical way round the problem is to introduce cooling at 6° above the PG, or rack the brew at 3–4° above the PG and chill it rapidly to at least 5°C. Such shock cooling arrests the fermentation and no more metabolisms of wort sugars take place. Once the brew is casked and slowly returned to cellar temperature, the yeast will revive and act on the residual sugars, conditioning the brew.

The reason for racking and resting is to allow the completion of fermentation without the brew sitting on a large deposit of old and decaying yeast. Secondly, and more importantly, a resting period of 48 hours, or perhaps longer in some cases, allows any excess of yeast in suspension, time to sediment. This enhances the fining action, and auxiliary finings can also be added at this stage if thought necessary. When employing true top yeast, racking and resting are not necessary as the yeast naturally flocculates into the closed head during the cleansing phase.

The secondary FV in the fridge.

HARVESTING YEAST

Should you acquire a good strain of yeast and intend to brew a series of beers to build up stocks, the yeast can be cropped from the FV during the 50 to 72 hour period. The yeast should be taken from under the surface with a sterilized nylon tea strainer or similar, so that it drains as it is being removed and added to a small sterilized container of about 250ml capacity. Fill the jar to the brim, close the lid and wipe it clean with a cloth soaked in sodium metabisulphite.

Store the sample in the fridge at 1–4°C, and it should remain fresh for up to seven days, although ideally it should be re-pitched within 48 to 72 hours. The jar should be vented daily to release any build-up of CO_2. Before reuse, the sample should be allowed to come to the ambient temperature, or the same temperature as the wort. I have pitched some samples directly into the wort, but lag times can be variable, and it is better if the sample is made up into a starter culture with 500ml of wort or malt extract, to an OG of 1040, and left to grow for about 48 hours. This will activate the yeast's enzyme system, and fermentation should get off to a quick start.

Agar slants can be acquired from 'Brulabs', and in this case we transfer some of the harvested yeast by scratching it into the slant with a sterile wire loop or cocktail stick. To propagate a Brulabs culture, or saved sample from the slant, we first make up a starter medium with 2 tablespoons of Spraymalt in 200ml of pre-boiled water to a gravity of 1045. Cool the sample to 25°C. Now open the agar slant and almost fill the container. Shake it gently for a few minutes, and you will notice the yeast cells coming off the slant. Add this to the starter medium, and seal with a bored cork plugged with cotton wool. Shake the starter regularly to drive out the CO_2, and after 48 hours, add another 200ml of extract. After a further 24 hours, the starter is ready for pitching. Pitch at the same temperature as the wort.

FREEZING YEAST

This method of preserving yeast for future brews is straightforward, but this does not mean that we can simply chuck it in the freezer and all will be well! For the process to be successful it is necessary that the yeast is frozen as quickly as possible, and in a medium that will ensure the yeast stays healthy. Yeast that is frozen *slowly* will be affected by a process known as lysing, where the mechanical forces of shearing exerted on the cells' membranes by the formation of large ice crystals, causes them to rupture. High concentrations of salts are also formed which are destructive to the cell.

Yeast, therefore, should ideally be quickly frozen to secure optimum results. The following freezing medium helps produce smaller ice crystals, limits the formation of salt concentrations and regulates the pH of the cell:

Freezing medium

$K_2 HPO_4.$	6.0g
$KH_2 PO_4$	2.0g
$Mg SO_4 7H_2O$	0.1g
$(NH_4)_2 SO_4$	0.1g
Glycerol	200ml

Sterilized distilled water, to final volume of 500ml

Materials required for freezing the yeast

- 300ml Vodka or Polish spirit/or freezing solution.
- Aseptic sample bottles of 20ml capacity, or better still, glass vials of 10ml capacity.
- Small plastic open-topped container of about 200ml capacity.
- Small tweezers.
- Gloves.
- 20ml syringe.

Add the first four chemicals to 300ml of distilled water and boil for 15–20min to ensure sterility (or microwave on high for 5min). The glycerine should be quite sterile and added to the water as quickly and as aseptically as possible. Funnel into a sterile bottle and apply the cap loosely. When the medium has cooled to room temperature, tighten the cap and store the medium in the fridge.

Meanwhile, place the spirit in a small sealed container and leave it in the freezer for at least 24 hours. The spirit will chill to –20°C, but will not freeze. For first-time use, the sample bottle or vial

and syringe will be in a sterile package and safe to use; thereafter they must be sterilized by boiling in water for 15–20min. Now, mix equal amounts of the freezing medium and thick yeast slurry and, using the syringe, fill each container to 0.75 per cent to allow for expansion. Put on your gloves and remove the spirit from the freezer. Using the tweezers, immediately lower the vial into the alcohol, and the solution will rapidly form an ice-cold slush. Quickly add the caps and store in the freezer.

Alternative freezing solutions (described in *How to Make Wines with a Sparkle*) are as follows:

–21°C = 33 parts common salt
 + 10 parts finely crushed ice

–55°C = 10 parts hydrated calcium chloride + 7 parts finely crushed ice

–30°C = 77 parts methylated spirit
 + 73 parts finely crushed ice

–72°C = Methylated spirits
 + Solid CO_2

The finely crushed ice is collected by scraping the wall of the freezer.

Some sort of identification should be used for each strain of yeast. For best results, the use of frost-free freezers should be avoided, as their fluctuating temperatures can have an adverse effect on the yeast's long-term viability.

Theoretically, yeast may be stored in this way for years, but the home brewer is advised to limit this to about a maximum of one year. Should any difficulty be experienced in acquiring the chemicals for the freezing medium, then just add a ratio of 0.4ml of glycerol to 0.6ml of fresh thick yeast, and freeze immediately. The thick slurry enhances the survival rate. In this case, it is not advisable to store the yeast for more than 6 months.

Specific Yeast Cultures

Bottle-conditioned beers are a good source of yeast, and these can be propagated as previously explained. Wyeast Laboratories and Whitelabs of America produce a range of pure yeast cultures for all styles of beer. The cultures for brews such as Berliner Weisse, Kölsch, Wheat beers and Belgium Lambics are essential if the true character of such brews is to be obtained. Brulab Yeast Service, University of Sunderland, also produces a good range of British brewing cultures, plus Belgium and Bavarian Pilsner strains.

To resuscitate the yeast for brewing, it is best activated with the same urgency with which it was frozen. To do this, make up a starter medium with unhopped malt extract, diluted to a gravity of 1040 with water and boiled for 15–20min. Be careful that the wort does not boil over. Allow to cool to 20–25°C and aerate it well. Place the vial in between your thumb and forefinger and it will quickly thaw out. Now invert it above the wort until the yeast slips out into the starter.

Do not place the sample bottle directly into the wort as this might introduce contamination into the brew. Maintain a temperature of 20–25°C until a strong colony of yeast is built up. This might take several days, depending on the quantity of yeast. The starter should be shaken and agitated as often as possible to aerate the wort and drive out CO_2, which inhibits growth. When vigorous growth is underway, adding more malt extract, or wort, prior to pitching can increase the starter medium. Always pitch at the same temperature as the wort.

If, for any reason, the yeast was frozen *slowly*, the culture should also be allowed to defrost *slowly* before adding to the wort medium. Finally, if at any time you suspect that your yeast is infected or not up to scratch, discard it immediately!

CHAPTER 11

BEER FININGS

Finings are added to beer to accelerate the natural sedimentation of yeast and nitrogenous debris. Whilst it is true that beer will eventually fall bright in cask without the use of finings, particularly if copper finings are used, it does take a long time. A brew that is not fined runs the risk of the yeast and protein matter settling to about tap level where it can stubbornly loiter, sometimes for weeks! This phenomenon led to the invention, by Bob Pritchard, of the float take-off, so that clear beer could still be drawn off the surface of the brew. Beer finings are therefore recommended to bring about a rapid precipitation of all suspended matter, and to ensure that such residuum settles firmly. This will allow clear beer to be drawn off without incurring any problems.

ISINGLASS

The traditional fining agent used in British breweries is isinglass, produced from the swim bladder of tropical and subtropical fish. The swim bladder, sometimes called maws or sounds, is an air sack that runs under the backbone and which is inflated or deflated as required by the fish to control its buoyancy. Before the bladders can be used to clear beer, they are first dried, shredded and steeped in an acidified solution producing a viscous paste resembling wallpaper adhesive.

The active ingredient of isinglass is solubilized collagen, a high molecular-weight protein consisting of triple polypeptide helices. Isinglass is temperature sensitive and should ideally be stored at 4–10°C, although it can survive up to 25°C for very limited periods. Over 25°C, the collagen is rapidly denatured into gelatine that is not nearly so effective at clearing beer.

Although brewers have used isinglass for centuries, and despite much research into its behaviour, the precise manner in which it works is not yet fully understood. In 1905, T. W. Bridge theorized that solubilized isinglass collagen sedimented rapidly at the pH of beer as it was close to its iso-electric point. As the collagen precipitates, it collected yeast and nitrogenous matter that formed a coagulum and settled out rapidly.

The traditional hypothesis first mooted in 1927, and which was accepted until 1991, was that electrostatic interaction of positively charged isinglass and negatively charged yeast cells cancelled each other out so that neutral flocs formed and rapidly settled out. However, recent studies show that when isinglass is added to bright beer, flocs still formed. The evidence suggests initial electrostatic action, which may be accompanied by hydrophobic interactions, with soluble constituents of nitrogenous matter, to form flocs. These flocs first mechanically ensnare and then chemically bind with yeast and fine matter to form large flocs that sediment rapidly.

Commercially prepared isinglass is readily available either on its own or as part of two-stage finings. For best results, the beer should be chilled to produce the protein-tannin and chill-haze complexes that will become entrapped within the network of flocs. As the beer warms up, the collagen reactions are also speeded up and are most active from 13°–15°C, ensnaring the chill haze particles, and so the beer falls bright. Warm beer fined with soluble collagen does not entrap the chill haze particles, and so when such brews are stored in a cold environment, they will display a degree of opalescence. Isinglass also removes fatty acids from the brew and so enhances head retention.

The typical rate of addition is 11–14ml/ltr. As liquid isinglass contains some 250–500ml/ltr of sulphur dioxide it should not be added to lager beer.

Harris Filters produce Beer Brite finings, and these are made from silica-hydrolyzed isinglass collagen that is freeze-dried using the latest scientific techniques. The main advantage of using this stable fining material is that it only takes 15min to prepare for use. It removes chill haze and produces compact sediment in the bottle or cask, thereby keeping waste to a minimum. The beer clears very quickly and the product has a long shelf life without the risk of becoming denatured by temperature. It is a sensible precaution to keep it in the fridge. Isinglass should be used as per the manufacturer's instructions.

POLYCLAR

Polyclar is made from polyvinylpolypyrrolidone (PVPP) and is a popular clarifying agent among American home brewers. It works by absorption and is used commercially in beer filters as it reduces the effects of oxidation and absorbs polyphenols, thereby removing chill haze. To clear 25ltr

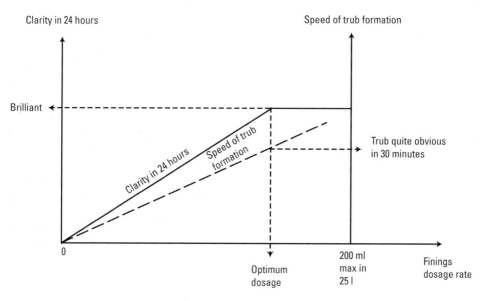

Optimum fining reaction. (G.B. Dallas)

of beer, mix 15g with 2ltr of wort to produce slurry and rouse it thoroughly into the brew. The beer should drop bright within 24 hours but it can be left, under suitable conditions, for up to a week.

GELATINE

Gelatine is produced by solubilizing animal tissue in alkaline solutions. Such denatured proteins have an iso-electric point of pH 4.7 and a net positive charge at the acidity of beer. Gelatine works by ionic bonding, in the same way as isinglass, but it is much less effective and so the procedure takes longer. To prepare the finings, sprinkle one sachet (15mg) of the granules into one cup of very hot water, stirring the mixture until dissolved. Prior to fining, thoroughly mix the gelatine with 500ml of beer and then rouse it into the brew. Take care not to introduce too much oxygen into the beer.

AUXILIARY FININGS

Auxiliary finings are employed to create the right environment for the successful clarification with isinglass. There are two basic types. Acidic polysaccharide is produced from gum acacia, and is negatively charged at the pH of beer. It has limited fining power when used on its own, but it is most important in enhancing the fining action of isinglass. The dosage is about 3.5ml/ltr, and it is added at least 4 hours before the isinglass.

Mineral auxiliary finings such as acidified silicates react strongly with nitrogenous matter and produce large flocs that settle out rapidly. They are ideal for getting rid of excess yeast and nitrogenous matter in a separate vessel before the brew is treated with isinglass in the cask. Alternatively, they may be added after the isinglass, but results can only be determined by experience.

Studies into the effect of yeast and fine particle size show quite clearly that the net charge of beer to be fined depends on the degree of copper fining with Irish moss. It was previously believed that the net charge of the nitrogenous materials in wort was positive charged, and this would result in neutralization with the negatively charged auxiliary finings. This would then lead to the precipitation of the protein materials to leave a balance that would co-precipitate with isinglass. Research has shown that a brew that has been optimally fined in the copper will have precipitated a considerable amount of positively charged protein so that the net balance of proteinaceous matter remaining will have a negative charge. However, a brew that has not been optimally fined in the copper will have an overall positive charge.

As auxiliary finings carry a negative charge and the wort also has a negative charge, they will repel one another and cannot electrostatically bond and coagulate. This has now led to the theory that the auxiliary finings either react with positively charged soluble elements that would otherwise clash with the fining mechanisms of isinglass, or they operate in such a way that they produce complex reactions that encourage the flocculation of the isinglass. The theory of beer finings now awaits further elucidation.

Liquid auxiliary finings are stabilized with about 500–800mg/ltr of sulphur dioxide.

CHAPTER 12

TRADITIONAL DRAUGHT BEER

Since 1979 my practice has been to manage draught beer from the wood in an oak pin, a cask of 4½gal/20.4ltr, and to regularly store strong ales in it for up to 4 months. To prevent it drying out when not in use, it has been used as a fining container, a resting vessel, and has been kept full of clean water, changed every

Steam-cleaning my oak pin.

three days. But after a long and weary apprenticeship, in my opinion oak casks cannot be recommended for the amateur.

However, an aluminium pin has been more successful, internally treated with epoxy resin so that the brew does not become contaminated by the metal. Cleaning is very easy with any of the recognized home-brew cleaning agents without the risk of metal contamination. Epoxy linings on casks must be checked regularly for integrity before using caustic soda-based detergents, as they corrode the cask very rapidly and sometimes explosively, as hydrogen gas is liberated!

The following tips and techniques were primarily learned from the use of the oak cask, but they are also suitable for a metal pin and larger casks.

TOOLS OF THE TRADE

As illustrated, a robust stillage is necessary to support the cask. Do *not* throw out the rear-end cut-out piece, as this will form the tilting wedge that will bring the cask into a final position so that all its contents can be drained. The tilting wedge is secured to the stillage by a small brass hinge, and when required it is flipped over into position to tilt the cask. As we are going to use water-cooling techniques, a superior rot-free stillage can be made from 20mm UVPC fascia cladding. It can also be doubled and glued and screwed together for extra strength.

Shives These are circular plugs available in two types, soft wood or PVC, and are used to seal the bung aperture on the pitch of the cask. A wooden shive will swell up and fill in any imperfections in the shive boss, making a very tight seal, and is superior to PVC.

Pegs or Spiles Soft pegs were traditionally made from American black oak that has microscopic tracheas running the length of the grain. This allows the excess primary conditioning gas to escape, but at the same time prevents the ingress of bacteria from attacking the brew. Today, soft pegs are made from bamboo that has a similar structure. Hard pegs are made from various hardwoods, and these are turned so that the grain runs the length of the peg, making a good seal, retaining the beer's condition.

Tuts These are also circular wooden or plastic plugs designed to fit the keystone boss that will secure the tap.

Taps Brass taps are very attractive but are no longer used commercially, having been ousted by plastic and stainless steel. Wooden taps are best avoided as they are prone to leaking when the cask comes under pressure, and invite infection.

Mallet A small rubber-headed or wooden mallet is required for pounding home the shive, tut and taps. Do not use a metal-headed hammer or you will damage the tap.

Cask dipper A traditional dipper is made of slim bamboo in four parts, each connected to the next by brass screw threads; it is calibrated in gallons from pins up to hogsheads. Although a dipper is not absolutely essential with such a small cask, you can make your own from a short piece of good quality hardwood. Calibrate it by adding a pint at a time, and etching the level of the watermark. The dipper should be sterilized before use. An alternative is to keep a record of the number of pints drawn off after each session chalked on an old slate.

Tools of the trade.

PREPARING THE CASK

Mallet a tut into the keystone boss and add the cleaning fluid. Seal the shive aperture with a suitable cork, and soak the pin for 10min; turn it regularly to ensure that all parts of the interior get a good soak. Now drain the cask and rinse it out with clean water.

If the brew is to be matured for only a week or so, it makes life easier to fit the tap at this stage. After the cask has had its initial soak, a wooden tut will be a little more pliable and its centre more easily cut out with a small chisel. This must be done with care, otherwise there is a risk that the tut will be split, resulting in leakage and bacterial infections. Gently mallet in the tap and make sure that it is secure. PVC tuts should not split.

PREPARATION OF THE BEER

An important requirement of beer that is to be dispensed in the traditional manner from a pin is that it should contain ample residual sugars to sustain it with an adequate supply of secondary conditioning gas during its shelf life. The top-fermenting techniques previously mentioned should satisfy this demand, and this, coupled to the saturation effect of the primary conditioning gas provided by the priming sugars, ensures a lively beer in tip-top condition.

The other requirement is that the beer should be casked with the right amount of yeast and fine nitrogenous matter to co-precipitate with the isinglass. Such a beer, having rested under the closed head during the cleansing phase, should meet these requirements, and under such conditions, it should fall bright within 24 hours.

Should a brew not clear rapidly, or if it does not fall bright within a few days, the problem might be caused by poor hot break formation in the copper. This will result in an excess of positively charged trub clashing with the positively charged isinglass, and the brew will either fail to clear, or is very slow to clear. In this case we should consider adding silica-based auxiliary finings, whose rapid action should quickly clear the brew. Another reason for the brew not clearing is if it has been racked into the cask too clean of wort materials, so there are not sufficient left in suspension to react with the finings.

Overall it is desirable to ensure that the wort is optimally fined in the copper, as treatment with auxiliary finings can run the risk of depleting the head retention properties. Also, if the excess wort matter has to be cleared in the cask, this will result in an excess of unstable deposits that might give clarity problems when drawing off a pint.

A brew fermented with dried bottom-fermenting yeast will probably have fermented close to the PG, and so it might not contain sufficient residual wort products for a successful cask conditioning. This can be overcome if the beer is snap-chilled at some 3° above the PG to halt the fermentation, and it will be clear enough to be racked directly into the cask.

Dry hopping will elevate the spiciness of the bouquet, and the amounts increase with the gravity of the brew. It can take up to 3 weeks for the aromatic oils to be fully extracted, and unless the beer is going to be stored for this length of time, forget it. With beers for quick consumption, better results will be obtained by late hopping in the copper.

RACKING THE BEER

With top yeast, carefully remove the crop from the closed head in the FV and siphon the beer, or run it from the tap using PVC tubing into the pin. Do this carefully, keeping the end of the tubing below the surface of the beer at all times to restrict the uptake of oxygen. When the cask is about 0.75 full, rouse in the finings and continue to fill the cask to leave some 300ml of space for the primings. After some 6 hours, the primings are added and the cask should be full to the bung, so that the beer is just level with the underside of the shive boss. A degree of oxygen uptake is inevitable whilst we do this. Finings should be used as per the manufacturers' instructions. Isinglass is much preferred.

Now, mallet in the shive, and roll the cask to and fro for a minute to mix the contents. If the shive is wooden, place the cask on the stillage at an angle so that it becomes wet and swells up, making a good seal.

PRIMING THE BEER

Priming the beer is necessary to saturate the brew with CO_2 and bring it into condition for immediate drinking. It should be understood that we are *not* attempting to use the pin as a pressure barrel: the three residual degrees are only theoretical at this stage, and do not start to produce gas until the yeast has consumed all the cane sugar primings.

If such a brew were casked and hard-pegged without priming sugar, it would be ages before sufficient gas were generated to bring the brew into a state of condition. Depending on the circumstances, we might do this if the brew is to be matured for some time. Usually we add quick-acting priming sugar so that the brew can be pulled in a fresh and sparkling state shortly after casking.

As yeast will preferentially utilize the sucrose (inverted to glucose and fructose),

it will consume the primings quite quickly, say over 2 to 3 days at 13°–14°C. Thereafter, it will synthesize the permease carrier maltotriase so that it can feed on the slowly fermentable maltotriose, producing 2.5 volumes of CO_2, which will evolve over a week or so, at 13°–14°C. Ideally, cask beer should be brought to peak condition within 48 to 72 hours after casking, and consumed within 4 to 7 days after broaching, so that the generation of secondary conditioning gas keeps it in a state of freshness throughout. 56g of cane sugar is sufficient, and will produce ample condition to impregnate the brew with CO_2. This is spent super-saturating the beer during the primary conditioning period, and it will also reduce the risk of oxygenation. Any excess of gas not dissolved (due to the amount of CO_2 already in solution) in the beer is vented to the atmosphere by the soft peg, leaving the brew with an approximate gas ratio of 1:1 at 13°–14°C.

After the cask is hard-pegged at about 36 to 48 hours or so, the residual priming sugar will still produce a small amount of gas, bringing the cask into a state of slight pressure, possibly increasing the gas content to 1.3 volumes. The secondary conditioning phase starts to kick in by this stage, and after a further period of 24 hours, the beer should be bright and ready for supping.

CONDITIONING

After a brief rest the cask will now require to be vented to allow the excess CO_2 from the priming sugar to escape. This will be a regular requirement most of the time, but during a cold snap you might find that most of the gas is absorbed and so the cask can be left until the brew is clear and ready for drinking.

Re-position the cask so that the shive is uppermost, and if you have not pre-drilled out the centre of the shive, it can be knocked out with a 150mm nail. Now gently mallet in a soft peg and allow the brew to come into primary condition, preferably in an ambient of about 13°–14°C. When venting is complete, the soft peg should be discarded, as microbes might have invaded the pores of the wood and to re-use it would run the risk of infection.

Sometimes the primary conditioning can be quite frisky, with the beer gently oozing out through the peg. Should this happen and the fobbing is light, just wipe it off with a cloth soaked in sodium metabisulphite. In some cases the fobbing will be quite strong, and in this case it requires to be controlled.

You could use a short length of 8mm copper pipe that is secured in the shive but is not in contact with the beer, to avoid siphoning. The other end is bent over and attached to a small plastic bottle that is plugged with a winemaker's cork with a small hole drilled through it to allow venting; the tubing is secured in the airlock aperture.

After the initial conditioning has quietened down, the soft peg is replaced with a hard one, and this seals the cask so that any more conditioning gas is retained to keep the beer fresh and in good condition. The exact time to replace the soft peg cannot be predetermined, as so much depends on the ambient temperature a which will influence the rate of the yeast's activity on the primings. Experience and judgement must be relied on.

An easy way to learn and judge the timing of hard-pegging is to silicone an airlock into a PVC shive. Watch the rate of bubbles passing through the lock and when they slow down, hard-peg. With experience you should be able to judge this very accurately.

As a general rule, as soon as the primary fermentation appears to have quietened down, on average 36 hours after racking, the hard peg can be inserted. If this is done too early, it is common to see seepage or light frothing around the tut and shive. This might only last for a short period, and so there is no need to do anything except regularly clean the affected areas. If the conditioning continues to be fairly brisk, a wooden tut might appear to distort a little under the stress of the internal pressure, with the beer seeping out around the tut and shive. In this case it will be necessary to slacken off the hard peg to release the pressure. The peg should not be removed completely, but as soon as a hiss of escaping gas is heard, it should be pushed back in so that only a very light escape of gas is audible.

The flow of gas should be controlled to avoid an excessive loss of condition, and as soon as it quietens down, the hard peg should be replaced immediately. If the hard peg is inserted too late, the brew will be fairly flat until the secondary fermentation kicks in.

BROACHING A CASK

If the brew is not to be consumed for some time after racking, the tap should not be fitted initially. To broach a cask is a skilful operation and requires a degree of dexterity! To fit the tap, slowly vent the cask to avoid a gush of gas escaping from the brew, lifting the yeast sediment. Then carefully cut around the edge of the tut with a small chisel, taking care not to cut right through it or damage it. Now place the tap against the centre of the tut and give it a sharp blow with the mallet to force it fully home. Most likely, a further couple of gentle taps will be required to ensure that the tap is properly seated and sealed. Take care not to overdo it, however, or the tut might split.

The cask should now be hard-pegged and left for at least a day to let the sediment settle down again. The cask will most likely come back to a state of pressure, and you should keep watch on the tut for any signs of seepage. Should this occur, a sound but gentle knock with the mallet should tighten things up and seal the cask. With PVC tuts the tap is just malleted home, and very few problems should occur with leakage.

SERVING THE BEER

After primary conditioning, the beer should quickly drop bright and the cask should be vented to allow the beer to be drawn off. Always vent the cask slowly to prevent the gas coming out of solution rapidly, with the possibility of bringing sediment up with it. Once this stage is reached, the shelf life of the brew becomes limited to a few days due to oxygenation. In the early stages of oxygenation the beer starts to taste like cardboard, and should the staling continue, its aroma becomes sweet and honey-like.

Just how lively the beer will be depends on the cellar temperature, and as long as it remains relatively steady at about 13°–14°C, the secondary conditioning will slowly evolve from the residual malt products. If the temperature drops below 13°C, the evolution of gas slows down because of the subdued activity of the yeast.

Should the temperature rise above 15°C, the yeast will become somewhat frisky and produce lots of gas. Initially this will be a bonus, as much beer can be drawn off, although if it becomes too warm the beer will taste somewhat cloying on the palate. But after such a short burst of activity the brew will be very flat and lifeless. The cask lees might also become unstable and flocculate to cloud the beer. A similar activity might also be due to a wild yeast or bacterial infection, and in such circumstances the brew might not clear, and will produce acid and nauseating odours.

After supping, it is important to replace the hard peg to retain any further evolution of gas in the cask. This will help the brew retain some condition, and will keep a fairly inert atmosphere in the ullage, keeping the beer as fresh as possible.

We can now see why we need so much gas in the first place, as it is being continually lost by drawing off a few pints under natural pressure, or by venting to pull many pints. By the end of the brew's short

Drawing beer with the (obsolete) Simcup cask pump.

shelf-life, the gas produced from the residual malt products are exhausted, and the amount of dissolved CO_2 will have dropped to about 0.8 volumes, or perhaps 0.5 volumes should the beer be left sitting too long. Remember that managing cask beer is an art, not a science, and there is no substitute for experience!

It is also possible to restore the lost condition by repriming when the cask is half full by adding fresh wort, as per the krausen wort table or equivalent malt extract. Simply use a small funnel and add the wort to the cask through the shive opening. Do not attempt to mix the beer, as the wort sugars will slowly diffuse throughout the brew and be acted upon by the yeast. Keep the cask hard-pegged, and allow a few days for it to come into condition. Depending on the ambient temperature, a degree of flocculation might occur, but this will settle down again in a short space of time. A good tip at this stage is to stoop the cask so that the beer settles in its final position and the contents can be drained completely.

Cask Cooling
The traditional cask cooling method is by evaporation. Hessian sacking or an old woollen blanket or bath towel are ideal materials, and these should be draped over the pin and kept wet. As the water evaporates it causes cooling, and depending on the ambient temperature, results are usually pretty good.

A most satisfactory arrangement is to acquire a large plastic tray from a commercial freezer and fit a small plastic tap to it, to act as an overflow. I use pint-sized blocks of ice and these immediately freeze on to the wet towel and remain there, slowly melting over a period of hours. The cold meltwater also slowly soaks the towel and drains into the drip tray where it is still cold enough to be used again.

A further refinement is to fill a couple of freezer bags with the ice blocks and sling them over the shive on each side of the cask. Puncture each one along the bottom with a series of small pinholes, and as the ice melts, the water will keep the towel wet automatically. Alternatively, fill a couple of ice-cube bags, puncture each cube, and drape over the cask. The use of a fan will enhance the cooling by increasing the evaporation rate. An alternative to ice is to use freezer blocks, but then we lose the benefit of the meltwater.

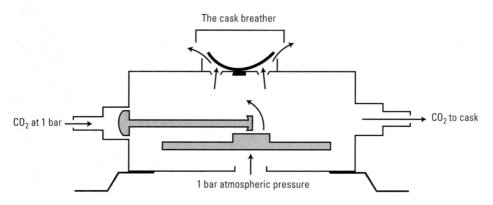

The cask breather.

The Homark Cask Breather

The cask breather is a simple device that maintains a sterile environment in the cask by supplying a quantity of CO_2, rather than air, into the ullage as beer is drawn off. While the beer is kept fresh throughout its shelf life, it does not restore lost condition and the beer should be consumed within a week.

The 'breather' is supplied with CO_2 at 1 bar (15 psi). When a pint of beer is drawn off, an initial slight drop in pressure inside the breather causes atmospheric pressure to enter the unit acting on a spring-loaded plunger that opens a valve allowing CO_2 to enter the cask. When the 'pull' stops, the spring-loaded plunger reasserts itself and the flow of gas stops, and any excess is immediately vented to the atmosphere via an exhaust port.

Temperature is also important in maintaining the 1:1 ratio, and should the beer warm up, it will lose condition that cannot be restored. It is important, therefore, that the cellar temperature remains relatively constant at 12°–14°C.

Cask Ventilator

This is a cheaper alternative to the 'breather'. When beer is drawn from the cask, the vacuum created inside the ventilator allows atmospheric pressure to force the small ball bearing in the left chamber of its seating, emitting air to replace the beer being drawn. The right-hand chamber is sealed by the heavier ball bearing being sucked downwards. When no beer is being drawn off, both ball bearings seal the cask, only retaining a very slight back pressure; should the internal pressure rise a little, the heavier ball bearing in the right-hand chamber is forced off its seating, allowing the cask to ventilate. The lighter ball bearing in the left-hand chamber is forced on to its seating, denying the ingress of air. This system retains a low level of natural CO_2 above the surface of the beer.

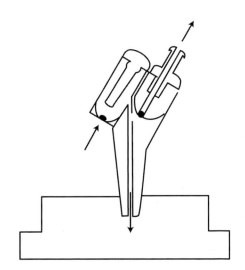

The cask ventilator.

Beer from the wood.

Using a Pressure Barrel

Pressure barrels can also be used to dispense beer in the traditional manner, but the cap will require some modification. A 15mm gas valve and copper pipe can be used, and these are secured to the cap by a tank connector (*see illustration*). The gas valve is strong enough to retain the internal pressure, and can be used as 'hard and soft pegs' to control the cask conditioning. I also fit the Homark cask breather to it. It can also be used to accept top pressure from a commercial CO_2 cylinder, via a pressure-reducing valve, and a sensible level of pressure that just keeps the beer flowing with a good head can be obtained. Without too much difficulty several barrels can be attached to one cylinder and the gas valve used to control the desired pressure to each one. A small pressure gauge fitted to the cap will ensure regular pressure.

Racking draught beer.

When using a pressure barrel, the cask beer racking method can still be used, but in this case the objective is to retain all the gas produced by residual wort products and the primings sugar. In this case reduce the racking gravity to about 2°, producing about 1.5 volumes of CO_2, and with the gas produced by the priming sugar, we have enough to condition the beer and push it out with a nice head. If this is done successfully there is no reason why virtually all of the brew cannot be dispensed before the need for extraneous CO_2. In this case a good robust barrel is recommended.

DEALING WITH PROBLEMS

Many home brewers experience flat draught beer, and there are many factors influencing this problem, such as leaky washers on caps and injectors; but it is primarily the fact that the brew is being racked at too low a gravity. This results in a lack of wort products to supply the essential conditioning gas, and as a result we have to rely on extraneous CO_2.

Cane sugar primings can also be replaced with glucose powder or syrup that is less sweet over a range of gravities.

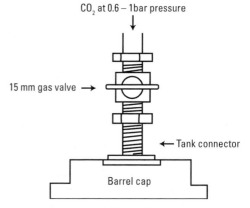

A domestic gas valve used for CO_2.

Draught beer in the fridge.

Table 26   Krausen wort for 25ltr brews
(For other volumes divide by 25 ×
new volume)

	Draught beer	Bottled beer (long term)	Bottled beer (short term)
OG	= 85g (3.4g/ltr)	= 72g (2.9g/ltr)	= 56g (2.24g/ltr)
1,030	Add 1,250ltr	Add 1,028ltr	Add 822ltr
1,035	1071	881	704
1,040	938	772	617
1,045	833	685	548
1,050	750	617	493
1,055	682	561	448
1,060	625	514	411
1,065	577	474	379
1,070	536	441	352
1,075	500	411	328
1,080	469	385	308

Should wort primings be used, the following table should add about 3.4g/ltr, over and above the 25 per cent or so of unfermentable materials, in 25ltr brews. In this case, the wort should be collected from the FV before fermentation.

Alternatively, if the beer is to be casked bright, then it will be necessary to prime it with some krausen wort to bring it into condition. In this case, the Krausen wort should be taken from the FV during the low Krausen phase and kept in a vented container in the fridge until required. We can also make up 'Krausen wort' with malt extract to the same gravity and volume, and add freshly fermenting yeast.

The columns for bottled beer in the table can also be used to prime draught beer, but the column for draught should not be used for bottled beer.

The brew should now be racked into the pressure barrel, and if necessary the auxiliary finings added. Leave the brew to rest for a further 4 hours to allow the coagulation of the proteins to take place, and then stir in the isinglass, or other fining material, and wait at least 6 hours before adding the primings. Seal the cask and leave it in an ambient temperature of about 18°C for 2 to 3 days. During this period of warm conditioning, the brew will come into primary condition and thereafter the cask should be moved to its final serving site. Ideally this should be 13–14°C, and the brew should fall bright within 24 to 48 hours.

Ullage
The ullage in draught containers will vary due to the size of the container and the volume of the brew. Some people worry about the deleterious effects of oxygen from the ullage, but this should

not be a problem: the ullage will only contain 21 per cent of oxygen, and due to the large surface area above the brew this is rapidly absorbed by the beer and reduced by the yeast as it ferments the priming sugars. The CO_2 produced rapidly charges the ullage with a protective inert atmosphere above the brew.

Extraneous CO_2

If the brew has been successfully racked at 2–3° above the PG, the gas produced from the residual wort products and the priming sugar will regularly dispense the brew over a period of weeks. If the brew is racked close to the PG, there will not be sufficient evolution of CO_2 to continually dispense the beer after the priming sugar has been exhausted. In this case it will be necessary to augment the brew with extraneous CO_2.

As a beer matures, the gases in the beer and headspace will equalize, but as beer is drawn off, more CO_2 will come out of solution into the headspace to maintain the balance of gases and, consequently, the beer becomes progressively flat. If a lot of beer is drawn off quickly, we run the risk of the gas coming out of solution fast enough to bring up with it the sedimented yeast and nitrogenous debris that will cloud the beer.

For best results the amount of gas in the ullage should be slightly in excess of the amount of gas in solution. Sensible use of a CO_2 injector system maintaining a slight head of pressure will keep the beer flowing in a fresh and lively state with a good head formation and retention. The best time to use the injector is when the brew is pouring 75 per cent beer and 25 per cent froth in the glass, and gentle top pressure is applied to maintain this.

Head Formation

To obtain a nice creamy top, take 100mm of food-grade PVC tubing, soften the end in hot water, and slip it over the tap outlet. When serving the beer with gentle top pressure, it is forced down the tube forming a turbulent vortex that shakes the gas out of solution, producing nice thick foam. Keep the tube well down in the glass at all times and as the glass fills up, the head becomes creamier. Keep pouring until the head is about 50mm high, and then stop pouring and let the beer rest. The head will now stabilize and can be topped up to 1cm. An alternative to the above is to fully vent the barrel so that at 13–14°C we obtain roughly the 1:1 ratio of gas. This makes the beer much softer on the palate and 'more-ish'.

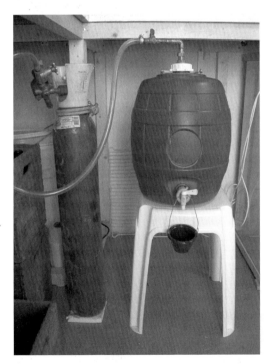

Top CO_2 pressure.

Serving draught beer from a pressure barrel.

The conventional CO_2 system for draught beer.

If you draw off the beer by gravity, do not expect great head formation or retention, and make sure that you flush out the ullage with CO_2 before resealing the barrel. Then bring the barrel back to fairly high pressure with more CO_2, and this will restrict any deterioration by oxygenation and keep the CO_2 in solution. Should a hand pump be used in conjunction with a cask breather, flushing out is not necessary although the barrel should be brought to pressure to keep the remaining dissolved gas in solution.

Cornelius Kegs

These kegs are made from stainless steel and are very popular with home brewers. The beer can either be conditioned in them, or racked bright. In the case of the former, the spear usually requires to be shortened by about 1cm to avoid sucking up the sediment as the beer is drawn. Racked beer needs to be conditioned by forced carbonation, discussed under bottling.

In the UK the keg is modified by fitting a pressure-barrel type CO_2 injector unit on top, and this is the most economical approach. A pressure gauge might also be fitted. The beer is served by a flexy-hose and tap. The fittings are 'quick release' and a pressure release valve vents the keg prior to opening.

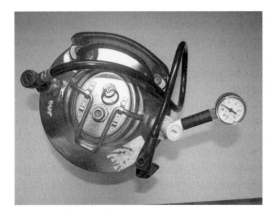

A bird's eye view of a Cornelius keg.

Cooling

Pressure barrels and kegs can be kept cool by evaporation by shrinking over them an old woollen sweater that is kept wet. A small fan blowing on them will also help. An ice ring can be made using a *savarin* mould that will sit over the narrow neck of a pressure barrel. Blocks of ice will sit on top of the soda keg and wide-necked barrels. The use of a fridge, adapted for cool and warm conditions, can also be used to keep draught beer at the correct serving temperature throughout the year.

Serving draught beer from a Cornelius keg.

CHAPTER 13

BOTTLED BEER

Whilst draught beer has a soft and quaffable character, bottled beer can be quite crisp, clean and refreshing. After a quick chill in the fridge, it makes an excellent thirst-quencher.

Bottled beer does demand more consideration than draught beer, and the strength of the beer, its racking gravity, bottling gravity and the anticipated time of storage, all have to be considered. Most important is the bottling gravity, as this affects the amount of residual dextrins and, consequently, in conjunction with primings, the amount of CO_2 produced.

THE BOTTLES

The bottles should be sound with no chips or cracks. Nowadays they come in all shapes, sizes and colours, and might be 'one-trip' or 'multi-trip', although the latter are becoming quite rare. One-trip bottles are designed to safely hold a pressure of 3.0 volumes of CO_2 and to be used once before being recycled. Although they are not made for continual use, they can be used with caution, and it is very important that priming rates are not exceeded. Multi-trip bottles are designed for continuous use and a stock should be acquired through your local home-brew outlet, or commercial returnable bottles.

Bottle sizes vary from imperial pints to a range of metric sizes from 250ml to 1500ml. Screw stoppers are now rare,

crown caps are most common, and screw-on crown types are becoming popular commercially; some continental bottles have swing stoppers. Traditionally, strong ales were bottled in nips – bottles of $\frac{1}{3}$ pint – and roughly 200ml. The alternative is to use 200ml multi-trip soft drink bottles. 250ml bottles are also fine, but as such brews are 'special' beers, why not bottle them in champagne bottles for that memorable occasion?

The colour of the glass is also important to cut down on the adverse effects of ultraviolet light reacting with iso-α-acids from the hops and the sulphur constituents of beer. Such photochemical reactions develop mercaptans, and these produce a garlic, or leek-like flavour and aroma. While all beers can suffer, light lagers are particularly prone to such light-struck, or sun-struck, reactions. Brown bottles are superior in restricting the actinic effects of light.

Obviously clear glass is not going to restrict the sunlight reactions, but commercial brewers now chemically modify the iso-α-acids by adding hydrogen atoms. Such tetra and hydroiso-α-acids are not sensitive to daylight; they also improve bitterness and enhance head retention. It is to be hoped that such hops might eventually trickle down to home brew outlets. All bottled beer should be protected from sunlight.

Bottles are best cleaned by filling them with a cleaning/sterilizing solution and soaking for 30min. Thereafter they can be flushed out with tap water, or by using the Rinse Master Mk 11. There is no need to drain them, as the hydrophobic nature of glass means that very little water remains, and they should be filled immediately. Bottles with stubborn deposits and surface films can initially be cleaned using the rotary brush attachment. Bottles that are flushed out after pouring a pint should not need such drastic treatment.

Bottling the beer must be done with care to prevent the brew picking up too much oxygen. This is best done by keeping the height between the beer container and the bottles as close as possible, so that the flow of beer is slow and turbulence is restricted. Also, the siphon tube should be kept below the surface of the beer to minimize oxygenation. Racking rods reach to the base of the bottle, and the flow of beer is controlled by a spring-loaded plunger that opens when depressed and closes when released.

By using a short piece of PVC tubing and a smear of silicon, the racking rod can be attached to tap on the FV or pressure barrel. When not in use, the rod is turned up out of harm's way and brought down for bottling; this allows ease of bottling at worktop height.

The headspace, or ullage, should not be more than 1cm, to cut down on the risk of oxidation. Too large a headspace encourages oxidation, with the consequential formation of cardboard-like notes and later, catty/elderflower taints.

Briggs *et al.* report that as little as 1ml of air in a 300ml bottle will have 1mg/ltr of oxygen, which can neutralize all the reductones in light lager. Commercial crown caps are now lined with oxygen-scavenging materials (sulphites and ascorbates), which limit the oxidative damage. Eventually these might be available to us.

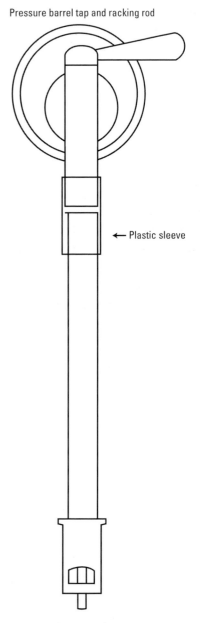

Pressure barrel tap and racking rod

← Plastic sleeve

The racking rod.

With home-brewed beer such risks are greatly reduced as CO_2 is liberated from the beer, and this helps dispel air in the headspace before the bottle is capped. As

The racking rod turned up out of harm's way.

the brew is bottled-conditioned, the strongly reducing power of the yeast will consume all the available oxygen, and as the beer becomes saturated with gas, the ullage, too, becomes pressurized with CO_2; this more than compensates for the slight uptake of oxygen during bottling, and the brew should be quite sound.

As recommended by Pasteur, it is advisable to lay the bottles on their sides for the first 24 to 36 hours of warm conditioning; this will create a larger surface area for the beer to absorb the oxygen, and be rapidly reduced by the yeast. Before placing them upright, give each bottle a couple of sharp twists to dislodge the yeast deposit.

Home-brewed beer can show remarkable stability of storage. In 1979 I brewed and bottled 10ltr of Russian stout, OG 1095 (loaded with reductones); there are still a few bottles left, and one was consumed in good condition at Christmas 2005!

REGULAR BREWS

These brews are OG 1030–1040, of short-term maturation.

Due to the powdery nature of dried yeast in the past, it was sound advice not to bottle direct from the FV as the heavy yeast deposit risked off-flavours and cloudiness on pouring. Such brews required fining in a secondary closed FV so that the brew could be bottled with the minimum of bottle sediment. Using the high quality dried yeast cultures available today results in a brew that is virtually clear by the end of the fermentation; this allows beer to be bottled direct from the FV after fermentation, without producing thick yeast deposits. In this case, as soon as the brew has attenuated to its PG, add three to five Campden tablets, and cover the beer to protect it from aerial infection. Wait a further 24 hours, and bottle.

Alternatively, we may rack the brew into a closed secondary FV, add Campden tablets, and 48 to 72 hours later add the bulk primings and bottle. Mature for 4 to 6 weeks. If using top-fermenting yeast, rack the brew just above the PG; allow it to attenuate to a stable PG, and clarify prior to bottling. Ideally the brew should only display a degree of opalescence. If the brew is bright, treat with Krausen.

MEDIUM-STRENGTH BREWS

These brews are 1040–1050, of medium-term maturation.

Ideally the brew should be racked into the secondary FV, with 2° of gravity above the PG. The secondary FV may be an oak or metal pin, or a pressure barrel. Dry hops may be added; the quantity varies with the gravity of the brew, and it is largely a matter of experimentation to find out the most desirable amount. Dry hops also assist clearing by acting as an attraction site for yeast and nitrogenous debris. An initial trial in 25ltr brews might be OG 1030–1040, 15–20g; OG 1040–1050, 21–28g; and OG 1050–1070+, 30–35g. The brew is now left for 3 to 4 weeks, preferably at 13–14°C; it will slowly condition and clarify without recourse to finings.

During maturation the yeast will slowly feed on the residual maltotriose sugars, and the beer becomes impregnated with CO_2, which prevents oxygenation and infection by aerobic bacteria. A pin should be soft-pegged to vent the excess conditioning gas; thereafter, it should be hard-pegged to retain the condition and protect the brew. Pressure barrels can be vented by unscrewing the cap.

By the end of the maturation period the fermentable sugars should have been consumed, and the brew should have reached a stable PG. This is desirable so that we achieve a constant and safe gas pressure from the priming sugar. Attempting to bottle the brew a couple of degrees above the PG is fraught with difficulties, and due to slight discrepancies in saccharometer readings, the gas pressure will be variable, causing gushing.

The unfermentable sugars remaining in the brew are termed 'stable dextrins' (maltotetraose, maltopentaose, malto-hexaose, and so on). Most unattenuating yeast strains will not ferment maltotriose, and some super-attenuating types will partly utilize maltotetraose. Such residual saccharine matter provides the brew with its fullness and character. After maturation it is necessary to prime the brew with some Krausen wort before bottling.

HIGH GRAVITY BREWS

These brews are 1050–1070+, of long-term maturation.

Traditionally, the mash heats in such brews were slightly above the regular mash temperature to ensure an ample supply of maltriose sugars to sustain the yeast during the long maturation period necessary to clarify and mature the beer. The PG will also be higher than normal, and this usually requires more hops to counteract the residual sweetness. If you do not care for strong bittersweet beers, then stick to regular mash heats and hopping rates; thereafter, follow the above procedures. It is advisable to follow traditional practices, brewing in October and bottling in the spring, and very good results can be achieved with an oak pin, the brew acquiring a mellow, oaky/nutty character.

Maturation can also be conducted in brown glass demi-johns sealed with a Hambleton Bard safety cork, which is a plastic bung fitted with a one-way valve. A stainless-steel pin or 'Corny' keg will also do for the total maturation period.

When such brews have matured for several months they will be starbright, and require primings with Krausen wort, as in Table 26 on page 121. Before we add the Krausen, the brew should be gently racked into another container to avoid rousing up the sediment. The inevitable small loss of beer by doing so is made up with the Krausen. Protect the brew with an air lock, and when it shows signs of fermentation, bottle it. Mature for at least 8 weeks at 12°C.

YEAST

The choice of yeast for bottled beer has a profound influence on the quality of the brew. A strongly bottom-fermenting dried

Bottling beer using the racking rod.

the brew. We can expect more fermentable products in a brew that is bottled at the end of the fermentation, and less fermentable material in a brew that has been matured for some time. The priming rate should reflect this.

After a series of tests using laboratory gram scales the average weight of a 0.5tsp of cane sugar weighs 1.65g, the traditional priming weight per pint (1.45g/0.5ltr). Priming individual bottles with such small amounts presents us with the difficulty of regularity. Bulk priming is to be preferred as the sugar is equally distributed, and regardless of the size, or variety of sizes of the bottles, we retain the same priming ratio.

Regular brews (1030–40) that are to be bottled after a short rest in the FV will still retain a fair amount of residual fermentable products and so the priming rate should be kept on the low side, typically 1.12g/0.5ltr (1.27g/pt). A longer rest of forty-eight to seventy-two hours will attenuate the brew close to its PG, and so the primings can be increased to 1.3g/0.5ltr (1.47g/pt). Heavier ales (1040–50) matured for four to six weeks should only retain a minuscule amount of fermentable material, and so the primings can be safely increased to 1.45g/0.5ltr (1.65g/pt). Alternatively we may use Krausen wort. High gravity beers (1050–1070+) stored for months should have reached a stable PG and be virtually devoid of fermentable matter; these are best Krausened.

yeast is better than a highly flocculating brewery culture that will require prolonged rousing to get the brew to attenuate to the PG. Different types of yeast will influence individual characteristics of the brew on maturation, and the choice can only be judged by experience.

We can also consider carrying out the primary and secondary fermentations with a brewery yeast, and Krausen the brew with a bottom-fermenting dried yeast starter. This should give light sedimentary deposits that will resist rising when the beer is poured.

PRIMING

The amount of residual fermentable matter remaining after fermentation and maturation will vary with the gravity of

Bulk Priming

For example, a 25ltr ale (1045) would require 50 × 0.5ltr bottles × 1.45g = 72g of cane sugar (or 44 pints × 1.65g = 72g). Dissolve the sugar in 500ml of beer and add to the brew. Alternatively add Krausen wort.

As rousing primings into the brew will inevitably flocculate the sediment, the brew should be racked into another vessel. A degree of oxygenation will be inevitable, but the addition of five Campden tablets 24 hours before racking will help keep it in check. After a few hours the primings should be dispersed throughout the beer, and so it can be bottled. Once bottled, lie each bottle on its side for the first 24 to 36 hours.

An alternative is to use a small syringe and add 500ml/50 = 10ml per 0.5ltr bottle, or reduce the volume to 440ml/44 bottles = 10ml/pt. To convert cane sugar to alternative primings we may use the following formula that takes account of the differences in LDK and the percentage of unfermentables:

$$\frac{\text{Cane sugar primings} \times \begin{pmatrix} 1 + \% \text{ of} \\ \text{unfermentables} \\ \text{in new priming} \end{pmatrix}}{\text{Alternative sugar LDK/cane sugar LDK}}$$

In this case we are converting 60g of cane sugar to liquid malt extract containing 25 per cent unfermentables.

$$\text{e.g.} \quad \frac{60\text{g} \times (1 + 0.25)}{303 \text{ LDK} / 385 \text{ LDK}} = \frac{75}{0.787}$$

= 95g of liquid malt extract

Krausen Wort

The quantities in Table 26 on page 121 under 'draught beer' are based on an average PG of 25 per cent. We may add the stated quantity to prime the present brew, or use a quantity from the present brew to prime a previous brew ready for bottling; for example, when brewing a 1045 ale, take 910ml to prime a 1030 ale ready for bottling. It should also be understood that the Krausen wort in Table 26 refers to the time the brew has undergone maturation, and not the time it should be matured in bottle.

The residual sweetness of a brew can be increased by adding Aspartame (Candarel). This artificial sweetener is 200 times sweeter than sucrose, and one tablet, or one teaspoon of powder, equals one teaspoon of sucrose. The tablets contain lactose, and makes adjustments easy by initially adding one per bottle. The powder contains maltodextrins and is more suitable for bulk treatments.

BOTTLING

Yeast-Free Bottled Beer

Yeast-free beer can be achieved in two ways. A method that has been used successfully for light- to medium-strength brews is to ferment the brew as for draught, and after it has been racked, fined and primed in a pressure barrel, it is allowed to mature and come into full condition over a couple of weeks at 12–14°C. Thereafter the barrel is placed in a refrigerator, and the temperature is slowly brought down to about 5°C and held there for a further 48 hours. By this time the CO_2 will be well dissolved in the beer and can be bottled. The barrel should be slowly vented prior to bottling.

If possible, chill the bottles as this will help the brew retain its condition during bottling. To fill the bottles successfully with the minimum of turbulence and loss of gas, the end of the siphon, or racking rod, should be kept below the surface of the beer at all times, preferably at the bottom of the bottle. Fill each bottle slowly and cap immediately. A helping hand at this stage is welcome, and this is a good time to introduce your partner to the delights of craft brewing!

Counter-Pressure Bottling

There are various models available and they all work on the same principle of maintaining equal pressure in the beer keg and bottle. By opening a bleed valve on the filler head, the CO_2 escapes from the bottle, and the beer is forced into it by gas pressure entering the keg. Fobbing should be minimal, and the beer bottled under inert conditions. For best results, the beer should be chilled to 5°C. The system requires a CO_2 cylinder with a pressure-regulating valve and an accurate pressure gauge. The manufacturers' instructions should be followed closely.

Forced Carbonation

To produce artificially carbonated beer for bottling (or draught), the beer must be fined and racked clean of yeast into a pressure barrel. The temperature of the brew should be lowered to 0–5°C and held

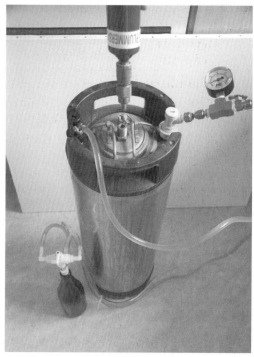

Bottling beer with a counter pressure CO_2 system.

131

there for at least 24 hours. Now introduce CO_2 from the injector unit, in short bursts, rocking the barrel as you do so, until the barrel comes to full pressure. The waves produced by rocking the barrel increase the surface area of the brew and so it readily absorbs more CO_2. Return the barrel to the fridge and chill again. After a few hours, repeat the process, although the barrel will not accept a great deal more gas as the rate of absorption decreases as the equilibrium is reached. If the barrel cap has a pressure relief valve, cautiously pressurize the barrel until this blows off.

We now have a fully carbonated beer, and as long as it can be kept chilled, the gas will remain in solution and it can be bottled as previously described for yeast-free beer. The barrel must be slowly vented before bottling and the use of a counter-pressure filler would also be an advantage. If using a commercial CO_2 cylinder for the process, a pressure regulator is essential, and this should be set to the safe working pressure of the barrel.

A refinement to the process is to make a 'carbonating spear' from 8mm copper pipe secured to a 15mm tank connector by the compression fitting. The blank end of the tank connector is prepared by cleaning the opening with steel wool and inserting a short length of 15mm copper pipe. Clean the pipe end and apply flux; now apply heat with a blowtorch, and tin the pipe with solder. Allow to cool, and apply more flux. Insert the pipe into the tank connector and apply heat until the solder runs free and makes a silver ring around the fitting.

Now secure a 15mm gas valve to the pipe and add another short length of pipe

Bottled beer undergoing warm and cold conditioning in the fridge.

Table 27   Working pressures for bottling

CO₂ volume required	Temperature °C		
	0.0	2.5	5.0
2.0 volumes	0.3 bar	0.4 bar	0.5 bar
2.5 volumes	0.4 bar	0.7 bar	0.9 bar
2.7 volumes	0.7 bar	0.9 bar	1.0 bar
3.0 volumes	0.9 bar	1.0 bar	1.2 bar

to this to take the CO_2 hose. The 8mm pipe should reach to the bottom of the barrel and is sealed. Two 0.5mm holes are drilled just above the base. A pressure gauge fitted to the cap would also be an advantage. Set the regulator valve at the safety limit of the barrel, and then slowly

A pressure gauge is useful for controlling pressure.

crack open the cylinder, but control the flow of gas into the barrel by the gas valve. The CO_2 will emit from the copper pipe in a fine spray, creating microbubbles that present a very large surface area for the transfer of gas, and superior absorption will take place. Bring the barrel to full pressure as before, and bottle as previously described.

CHAPTER 14

HEAD FORMATION AND RETENTION

'Landlord, charge the flowing bowl!'
Prof. J. S. Hough.

Head formation and retention are best considered together, as we cannot have one without the other. The head on a pint is very pleasing to the eye and imparts a smooth and even flavour. The products that contribute to good foam are formed throughout the brewing process.

MALTING

As the piece is germinating, the maltster has to strike a balance between sufficient proteolysis to provide FAN for yeast growth, and to reduce the potential of nitrogenous haze. At the same time, we must ensure that ample nitrogenous material remains to eventually produce palate fullness and head retention.

Under-modified malt, or chit malt, produces liberal amounts of nitrogenous products, but they require a protein rest to release the soluble nitrogen, reduce the haze potential, and enrich the wort with ample glycopolypeptides to produce good foam. Well modified malt has undergone sufficient protein digestion to satisfy these conditions. Over-modified (over-shot) malt has had its nitrogen and carbohydrate depleted, and is not accepted for brewing.

Kilning induces the formation of melanoidins that have been shown to enhance head retention by slowing down the rate at which foam collapses. They help protect the head from the detrimental effects of fatty acids, and promote the formation of foam: hence the tight, creamy head so obvious in stouts.

MASHING

The mash heat also has important consequences for the head on a beer. A mash at 68–70°C will produce more dextrins and hence better head retention than maltose-rich wort mashed at 62–64°C. Mashing at low temperatures, particularly for long periods, is detrimental to head retention. The over-zealous use of nitrogen-diluting adjuncts will deplete the wort of foam-positive materials.

Sparging should be halted at 1005–03 for ales and stouts, and 1005 for light ales and lagers, to restrict the extraction of foam-damaging lipids. Many commercial brewers actually stop sparging at 1010 to obtain superior worts.

COPPERING

Coppering precipitates significant amounts of polypeptide-polyphenol complexes, and so a balance has to be struck between the time of coppering and its effects on palate fullness, clarity and head retention. Beer with a low tannin content shows improved head retention. Short boiling times produce improved head retention, but long-term microbial stability might also be compromised. Light gravity brews, boiled for 60min, will retain ample foaming materials as long as the hot break and adequate hop utilization are also secured. Medium-strength brews usually obtain all of the above within a 90min boiling. High gravity brews might require coppering for up to 2 hours, and although substantial amounts of polypeptides are precipitated as break, more than sufficient remain for palate fullness and, theoretically, head retention.

The time of coppering also affects the isomerization of the hop resins, although there appears to be little difference between the type of hop products employed with respect to head retention. Coppering for 60 to 90min is usually quite adequate. The hydrophobic α-acids and iso-α-acids are responsible for foam rigidity, and the lacing effect of the foam as it clings to the side of the glass. Chemically modified hops (tetra and hydroiso-α-acids) promote good foam and, in conjunction with the hydrophobic glycopolypeptides, peptides and polypeptide-β-glucan complexes, contribute to the overall development of good head formation and retention.

High levels of hop oil are ruinous to head retention, but small quantities can inhibit potential gushing in beer. In general, lipids are destructive to beer foam and the eye-catching lacing effect. Most of the lipids are, however, precipitated with the hot break and filtered out through the bed of spent hops. The hop sparge will wash some of this through, and when we consider the overall quality of wort, we might well question if a hop sparge is necessary. Yeast consumes fatty acids (oleic and linoleic acids) during fermentation and so beer only retains a small amount of lipids. Due to the formation of staling fatty acids in hops during storage, old hops are not as foam positive as fresh hops.

FERMENTATION

Ethanol has the effect of lowering the surface tension, and at gravities up to 1050–55, enhances good foam and the lacing on the glass. Ethanol above 5 per cent ABV has a deleterious effect on foam; hence strong ales and barley wines do not usually exhibit long-lasting foamy heads.

Other factors that have a detrimental effect on foam are elevated fermentation temperatures and excessive yeast growth, which cause racing fermentations and low attenuation, depleting the beer of viscosity and saccharine matter. Cool fermenting temperatures and a low beer pH are most positive. More foam-stabilizing products are lost into the yeast head with top-fermenting yeasts than with bottom-fermenting yeast. Beer left in contact with large amounts of yeast deposits runs the risk of poor head retention and yeast bite due to the release of fatty acids during autolysis.

Foam forms readily from CO_2, Nitrogen (N_2) and air. CO_2 is very soluble and it readily dissolves in beer. On serving, it comes out of solution in large bubbles that produce a substantial, but rather coarse foam. N_2, on the other hand, is less soluble and comes out of solution in much finer bubbles, producing a tight-knit creamy head. Small bubbles also rise more slowly in the beer, and attract and collect more foam-stabilizing materials. Thus the foam produced is much richer and creamier, and better reflects light from the gases trapped therein; hence the smooth white creamy tops on nitro-beers and stout.

Air has an adverse effect on beer stability and it is only used to serve the beer, particularly in Scotland. In the air-pressure dispense system, working on the Venturi principle, beer in the drip tray is continually recycled with beer coming from the cask in the cellar. As the air is entrained with the beer, the CO_2 is agitated out of solution, and both form microscopic bubbles that produce a fine creamy top on the beer. A hand-pump with the sparkler screwed up tight will produce a similar effect.

The Head

Gas in a bottle or can of beer is held in a state of supersaturation, and beer has the ability to retain this. When a bottle is opened, the gas does not immediately gush out to re-establish the equilibrium of gases: it starts to come out of solution in small bubbles slowly, and more rapidly when larger bubbles form, and so a correctly primed bottle of beer, slightly chilled, should not foam excessively.

Bubble formation requires a nucleation site, typically a rough surface, and the base of some beer glasses is dimpled, or etched, to facilitate this. This is to please the consumer, so that the gas slowly evolves during consumption and retains a head. Also, beer in a glass does not evenly wet the surface with which it is in contact. Consequently it forms arches over any minuscule indentation, scratches, or dirt on the glass surface, forming minute air pockets. The saturated gas in solution is quickly driven into such microscopic air sacs that these become 'seed' bubbles.

The seed bubble continues to grow to a point at which its buoyancy drags it away

to the surface, leaving behind a minuscule air sac to seed the next bubble. This phenomenon can often be observed, as the gas evolves from a fixed point on the side of the glass, forming a fast-rising bead.

As the gas scurries to the surface, the walls of the bubbles are absorbing the hydrophobic foam-forming complexes, which give rigidity and structure to the foam. As the bubbles collect and collide at the surface, the foam quickly builds into a head, but slowly starts to collapse as it drains of beer and changes from a wet to dry, or liquid to solid state. N_2 has a tendency not to re-dissolve and so bubble drainage is slower. The continual evolution of bubbles builds up underneath the head, compensating for the rate of foam collapse from bursting and draining, maintaining the equilibrium.

The rate of drainage is restricted by melanoidins and the tails of the polypeptides worming their way into the frothy matrix, creating a more viscous foam. The iso-α-acids also form salts with some of the heavy metals in beer, particularly nickel, and further cross-linking with polypeptides and residual carbohydrates enhances a good head.

Foam is more stable when the internal and external pressures of the bubbles are equal, and the beer has a low and constant surface tension. The seasoned tippler knows all about this from experience, because when he goes to throw some darts, for example, he covers his pint with a beer mat. Consequently, the vapour pressure increases and so does the foam stability. A lidded beer stein achieves the same end.

As the head is forming, the foam is pressed against the side of the glass and the hydrophobic nature of the glass ensures that the beer quickly drains away. The head-retaining products that give the froth cling, stubbornly remain, so that the skeleton of the foam remains to produce the lacing effect.

Commercial brewers may add propylene glycol alginate to their beers to enhance head retention. This product is also available to home-brewers, although I have never found it necessary.

GUSHING BEER (WILD, OR JUMPING BEER)

This is an infuriating phenomenon that causes beer to foam uncontrollably as soon as a bottle is opened or a cask vented. There are many reasons for gushing beer, and we have already touched on the effect of microcrystals of calcium oxalate extracted during mashing, acting as nucleation sites causing beer to gush.

When we think of hops, home brewers naturally think of bitterness and aroma. Hops in various ways, however, can induce wild beer, and can also inhibit it! The oxidized products of humulone and its derivatives, for example, can induce gushing, and it was also recognized in the earlier forms of hop extracts that dehydrated humulinic acid was a powerful promoter of wild beer. Saturated long-chain fatty acids are known gushing agents, but most of the lipids are removed from extracts and hop oil.

Fungal infections are common on wet or weathered barley, and this was prevalent in the past when grain was stooked in the field to dry before storage. Microflora such as *Fusaria* (red mould) and *Alternaria* require a moisture content of around 25 per cent for growth and were known to promote gushing, but the reasons were obscure.

In early experiments a mash was infected with *Fusaria*, but the resultant beer did not gush. This led to the theory that the gushing was caused by a polypeptide extracted from the grain by the fungus, and this has now been confirmed. Improvement in agricultural methods and close laboratory analysis ensures the microflora is within very tight limits before the barley is accepted for malting.

The storage fungus, *Aspergillus*, will grow at 13 per cent moisture and will also promote gushing, and so barley is dried before storage.

Gushing can be inhibited if the fatty acids present are unsaturated – but of course, this is not something that we will be aware of. By increasing the hop rate, the unconverted α-acids and hulupones remaining after coppering help suppress gushing. Small quantities of hop oil, principally the faction caryophyllene, help keep wild beer in check. Presumably, as craft brewers generally use hops quite liberally in their brews, this suppresses any potential gushing and it is not a serious problem for us.

Gushing is not a difficulty reported by the micro-brewing industry, and for most home brewers the problem is occasionally caused by poor sanitation or the inexperienced over-priming or bottling of beer before it has reached a stable PG. The American Homebrewers Association does not report any significant problems with gushing at their annual beer competition, which attracts hundreds of entries.

CHAPTER 15

BEER RECIPES

RECIPE NOTES

Before we move on it should be noted that, with the exception of Berliner Weisse, Kölsch beer, wheat beers and Belgium beers, the yeast cultures recommended in the recipes should be taken as 'first choice' only. Whilst such specialist yeast will enhance the character and quality of palate of a well-formulated and brewed beer, they will not convert a bad recipe or a poorly brewed beer into a prize-winner!

Those who prefer dried yeast will still produce high quality ale and it is heartening to note that many microbrewers use dried yeast with complete satisfaction! The fermentation profiles are quite sound, but should the specialist yeast instructions differ then it is wise to follow the profile recommended.

The mashing efficiency is based on 275 LDK. Should your value of extract recovery be less then increase the malt contents of the recipe accordingly. Keep the mashing rate the same but limit the sparging to collect no more than 28–32ltr.

The type of hops need not be rigidly adhered to, so do not feel inhibited by trying various varieties should the recommended type not be available. The IBUs will also vary with the percentage utilisation in the copper, and the type of brewing liquor.

ENGLISH ALES

'Beer drinking don't do have the harm of lovemaking'.
Eden Philpotts, from The Farmer's Wife.

20ltr Burton Ale 1090

Grist & Sweet Wort			
Pale malt	4.600kg		
Mash liquor	10–12ltr		
Strike heat	72°C		
Grist heat	30°C		
Initial	66–67°C		
Mash stand	90min		
Sparge volume	22–24 litters		
Sparge heat	72°C 10min		

Bitter Wort & Beer		
Maximum wort	34ltr	
Copper hops	35 IBU Goldings	2–3hrs
	35 IBU Fuggles	2–3hrs
Aroma hops	30g Goldings, dry hopped.	
Copper adjunct	1.5kg pale malt extract	20min
	0.300g glucose powder	20min
% utilisation	18%	
Irish Moss	2 grams	10min
Yeast	Brulabs Burton 2556	
Ferm. profile	17–23°C	
Racking gravity	2° above P.G. into cask.	
Maturation	9–12 months	

25ltr 'Iced in India' IPA 1075

Grist & Sweet Wort

Pale malt	3.600kg
Carapils	1.000kg
Mash liquor	10ltr
Strike heat	72°C
Grist heat	32°C
Initial	68°C
Mash stand	90min
Sparge vol.	24ltr
Sparge heat	76°C

Bitter Wort & Beer

Maximum wort	34ltr	
Copper hops	30 IBU Northdown,	90min
	25 IBU Fuggles	90min
Aroma hops, 30g Goldings, dry hops in cask		
Utilization	18%	
Copper adjuncts, 500g Demerara		90min
	1.5kg lager malt extract	15min
Irish Moss	1.5g	10min
Yeast. Brulabs Burton 2556. Wyeast 1028. WLP005		
Fermentation profile	15–21°C	
Racking gravity, 2° above the PG		
PG	1018–22	
ABV	7%	
Maturation	6–12 months	

25ltr The Squire's Ale 1055
(Best bitter)

Grist & Sweet Wort

Pale malt	4.400kg
Crystal malt	0.100kg
Amber malt	0.100kg
Mash liquor	12ltr
Strike heat	72°C
Grist heat	32°C
Initial	66–67°C
Mash stand	90min
Sparge liquor	22ltr
Sparge temp.	75.5°C

Bitter Wort & Beer

Maximum wort	34ltr	
Copper hops	30 IBU Goldings,	90min
	20 IBU Fuggles	90min
Aroma hops	25g Goldings, hot soak	15min
Copper adjunct	450g Golden Syrup	15min
Irish moss	1.5g	10min
Utilization	22%	
Yeast. Brulabs Thames Valley 1508. WLP005		
Ferm. profile	15°–21°C	
Racking gravity	1017	
PG	1014	
ABV	5.2%	

25ltr Heritage Pale Ale 1048

Grist & Sweet Wort

Pale malt	4.300kg
Crystal malt	0.200kg
Mash liquor	11ltr
Strike heat	72°C
Grist heat	32°C
Initial	66–67°C
Mash stand	90min
Sparge liquor	22ltr
Sparge heat	76°C

Bitter Wort & Beer

Maximum wort	33ltr	
Copper hops	45 IBU First Gold	90min
Aroma hops	20g Styrians, hot soak	15min
Irish Moss	1.5g	10min
Utilization	22%	
Yeast. Brulabs Yorkshire 3524. Wyeast 1968		
Ferm. profile	15–21°C	
Racking gravity	1015	
PG	1012	
ABV	4.6%	

25ltr Hopsack Bitter 1040

Grist & Sweet Wort

Pale malt	3.500kg
Crystal malt	0.250kg
Mash liquor	9ltr
Strike heat	70°C
Grist heat	32°C
Initial	65–66°C
Mash stand	90min
Sparge liquor	20ltr
Sparge heat	76°C

Bitter Wort & Beer

Maximum wort	29ltr	
Copper hops	20 IBU Progress	90min
	15 IBU Fuggles	90min
Aroma hops	15g Goldings, hot soak	15min
Irish Moss	1g	10min
Utilization	22%	
Yeast. Brulabs Thames Valley 1500		
Ferm. profile	15°–21°C	
Racking gravity	1013	
PG	1010	

25ltr Dibnah's Mild Ale 1039

Grist & Sweet Wort

Mild malt	3.300kg
Torrified wheat	0.300kg
Mash liquor	9ltr
Strike liquor	70°C
Grist heat	30°C
Initial	64–65°C
Mash stand	90min
Sparge liquor	18ltr
Sparge heat	76°C

Bitter Wort & Beer

Maximum wort	27ltr	
Copper hops, 25 IBU Target/Northdown,		90min
Copper adjuncts, 40ml of gravy browning		20min
Utilization	22%	
Irish Moss	1g	10min
Yeast. Brulabs East Midlands 2540		
Ferm. profile	17–19°C	
Racking gravity	1013	
Sparge heat	75.5°C	
PG	1010	
ABV	3.8%	

25ltr Bottled Family Light Ale 1036

Grist & Sweet Wort

Pale malt	3.000kg
Wheat malt	0.200kg
Crystal malt	0.200kg
Mash liquor	9ltr
Strike liquor	70°C
Grist heat	30°C
Initial	66°C
Mash stand	90min
Sparge liquor	16ltr
Sparge heat	76°C

Bitter Wort & Beer

Maximum wort	top up to 32ltr	
Copper hops	25 IBU WGV	90min
Aroma hops	15g Fuggles, hot soak	15min
Irish Moss	1g	10min
Utilization	22%	
Yeast. Muntons Gold/Nottingham		
Ferm. profile	15°–21°C	
Racking gravity	1012	
PG	1009	
ABV	3.4%	

25ltr 'Broon Yil' 1048

Grist & Sweet Wort		*Bitter Wort & Beer*		
Mild ale malt	4.400kg	Maximum wort	34ltr	
Roast malt	0.025kg	Copper hops	25 IBU Fuggles	90min
Amber malt	0.100kg	Utilization	22%	
Mash liquor	10ltr	Yeast. Brulabs Tyneside Bitter 4008		
Strike heat	70°C	Ferm. profile	17°–19°	
Grist heat	30°C	Racking gravity	1014	
Initial	66°C	PG	1011	
Mash stand	60min	Bottling gravity	1011	
Sparge liquor	21ltr	ABV	3.9%	
Sparge temp.	78°C			

25ltr Buzz Ale 1040
(Honey beer)

Grist & Sweet Wort		*Bitter Wort & Beer*		
Pale malt	3.000kg	Maximum wort	25ltr, top up to 30ltr	
Wheat malt	0.200kg	Copper hops	30 IBU Hersbrucker	90min
Crystal malt	0.100kg	Aroma hops	21g Tettnang	10min
Mash liquor	8ltr	Adjunct	500g honey added to the FV*	
Strike heat	70°C	Irish Moss	1g	10min
Grist heat	30°C	Utilization	22%	
Initial	66°C	Yeast	Dried ale yeast	
Mash stand	60min	Ferm. profile	15–21°C	
Sparge liquor	17ltr	Racking gravity	1013	
Sparge heat	75°C	PG	1010	
		ABV	3.8%	

*Try various type for flavour and aroma.

25ltr Autumn Glory 1036
(Fruit beer)

Grist & Sweet Wort		*Bitter Wort & Beer*	
Pilsner malt	1.500kg	Maximum wort	27ltr
Wheat malt	2.100kg	Copper hops, 30 IBUs of mixed aroma hops 90min	
Mash liquor	9ltr	Add 2kg of blackberries/raspberries to the FV Strain	
Strike heat	70°C	onto the hot wort and pitch the yeast when cool[1]	
Grist heat	30°C	Ferment on the pulp at 15°–21°C for 4 days. Strain into	
Initial	60°C	Secondary FV at 1012[2]	
Sparge liquor	18ltr	Yeast	Dried yeast
Sparge heat	76°C	PG	1009
		ABV	3.5%

[1]Prior to fermentation add 2 tbsp. of winemakers pectic enzyme to counteract pectin haze.
[2]Try cautiously adding some raspberry/cider vinegar for a touch of 'Lambic' sourness.

25ltr Best Scotch 1038

Grist & Sweet Wort		*Bitter Wort & Beer*		
Pale malt	3.200kg	Maximum wort	28ltr	
Torrified barley	0.500kg	Copper hops	15 IBU WGV	90min
Crystal malt	0.225kg		15 IBU Fuggles	90min
Mash liquor	10ltr	Aroma hops	20g Goldings, hot soak	15min
Strike heat	70°C	Irish Moss	1g	10min
Grist heat	30°C	Utilization	22%	
Initial	66–67°C	Ferm. profile	15–21°C	
Mash stand	60min	Racking gravity	1013	
Sparge volume	18ltr	PG	1010	
Sparge heat	76°C	ABV	3.7%	

TRADITIONAL SCOTTISH BEERS

25ltr 3 Guinea Ale 1030

Grist & Sweet Wort		*Bitter Wort & Beer*		
Mild ale malt	2.700kg	Maximum wort	top up to 31ltr	
Crystal malt	0.200kg	Copper hops	22 IBU Northdown	90min
Roast malt	0.030kg	Utilization	22%	
Mash liquor	9ltr	Yeast. Brulabs Scottish Borders 4500. Wyeast 1728		
Strike heat	72°C	Ferm. profile	15°–19°C	
Grist heat	30°C	Racking gravity	1012	
Initial	67°C	PG	1009	
Mash stand	60min	ABV	2.7%	
Sparge liquor	18ltr			
Sparge heat	78°C			

25ltr 4 Guinea Ale 1042

Grist & Sweet Wort		*Bitter Wort & Beer*		
Scottish pale malt	3.500kg	Maximum wort	29ltr	
Crystal malt	0.200kg	Copper hops	25 IBUs Goldings	90min
Amber malt	0.200kg	Utilization	22%	
Mash liquor	10ltr	Irish Moss	1g	10min
Strike heat	70°C	Yeast	Brulabs Scottish Borders 4500	
Grist heat	30°C	Ferm. profile	15–19°C	
Initial	66°C	Racking gravity	1013	
Mash stand	60min	PG	1010	
Sparge liquor	19ltr	ABV	4%	
Sparge heat	76°C			

25ltr 5 Guinea Ale 1055
(Strong mild)

Grist & Sweet Wort		*Bitter Wort & Beer*		
Scottish pale malt	4.100kg	Maximum wort	30ltr	
Crystal malt	0.300kg	Copper hops	30 IBU Fuggles	90min
Amber malt	0.100kg	Copper adjunct	500g Barley Syrup	20min
Roast barley	0.030kg	Utilization	22%	
Mash liquor	10ltr	Yeast. Brulabs East Midlands 2540. WLP 002		
Strike heat	70°C	Ferm. profile	15°–19°C	
Grist heat	30°C	Racking gravity	1017	
Initial	66°C	PG	1014	
Mash stand	75min	ABV	5.2%	
Sparge liquor	20ltr			
Sparge temp.	76°C			

20ltr Highland Fling 1090
(10 Guinea Ale)

Grist & Sweet Wort		*Bitter Wort & Beer*		
Scottish pale malt	4.600kg	Maximum wort	34ltr	
Mash liquor	10–11ltr	Copper hops	30 IBU Northdown	2hr
Strike heat	73°C		25 IBU Fuggles	2hr
Grist heat	35°C	Copper adjunct	1.5kg pale malt ex.	20min
Initial	68°C		0.454kg Golden Syrup	20min
Mash stand	90min	Irish Moss	2g	10min
Sparge liquor	22–23ltr	Utilization	18%	
Sparge temp.	78°C	Yeast. Brulabs Burton 2556. Wyeast 1028		
		Ferm. profile	16°–23°C	
		Racking gravity, 2° above the PG into cask		
		PG	1028–32	
		ABV	7.5–8%	

25ltr Cavalier 80/- Ale 1044

Grist & Sweet Wort		*Bitter Wort & Beer*		
Scottish pale malt	3.600kg	Maximum wort	30ltr	
Flaked maize	0.400kg	Copper hops	25 IBU Goldings	90min
Roasted barley	0.050kg	Irish Moss	1.5g	10min
Mash liquor	10ltr	Utilization	22%	
Strike heat	71°C	Yeast. Brulabs Scottish Borders 4500. Wyeast 1728		
Grist heat	30°C	Ferm. profile	15°–20°C	
Initial	67°C	Racking gravity	1015	
Mash stand	90min	PG	1012	
Sparge liquor	20ltr	ABV	4.2%	
Sparge temp.	76°C			

25ltr Edinburgh Gold Tankard 1042
(80/-)

Grist & Sweet Wort		*Bitter Wort & Beer*		
Scottish pale malt	3.600kg	Maximum wort	30ltr	
Carahelle	0.400kg	Copper hops	25 IBU Challenger	90min
Crystal malt	0.100kg	Aroma hops	10g Goldings	15min
Mash liquor	10ltr	Irish Moss	1.5g	10min
Strike heat	70°C	Utilization	22%	
Grist heat	30°C	Yeast. Brulabs Scottish Borders 4500		
Initial	65°C	Ferm. profile	15–20°C	
Mash stand	90min	Racking gravity	1014	
Sparge liquor	20ltr	PG	1011	
Sparge temp.	76°C	ABV	4.3%	

25ltr 70/- Ceilidh Ale 1040

Grist & Sweet Wort		*Bitter Wort & Beer*		
Scottish pale malt	3.300kg	Maximum wort	28ltr	
Crystal malt	0.300kg	Copper hops	23 IBUs Challenger,	90min
Mash liquor	9.5ltr	Irish Moss	1.0g	10min
Strike heat	71°C	Utilization	22%	
Grist heat	30°C	Yeast. Brulabs Scottish Borders 4500. WLP028		
Initial	67°C	Ferm. profile	15°–19°C	
Mash stand	90min	Racking gravity	1014	
Sparge liquor	19ltr	PG	1011	
Sparge temp.	78°C	ABV	3.7%	

25ltr The Grousebeater's 60/- Ale 1035

Grist & Sweet Wort		*Bitter Wort & Beer*		
Pale malt	2.600kg	Maximum wort	24ltr, top up to 30˙l	
Crystal malt	0.500kg	Copper hops	20 IBU Northdown	90min
Amber malt	0.200kg	Irish Moss	1g	10min
Mash liquor	8ltr	Utilization	22%	
Strike heat	71°C	Yeast. Brulabs Scottish Borders 4500. Wyeast 1728		
Grist heat	30°C	Fermentation profile	15°–18°C	
Initial	67°C	Racking gravity	1012	
Mash stand	60min	PG	1009	
Sparge vol.	19ltr	ABV	3.4%	
Sparge temp.	78°C			

25ltr Session Sixty Shilling Ale 1037

Grist & Sweet Wort		*Bitter Wort & Beer*		
Mild ale malt	3.000kg	Maximum wort	26ltr	
Amber malt	0.250kg	Copper hops	20 IBUs Fuggles	90min
Oat malt	0.170kg	Utilization	22%	
Mash liquor	9ltr	Irish Moss	1g	10min
Strike heat	71°C	Yeast. Brulabs Scottish Border		
Grist heat	30°C	Fermentation profile	15–18°C	
Initial	67°C	Racking gravity	1012	
Mash stand	60min	PG	1010	
Sparge liquor	17ltr	ABV	3.4%	
Sparge heat	78°C			

25ltr Scottish Brown Ale 1040

Grist & Sweet Wort		*Bitter Wort & Beer*		
Scottish pale malt	3.300kg	Maximum wort	28ltr	
Crystal malt	0.500kg	Copper hops	20 IBUs WGV	90min
Chocolate malt	0.050kg	Irish Moss	1g	10min
Mash liquor	10ltr	Utilization	22%	
Strike heat	71°C	Yeast. Brulabs Scottish Borders 4500/Wyeast 1728		
Grist heat	30°C	Fermentation profile	15–18°C	
Initial	66°C	Racking gravity	1013	
Mash stand	60min	Bottling gravity	1010	
Sparge liquor	18ltr	PG	1010	
Sparge heat	78°C	ABV	3.8%	

25ltr Big Tam Scotch Ale 1075

Grist & Sweet Wort		*Bitter Wort & Beer*		
Scottish pale malt	4.500kg	Maximum wort	33ltr	
Mash liquor	10ltr	Copper hops	20 IBU Challenger	90min
Strike heat	73°C		20 IBU Goldings	90min
Grist heat	30°C	Copper adjunct	1.800kg light malt extract	20min
Initial	68°C		0.500kg soft brown sugar	90min
Mash stand	90min	Irish Moss	2g	15min
Sparge liquor	23ltr	Utilization	18%	
Sparge temp.	78°C	Yeast. Brulabs Scottish Borders 4500. Wyeast 1728		
		Ferm. profile	12°–18°C	
		Racking gravity	2° above the P.G.	
		PG	1018–22	
		ABV	6.7%	

25ltr Heather Ale 1045

Grist & Sweet Wort		*Bitter Wort & Beer*		
Scottish pale malt	3.100kg	Maximum wort, top up to 30ltr		
Carahelle	0.300kg	Copper flavour, 20 IBU Goldings*		90min
Mash liquor	9ltr		3ltr Bell heather tips	45min
Strike heat	73°C	Aroma	2ltr Bell heather tips	10min
Grist heat	35°C	Adjunct 454g Heather honey added to the FV		
Initial	67–68°C	Utilization	22%	
Mash stand	60min	Yeast	Dried yeast	
Sparge liquor	18ltr	Ferm. profile	15°–21°C	
Sparge heat	78°C	ABV	3.8%	

*Try adding some bitter Bog Myrtle (Sweet gale) with its Eucalyptus-like aroma.

STOUT, 'begorrah'!

25ltr Toucan Stout 1045

Grist & Sweet Wort		*Bitter Wort & Beer*		
Pale malt	3.800kg	Maximum wort	34ltr	
Roast barley	0.500kg	Copper hops	20 IBU Northern Brewer	90min
Flaked barley	0.500kg		15 IBU Fuggles	90min
Mash liquor	12ltr		5 IBU Target	90min
Strike heat	71°C	Utilization	22%	
Grist heat	30°C	Yeast. Wyeast Irish 1084 or Whitelabs WLP004		
Initial	65°–66°C	Ferm. profile	15°–19°C	
Mash stand	90min	Racking gravity	1015	
Sparge liquor	22ltr	PG	1012	
Sparge heat	78°C	ABV	4.2%	

25ltr Toucan Foreign Extra 1075

Grist & Sweet Wort		*Bitter Wort & Beer*		
Pale malt	4.300kg	Total wort	34ltr	
Roasted barley	0.500kg	Copper hops	30 IBUs Target	90min
Amber malt	0.200kg		30 IBUs Northdown	90min
Mash liquor	12ltr	Copper adjunct, 1.8kg pale malt extract 0.300kg		20min
Strike heat	71°C	Utilization	18%	
Grist heat	30°C	Yeast	Wyeast/Whitelabs Irish ale	
Initial	65–66°C	Fermentation profile,	15–19°C	
Mash stand	60min	Racking gravity	1023	
Sparge liquor	22ltr	Bottling gravity	1020	
Sparge heat	78°C	PG	1020 (Check for stability)	
		ABV	7%	

25ltr Old Fartalot's Oatmeal Stout 1038

Grist & Sweet Wort		*Bitter Wort & Beer*		
Mild ale malt	2.800kg	Maximum wort	27ltr	
Pinhead oatmetal	0.500kg*	Copper hops	40 IBU Progress	90min
Roast malt	0.200kg	Utilization	22%	
Amber malt	0.200kg	Yeast. Brulabs East Midlands 2540		
Mash liquor	10ltr	Ferm. profile	17°–19°C	
Strike heat	70°C	Racking gravity	1012	
Grist heat	30°C	PG	1009	
Initial	64°–65°C	ABV	3.3%	
Sparge liquor	17ltr			
Sparge temp.	78°C			

*Or porridge oats.

25ltr Thistle Stout 1040

Grist & Sweet Stout		*Bitter Wort & Beer*		
Pale malt	3.300kg	Maximum wort	31ltr	
Amber malt	0.300kg	Copper hops	25 IBUs Target	90min
Black malt	0.400kg		15 IBUs Fuggles	90min
Flaked oats	0.250kg	Utilization	22%	
Mash liquor	11ltr	Yeast	Whitelabs Irish WLP004	
Strike heat	70°C	Ferm. profile	15–19°C	
Grist heat	30°C	Racking gravity	1013	
Initial	65°C	PG	1010	
Mash stand	60min	ABV	3.8%	
Sparge liquor	20ltr			
Sparge heat	78°C			

25ltr Milk Stout 1047

Grist & Sweet Wort		*Bitter Wort & Beer*		
Pale malt	3.250kg	Maximum wort	29ltr	
Crystal malt	0.500kg	Copper hops, 25 IBU WGV		90min
Chocolate malt	0.100kg	Copper adjunct, 500g lactose[1][2]		90min
Roast malt	0.085kg	Utilization	22%	
Mash liquor	10ltr	Yeast. Brulabs East Midlands 2540		
Strike heat	73°C	Ferm. Profile	17°–19°C	
Grist heat	30°C	Racking gravity	1019	
Initial	67°–68°C	PG	1016	
Mash stand	60min	ABV	3.9%	
Sparge liquor	19ltr			
Sparge temp.	78°C			

[1]Will add some 5° to the O.G. and P.G.
[2]Or try adding 1–2 Candarel tablets per bottle.

25ltr Paddy's Porter 1055

Grist & Sweet Wort		*Bitter Wort & Beer*		
Pale malt	4.000kg	Maximum wort	34ltr	
Brown/amber malt	0.250kg	Copper hops	40 IBU Fuggles	90min
Roast malt	0.250kg	Copper adjunct	1kg pale malt extract	20min
Mash liquor	11ltr	Utilization	22%	
Strike heat	70°C	Yeast. Wyeast 1084. Whitelabs WLP023		
Grist heat	30°C	Ferm. profile	15°–19°C	
Initial	65°C	Racking gravity	1016	
Mash stand	75min	PG	1013	
Sparge liquor	23ltr	ABV	5.4%	
Sparge temp.	78°C			

25ltr Scottish Porter 1050

Grist & Sweet Wort		*Bitter Wort & Beer*		
Pale malt	4.000kg	Maximum wort	34ltr	
Crystal malt	0.500kg	Copper hops	35 IBUs Northdown	90min
Black malt	0.300kg	Copper adjunct	0.300kg dark Spraymalt	20min
Mash liquor	12ltr	Utilization	22%	
Strike heat	70°C	Yeast	Wyeast Irish 1084	
Grist heat	30°C	Ferm. profile	15–19°C	
Initial	65°C	Racking gravity	1016	
Mash stand	60min	PG	1013	
Sparge liquor	22ltr	ABV	4.7%	
Sparge heat	78°C			

25ltr Rye Stout 1044

Grist & Sweet Wort		*Bitter Wort & Beer*		
Pale malt	2.000kg	Maximum wort	31ltr	
Rye malt	2.000kg	Copper hops	35 IBU Northern Brewer	90min
Roasted barley	0.500kg	Utilization	22%	
Mash liquor	11ltr	Yeast. Wyeast Irish 1084		
Strike heat	70°C	Ferm. profile	15–19°C	
Grist heat	30°C	Racking gravity	1013	
Initial	65–66°C	PG	1010	
Mash stand	75min	ABV	4.2%	
Sparge liquor	20ltr			
Sparge temp.	78°C			

10ltr Tsar Russian Stout 1095

Grist & Sweet Wort		*Bitter Wort & Beer*		
Pale malt	3.500kg	Maximum wort	18ltr	
Roast malt	0.500kg	Copper to reduce volume to just over 10ltr		
Mash liquor	9ltr	Copper hops, 85 IBU Target		90min
Strike liquor	70°C	Copper adjunct, 500g pale Spraymalt		20min
Grist heat	30°C	Utilization	18%	
Initial	64°–65°C	Yeast	Wyeast Irish 1084	
Sparge liquor	9ltr	Ferm. profile	15°–21°C	
Sparge heat	78°C	Racking gravity	1033–1037	
		PG	1030–1034	
		ABV	10%	

25ltr Ginger Stout 1035

Grist & Sweet Wort		*Bitter Wort & Beer*		
Pale malt	3.000kg	Maximum wort	28ltr	
Crystal malt	0.500kg	Copper hops	38 IBU Goldings	90min
Roast malt	0.200	Copper adjunct 1X 350g jar of stem ginger		15min*
Mash liquor	9ltr	Utilization	22%	
Strike heat	70°C	Yeast	Dried yeast	
Grist heat	30°C	Ferm. profile	15–21°C	
Initial	65°C	Racking gravity	1011	
Mash stand	60min	PG	1008	
Sparge liquor	19ltr	ABV	3.5%	
Sparge heat	78°C			

*Also try 100mm of peeled and chopped root ginger.

25ltr Chocolate Stout 1040

Grist & Sweet Wort		*Bitter Wort & Beer*		
Pale malt	3.200kg	Maximum wort	30ltr	
Crystal	0.400kg	Copper hops	25 IBU Fuggles	90min
Chocolate	0.200kg	Copper adjunct	300g, Belgium chocolate*	20min
Black	0.100kg	Utilization	22%	
Mash liquor	10ltr	Yeast	Dried ale yeast	
Strike heat	72°C	Ferm. profile	15–21°C	
Grist heat	30°C	Racking gravity	1013	
Initial heat	65°C	PG	1010	
Mash stand	60min	ABV	3.8%	
Sparge liquor	20ltr	Sparge heat	75°C	
Sparge heat	75°C			

*At least 70% cocoa solids, preferably 80%. Also try 300g cocoa powder.

25ltr Hibernian Red Ale 1045

Grist & Sweet Wort		*Bitter Wort & Beer*		
Pale malt	4.400kg	Maximum wort	33ltr	
Roasted barley	0.040kg	Copper hops, 25 IBU Target hops		90min
Mash liquor	12ltr	Irish Moss	1.5g	10min
Strike heat	72°C	Utilization	22%	
Grist heat	30°C	Yeast	Wyeast Irish 1084	
Initial	66°–67°C	Fermentation profile	12°–18°C	
Mash stand	90min	Racking gravity	1015	
Sparge liquor	21ltr	PG	1012	
Sparge heat	78°C	ABV	4.2%	

CHAPTER 16

CONTINENTAL BEERS AND BEER RECIPES

CONTINENTAL BEERS

Pilsner

The Czech Pilsner is a light lager of about 3.5–5% ABV. It evolved at the Citizen's Brewery (est. 1832) at Pilsen in the Czech Republic in 1842. Legend has it that a monk smuggled the bottom-fermenting yeast from Munich, and the Czechs engaged the Bavarian brewer, Joseph Groll, to brew their golden lager. It is brewed with soft water, is very low in bicarbonate, and aged for 2 to 3 months; 30–43 IBUs of Saaz hops produce a medium hop flavour and a dry finish. German Pilseners are brewed from 30–40 IBUs, but the palate is crisper, influenced by a slightly harder liquor. The condition in both beers should be sparkling with a good running bead, forming good head formation and retention.

Dortmunder

This is a golden beer, with a deeper complexion than a Pilsner. It is a beer that attenuates well, has a clean and refreshing medium malt and hop flavour, and good head retention. Historically it is brewed with hard waters similar to Burton-on-Trent, but with less gypsum and almost twice the level of bicarbonate. Today the liquor is softened to less than 50mg/ltr of carbonate. Traditionally it is aged 3 to 4 months. ABV 55.5 per cent; IBUs 18–22.

Munchen Dunkel

This is a full-bodied, brown aromatic beer, brewed with the rich malty-flavoured Munich and Melanoidin-type malts. It has a very mild hop flavour and sweetish malty palate; it is lagered for 3 to 5 months. The water is moderately soft, with a bicarbonate content of 100–150mg/ltr. It is claimed to be similar to Dublin water, but today, the domestic supply in Dublin only supports some 14mg/ltr of bicarbonates. 24 IBUs; ABV 4–5 per cent.

Munchen Helles

Pale to deep gold in colour, this beer has a light, malty sweetness in the palate, balanced by a delicate hop flavour. It is best brewed with soft water, with 50mg/ltr carbonate. ABV 4–5 per cent; IBUs 18–25.

Bock Beer

This is a seasonal high gravity brew that is considered to be too full bodied for general consumption. Bock beer is brewed with a good percentage of roasted Munich and dextrin-rich malt that gives it its characteristic full malty-roasty flavour.

The ABV must not be less than 6 per cent. Brew with temporarily hard liquor at a maximum of 150mg/ltr of carbonate; IBUs 25–30. Dopplebocks are similar, with an ABV of 7–13 per cent, IBUs 18–30.

Vienna Style

This rich, amber-coloured beer was first brewed by the eminent brewer, Anton Dreher, in 1841, and made the Austrian capital famous as a brewing centre. The OG is 1050–60, the palate light dryish and malty, with 20–30 IBUs. Brew with Munich-type liquor supporting a maximum of 150mg/ltr of carbonates. Colour 15–30 EBC°, ABV 4.9–5.8. The Vienna style also includes the celebrated 'Marzen' and 'Octoberfest' beers.

Weizenbiers

Until the late twentieth century, 'wheat beers' were little known outside their birthplace, Bavaria. They fall into three categories: Weizenbiers or Weissebier (white beer), Dunkelweizen (dark beer) and the celebrated Berliner Weisse (*see below*).

Weizenbier may be straw to golden in colour, with a malty, but slightly estery-tart or phenolic palate and an ABV of 3–5 per cent. Hopping is at all times low, at 15 IBUs. By law, wheat beers should not contain less than 50 per cent malted wheat, the remainder being pale malt with perhaps a small proportion of melanoidin-type malts for flavour. They are best brewed with soft to medium hard liquor. The fermentation profile is around 25–30°C.

Dunkelweizen is similar, and must also have a minimum of 50 per cent malted wheat. The colour may be chestnut to rusty brown. Hop flavour is barely evident at 15 IBUs, and an ABV of 4.8 to 5.5 per cent rounds off this flavoursome beer style. The liquor may be soft to hard, and the fermentation profile is 15–21°C.

Wheat beers are fermented at elevated temperatures to enhance the formation of the fruity/estery palate. The spicy/clove-like or phenolic palate can only be achieved by using a true wheat beer yeast.

Berliner Weisse

A very dry beer with a low attenuation and a pH of about 3.3. The palate is distinctly sour, created by a mixture of *S. -cerevisiae* and *L-. delbruckii* cultures. The grist should contain 60–75 per cent malted wheat, the remainder being Pilsner malt. Hopping is very low at 3–5 IBUs, and the ABV is around 2.8–3.4 per cent. A hard liquor is best, and a fermentation profile of around 15°C should be observed. A special yeast culture is necessary to brew this beer successfully.

Kölsch Bier ('Keulsh')

Pronounced 'Keulsh', this beer is the speciality from the city of Köln (Cologne), northern Germany. A pale golden, top-fermented beer at 10–12 EBC°, it has a light, clean and refreshing palate with a hint of fruity tartness in the finish. It is mildly hopped at 20–25 IBUs, and an OG of 1040–46. It has an ABV of about 5 per cent. Lager for at least 6 weeks; Kölsch yeast is recommended.

Weizenbocks

The high gravity equivalents of wheat beers, with original gravities of 1066–80; they may be pale or dark, with 10–15 IBUs and an ABV of 7–10 per cent.

Rauchbier

The speciality smoked beer that evolved in Bamberg, northern Bavaria. Rauchbier should have a full, malty-rich palate with medium hop bitterness at around 20–30 IBUs. The smoke character should be in harmony with the malt and hops, the colour about 30 EBC° and the ABV 4.5–5 per cent. Rauchbier is a rather acquired taste. Brew with soft to medium-hard carbonate liquor.

Belgium Abbey Beers
In 1098 Benedictine monks, led by St Robert Molesme, formed an Order of Monks in the forest of Citeaux, or Cistercian. In the seventeenth century the order split into two communities of Common Observance and Strict (silence) Observance, the latter becoming the Cistercian of the Reformed Rule under the Norman, De Rance (1626–1700), who was the Abbot of La Trappe. Monasteries throughout Belgium brew beers for sale, but only abbeys of the Trappist order can label their beers 'Trappist'.

Trappist ales are top-fermented, bottle-conditioned and available in various characteristics. High fermentation temperatures are common to induce an estery palate. Hopping is usually light, at 20–30 IBUs. Candy sugar is preferred to influence flavour, and the water is soft, very low in calcium, and slightly acidic. Specialist yeast is necessary to brew this type of beer successfully.

Lambic Beers
These are sometimes referred to as 'wild beers' due to their natural inoculation with wild yeasts that produce an acidic sourness over the maturation period. As no hop character is required only aged hops are used as these retain their preservative power, but little or no bitterness or flavour.

BREWING LIQUOR

The chart shows the natural waters of the famous continental brewing localities. Dortmund and Munich water are softened when brewing pale lagers.

Soft Water
Soft water is considered to be best for Pilsner lager styles, although the palate can be a little insipid unless an adequate hopping rate is employed. Low acidic lager malts will not produce sufficient acidity in very soft water, and so it is desirable to acidify it with lactic acid, or acid malt, to produce a mash tun pH of 5.3–5.5. With well modified malts, the pH can be obtained by the addition of 0.2–0.5mg/ltr of calcium chloride or gypsum, the choice being one of beer flavour.

For a Dortmunder, try treating with the salts as described in the table, excluding the bicarbonate. Acidify with gypsum if necessary. For a dark Munchener, add the salts in the table, and for a Helles, reduce the bicarbonate to below 50mg/ltr and adjust with gypsum.

Table 28   Nineteenth-century water supplies

Salts, mg/ltr	Pilsen	Vienna	Dortmund	Munich
$CaSO_4$	3.5	307	278	27
$Mg|SO_4$	4	0	114	5.7
$MgCl_2$	0	24	0	14.3
$MgCO_3$	0	200	0	61
NaCl	8	34	174	0
$CaCO_3$	15	304	450	200
Total weights	0.030.5	0.869	1.016	0.281

Moderately Hard Liquors

These liquors are the most common, and so it is desirable to reduce the temporary hardness to 25mg/ltr when brewing Pilsners. If the carbonate levels remain between 25–50mg/ltr, the beer will have more of a German lager character. This can be achieved by boiling for *1h* with further adjustments with lactic acid, or acid malt in the grist, to get to a mash pH of about 5.5. If mashing well modified malts, the pH can be adjusted with gypsum and brought down to around 5.5–5.3. Alternatively, use lime treatment, or lime and lactic acid/malt to bring the pH to around 5.5.

To brew the more robust Dortmunder style of lager might only require a good boiling to precipitate the bicarbonates. Lime treatment may also be used, but any further acidification necessary to obtain the pH should be made with gypsum.

Untreated, moderately hard liquor supporting up to 150mg/ltr of bicarbonates is ideal for the dark Muncheners, and their rich aromatic quality is not secured when brewed with soft water. Reduce the temporary hardness to at least 50mg/ltr for Munich Helles.

Permanently Hard Waters

These waters are more problematical, and Pilsner styles can only be successfully brewed if the total hardness can be reduced. Boiling helps a little, and perhaps a grist of well modified malt, including a small percentage of adjuncts. Permanently hard liquor should be satisfactory for a Dortmunder, and well modified malt grist will also help.

Dark Muncheners, Helles and Vienna-style lagers should just be brewed with the untreated water, unless the permanent hardness can be diluted with rainwater.

DECOCTION MASHING

This developed as a pre-thermometer way of bringing the mash heat up to the saccharification rest. This entails raising the temperature of the goods by a series of steps and rests, from cold to the desired saccharification rest, so that the proteolytic and amolytic enzymes can operate at their optimum range.

The number and time of decoctions is dependent on the type of beer being brewed. Pale lagers are limited to a 15min boiling, to curb the extraction of undesirable husk material and reduce melanoidin formation, therefore keeping the colour light. The last decoction in dark lagers is boiled for up to 45min to extract full colour and the flavoursome melanoidin caramel-like products from the roasted malt.

Grist/Liquor Ratios

Traditionally, pale lager mashes are very fluid, with 3.8–4.7ltr/kg; dark lager mashes are much stiffer, with 2.3–3.2ltr/kg. Such volumes were necessary with decoction mashes, as much liquor was lost during the long boiling times. These volumes are not necessary for craft brewers, and you should find the following ratios satisfactory. For pale lager mashes use 2.7ltr/kg and sparge with 4.8ltr/kg. For dark lagers, mash with 2.4ltr/kg and sparge with 5.1ltr/kg; in both cases this will keep the total grist/liquor ratio to 7.5ltr/kg, and so we should not experience any difficulty with copper capacity.

Typical Three-Stage Decoction

Two-thirds of the cold liquor is initially mixed with the goods and rested for 30min. Meanwhile the remaining third of the liquor is brought up to boiling point and roused into the mash, and then stirred continuously to even out the temperature to between 35–41°C. An alternative approach is to use a strike heat of about 46°C to achieve these parameters, and in both cases the aim is to allow the grist to hydrate.

During this phase, the liquor absorbs phosphates, pre-formed sugars and enzymes extracted from the grist. Phytase will hydrolyze phytin to phytic acid (phosphoric acid), which acidifies the mash, and any water treatments including acid malt should bring the pH to below 5.8. Phytase also releases the vitamin inositol, essential for yeast nutrition and growth.

After 30min, one third of the thick mash is strained out, which allows the enzyme-rich wort to remain active in the mash tun to effect the next rest. The mash is pumped over to a mash copper and heated to 65°C for 20min to secure saccharification, and then boosted to boiling for 15min. The mash is now returned to the main mash tun and slowly mixed in to avoid introducing oxygen that will set up deleterious staling reactions with melanoidins and polyphenols that will darken the wort. The mash is now stabilized at 50°C and maintained for a further 30min to allow more acidification by phytase/phosphate reactions to a pH of about 5.5.

This is the protein rest, and the proteases digest the proteins, releasing peptides and amino acids. This provides the necessary nutrition that the yeast will use to build up its protoplasm. The enzyme β-glucanase, and any hemicellulases that survived the low temperature kilning cycle, demolish the remaining structure of the food store. Haze-forming materials are depleted, but sufficient polypeptides remain for palate fullness, and lager worts depend much more on soluble nitrogenous products for palate fullness than do infusion worts.

After the demolition of the endosperm, the other important function that takes place is the assault on amylopectin by the de-branching enzymes α-glucosidase and dextrinase.

Once the acid and protein digestion rests are complete, the next stage is to bring the mash heat up to the saccharification rest. This is typically 65–66°C, and again, this is done by straining out a third of the thick mash and bringing it to boiling for 15min, and then returning it to the mash, to raise the mash heat. It might take a couple of cycles to achieve the desired temperature, and a brief rest at about 62–64°C is usually required. In the case of dark lagers, the later boiling is extended to 45min to encourage the formation of melanoidins and a degree of caramelization of sugars.

At 65–66°C, the less thermostable enzymes, such as proteases, phytase, β-glucanase and peptidase, are de-activated and play no further role in the production of sweet wort. The length of time at this rest depends on the sugar ratio desired, but is usually about one hour. The mash thickness can also be diluted a little at this stage to encourage β-amylase should a more fermentable wort and drier beer be desired. β-amylase does not remain stable in such an environment, and it progressively weakens and dies off within an hour or so. For dark lagers it is usual to mash at 68°C, the optimum for α-amylase and, therefore, a more full-bodied dextrin wort is produced. This provides the necessary body and rich melanoidin-like flavours and aromas expected in dark lagers.

Finally the last decoction should be very fluid, typically 75 per cent wort and

25 per cent grist. This is boosted to 75°C to de-activate the enzymes, particularly α-amylase, which has a high thermal stability, and fix the sugar ratios. Once this stage is reached, the mash is transferred to a lauter tun for sparging.

Lautering

During decoctions, much of the air entrained in the goods is driven off, and consequently it does not float like an infusion mash does during sparging. To overcome this, the lauter tun is similar to an infusion mash tun, but is wider and shallower and filled with liquor as far as the mash screen. This cushions the weight of the grist as it falls in, preventing it compacting and clogging up the mash screen, causing a set mash.

The mash is now allowed to settle for about 30min, and the husk particles settle according to their size and specific gravity, descending from the heaviest to the lightest, with the flotsam-like proteinaceous material and spent embryos forming the top layer, producing the *marbled break*. The shallow lauter tun allows the grist to be rapidly sparged, efficiently washing out the extract but also limiting the amounts of silica, ash, polyphenols and lipids leaching into the wort.

Few brewers now employ the traditional three-stage decoction process, and a two-stage, or a variant of it, is now normal. The craft brewer should not be concerned about decoction mashing and should concentrate on the *quality of wort*, and a mashing method that produces this requirement. In fact, there is no experimental data to justify the belief that decoction mashing leads to better lager-style beers.

Programmed Infusion (PI)

(Also known as 'Rising Temperature Infusion'.) This is suitable for British two-rowed malts. The brewer, and not the maltster, dictates the degree of modification. Lager malts in the UK are usually slightly less modified than pale malts, with nitrogen around 1.65–1.7 per cent, and such malts are suitable for a PI mash. As sufficient acid phosphate has been produced during malting, the acid rest is dispensed with.

In this case, the strike liquor should be heated to 55°C to obtain an initial heat of about 50°C. At this rest, phytic acid is leached out into the goods and further calcium phosphate reactions bring the pH quite naturally below 5.5. A 15min rest at this temperature is all that is necessary to allow the proteases time to digest the limited amount of protein present. Next, a couple of 'decoctions' boosts the mash heat to 65°C for pale lagers, or 68°C for *dunkels*.

In this method we may raise the temperature of the goods from 50°C to boiling with a short saccharification rest, by the traditional decoction method. When boiling the mash portion, it will splutter quite a bit, but this can be quietened down by continuous stirring, or by using a hand-held food mixer, which will also restrict the wort caramelizing on the bottom. A splatter screen is also helpful.

Single Decoction

If the mash tun has a thermostatically controlled heating element below the mash screen we can, with trial and error, adjust the thermostat so that each portion of wort drawn off will be at the desired mash heat. By continually re-circulating the wort, the temperature of the goods will be raised quite quickly to the saccharification rest *in situ*. If the mash tun does not have a heating element, then just collect the wort in a saucepan and heat it to the required temperature before returning it to the mash. Alternatively, heat it to 65°C and hold for 15–20min to allow saccharification to take place, before boosting to boiling and returning it to the mash. If the malt is well modified, employ a single temperature infusion rest at 64–65°C for pale lagers, and 66°–68°C for dark lagers.

The Key to Good Brewing

As we can see, there are many variations possible with producing lager worts. Beginners to craft brewing should not panic if the initial low temperature rests are not accurate, as such mash heats are not critical. In traditional decoctions, the amount of mash taken from the tun can vary, as can the number of decoctions, including the temperature and the time at each rest for saccharification, before boiling and returning to the tun. The saccharification rest can also be varied, with or without a rest at 60°C, or at temperatures slightly above or below 65°C. Experimentation is the key to good brewing!

If sparging is initiated at 78°C in a closed mash tun, the temperature of the goods will rise dramatically. Consequently, we can forego the final rest at 70°C designed to destroy enzyme activity and secure the sugar ratio. If coppering is started as soon as the heating element is covered and the hops added to form a floating lid, the rapidly increasing temperature will destroy any enzymes washed through with the wort.

CONTINENTAL RECIPES

25ltr Bohemian Pilsner 1048

Grist & Sweet Wort		*Bitter Wort & Beer*		
Pilsner malt (2-row)	4.500kg	Maximum wort	34ltr	
Mash liquor	12ltr	Copper hops	36 IBU Saaz	90min
Strike heat	55°C	Aroma hops	30g Saaz	10min
Grist heat	25°C	Irish moss	1g	10min
Initial rest	50°C, 15min	Utilization	22%	
1st rest	60°C, 15min	Yeast. Wyeast Pilsen 2007. Whitelabs WLP 800		
2nd rest	65°C, 60min	Ferm. profile	7–12°C	
Sparge liquor	22ltr	Racking gravity, 1017 into closed secondary FV		
Sparge temp.	75.5°C	PG	1012	
		ABV	4.2%	

25ltr Dortmunder Export 1048

Grist & Sweet Wort		*Bitter Wort & Beer*		
Lager malt	4.100kg	Maximum wort	33ltr	
Carahelle	0.400kg	Copper hops	15 IBU Target	90min
Mash liquor	12ltr		15 IBU Mittlefruh	90min
Strike heat	55°C	Aroma hops	15g Mittlefruh	15min
Grist heat	25°C	Irish moss	1.5g	10min
Initial rest	50°C, 15min	Utilization	22%	
1st rest	60°C, 5–10min	Yeast	Wyeast 2040	
2nd rest	67°C, 60min	Ferm. profile	7–12°C	
Sparge heat	75.5°C	Racking gravity	1017 into secondary FV	
Sparge liquor	21ltr	PG	1012	
		ABV	4.6%	

25ltr Bavarian Helles 1045

Grist & Sweet Wort		*Bitter Wort & Beer*		
Lager malt (2-row)	3.300kg	Maximum wort	34ltr	
Munich malt	1.000kg	Copper hops, 25 IBU Hersbrucker		90min
Carapils	0.300kg	Aroma hops	10g Saaz	15min
Mash liquor	12ltr	Irish moss	1.0g	10min
Strike heat	55°C	Utilization	22%	
Grist heat	25°C	Yeast. Brulabs Bavarian Pils 5705		
Initial	50°C, 15min	Ferm. profile	7–12°C	
2nd rest	66°C, 60min	Racking gravity, at 1015 into secondary FV		
Sparge liquor	22ltr	PG	1010	
Sparge temp.	75.5°C	ABV	4.9%	

25ltr Bavarian Dunkel 1045

Grist & Sweet Wort		*Bitter Wort & Beer*		
Lager malt	3.400kg	Maximum wort	34ltr	
Munich malt	1.000kg	Copper hops	25 IBU Mittlefruh	90min
Melanoidin	0.200kg	Utilization	22%	
Crystal malt	0.150kg	Yeast. Wyeast 2206. Whitelabs WLP833		
Chocolate malt	0.020kg	Ferm. profile	7–12°C	
Mash liquor	12ltr	Racking gravity 1018 into secondary FV		
Strike heat	55°C	PG	1013	
Grist heat	25°C	ABV	4%	
Initial	50°C, 15min			
1st rest	68°C, 60min			
Sparge liquor	22ltr			
Sparge temp.	75.5°C			

25ltr Vienna Style 1048

Grist & Sweet Wort		*Bitter Wort & Beer*		
Vienna malt	4.400kg	Maximum liquor	33ltr	
Crystal malt	0.275kg	Copper hops, 25 IBU Target hops		90min
Mash liquor	12ltr	Irish moss	1.5g	10min
Strike heat	72°C	Utilization	22%	
Grist heat	30°C	Yeast.	Wyeast Vienna 2206	
Initial	66–67°C	Fermentation profile	12–18°C	
Mash stand	90min	Racking gravity	1015	
Sparge liquor	21ltr	PG	1012	
Sparge heat	78°C	ABV	4.2%	

25ltr Süd Deutsches Weizen Bier 1045

Grist & Sweet Wort		*Bitter Wort & Beer*		
Pilsner malt	2.000kg	Maximum wort	33ltr	
Wheat malt	2.000kg	Copper hops, 15 IBU Mittlefruh/Tettnang		90min
Carahelle	0.100kg	Irish moss	1.5g	10min
Mash liquor	11ltr	Utilization	22%	
Strike heat	55°C	Yeast. Wyeast Bavarian Wheat 3056/3638		
Grist heat	25°C	Ferm. profile	As per yeast instructions	
Initial	50°C, 10min	Racking gravity	1015 into secondary FV	
1st rest	60°C, 10min	PG	1009	
2nd rest	65°C, 65min	ABV	4.6%	
Sparge liquor	23ltr			
Sparge heat	75.5°C			

25ltr Süd Deutsches Dunkelweizen 1050

Grist & Sweet Wort		*Bitter Wort & Beer*		
Wheat malt	2.600kg	Maximum wort	34ltr	
Munich malt	1.600kg	Copper hops 15 IBU Mittlefruh/Tettnang		90min
Carahelle	0.200kg	Irish Moss	1.5g	10min
Crystal malt	0.400kg	Utilization	22%	
Mash liquor	11ltr	Yeast. Wyeast 2206. Whitelabs WLP833		
Strike heat	55°C	Ferm. profile	As per yeast instructions	
Grist heat	25°C	Racking gravity	1015 into secondary FV	
Initial	50°C, 10min	PG	1010	
1st rest	68°C, 65min	ABV	5%	
Sparge liquor	23ltr			
Sparge heat	75.5°C			

25ltr Holy Smoke! 1045

Grist & Sweet Wort		*Bitter Wort & Beer*		
Pale malt	2.000kg	Maxim wort	29ltr	
Rauchmalz	2.000kg*	Copper hops, 28 IBU Northern Brewer		90min
Crystal malt	0.240kg	Utilization	22%	
Chocolate malt	0.240kg	Yeast. Wyeast 2206. Whitelabs WLP833		
Mash liquor	11ltr	Ferm. profile	15–21°C	
Strike heat	70°C	Racking gravity	1015	
Grist heat	30°C	PG	1012	
Initial	65°C	ABV	4.2%	
Mash stand	60min			
Sparge liquor	18ltr			
Sparge heat	75.5°C			

*Adjust future brews to taste.

25ltr Biere Blanche/Witbier 1045
(Hoegaarden-style)

Grist & Sweet Wort		*Bitter Wort & Beer*		
Belgium pale malt	2.500kg	Maxim wort	33ltr	
Wheat malt	1.000kg	Copper hops, 20 IBUs Goldings		90min
Flaked wheat	0.700kg	Copper adjunct, 30g ground coriander		15min
Mash liquor	11ltr		25g Curacao orange peel	15min
Strike heat	55°C		15g split cardamom seeds	15min
Grist heat	25°C	Utilization	22%	
Initial rest	50°C	Yeast. Wyeast Belgian White 3944		
2nd rest	66°C	Ferm. profile	15–18°C	
Sparge liquor	22ltr	PG	1011	
Sparge heat	75.5°C	ABV	4.5%	

20ltr The Canon's Ale 1075
(A brew of high calibre!)

Grist & Sweet Wort		*Bitter Wort & Beer*		
Belgium pale malt	3.600kg	Maximum wort	33ltr	
Munich malt	0.850kg	Copper unhopped for		15min
Mash liquor	11ltr	Copper hops, 13 IBU Hersbrucker		75min
Strike heat	55°C		12 IBU Goldings	75min
Grist heat	25°C	Copper adjunct, 200g pale dried malt ext.		75min
Initial rest	50°C, 15min	600g candy sugar		75min
2nd rest	66°C, 65min	Utilization	22%	
Sparge liquor	22ltr	Yeast. Wyeast Belgian Trappist 3787.		
Sparge heat	75.5°C	Ferm. profile	25–30°C	
		PG	1018	
		ABV	7.3%	

25ltr Berliner Weisse 1033

Grist & Sweet Wort		*Bitter Wort & Beer*		
Pilsner malt, 2-row	1.400kg	Maximum wort	22.5ltr, top up to 30ltr	
Wheat malt	1.600kg	Copper hops, 60% of 5 IBU Hallertau		90min
Mash liquor	9ltr		40% of 5 IBU Hallertau	70min
Strike heat	55°C	Utilization	22%	
Grist heat	30°C	Yeast. Wyeast Kolsch		
Initial	50°C, 15min	Wyeat L-Delbrueckii (25G)		
1st rest	60°C, 20min	Ferm. profile	15–18°C	
2nd rest	64°C, 30min	Racking gravity	1010	
3rd rest	68°C, 30min	PG	1008	
Sparge liquor	13.5ltr	Maturation in bottle	6–24 months	

25ltr Kölsch bier Style 1044

Grist & Sweet Wort		*Bitter Wort & Beer*		
Pilsner malt	3.000kg	Maximum wort	30ltr	
Wheat malt	1.000kg	Copper hops	22 IBUs Hallertauer	60min
Mash liquor	11ltr	Utilization	22%	
Strike heat	55°C	Yeast. Wyeast Kölsch 2565. 13–16°C*		
Grist heat	30°C	or, Whitelabs Kölsch WLP029. 18–20°C*		
Initial	50°C, 15min	Racking gravity	1014 into secondary FV	
1st rest	65°C, 60min	Lagering	4 weeks	
2nd rest	68°C, 15min	PG	1011	
Sparge liquor	19ltr	ABV	4%	
Sparge heat	78°C			

*Top fermentation.

5ltr Lambic Style 1045

Grist & Sweet Wort		*Bitter Wort & Beer*	
Belgium pale malt	2.500kg	Maximum wort	38ltr
Crushed soft wheat	0.800kg	Hops, 50g of 2-year-old aroma hops	150min
Wheat malt	0.800kg	Utilization	22%
Mash liquor	12ltr	Yeast. Wyeast Belgium Lambic blend, 3278	
Strike liquor	55°C	Ferm. profile, 17–24°C	
Grist heat	30°C	Rack at 1018 into oak cask. Ferment and mature	
Initial	50°C, 30min	for at least 2 years. For a fruit Lambic, rack into	
1st rest	60°C, 45min	a carboy and add 4kg of whole raspberries or	
2nd rest	70°C, 15min	cherries. Allow to ferment at 18°C for 6 months	
Sparge liquor	26ltr	PG	1010 to 1012
Sparge heat	85°C	ABV	4–4.5%

LAGER FERMENTATION

Lager fermentations show similar profiles and characteristics to top-fermenting yeast, but not quite so dramatic, the main differences being that they precipitate at the end of the fermentation and operate at much lower temperatures. The latter keeps the formation of vicinal diketones, principally the butterscotch-like diacetyl, on the low side. The formation of various esters, which give rise to unwanted fruitiness, are also subdued, leaving the beer with a clean and refreshing palate.

Yeast starters are recommended for dried and cultured lager yeast, and these are best prepared from unhopped malt extract with a gravity of about 1045, made up to at least 500ml, and acidified with lactic acid/citric acid to pH 5.1–5.4. Once the starter is fully active, it should be acclimatized in the fridge at 5°C for up to 72 hours.

Primary Fermentation

Aerate the wort and pitch the yeast starter at about 7°C and cover the FV. Apply gentle warmth and allow the temperature to rise by about 2–3°C over the next 24 hours. This is the lag phase, and after some 12 to 15 hours, a light frothy coat of foam slowly starts to cover the surface of the brew. The brew now enters the *low Krausen* phase, which lasts for about 48 hours with a pH of about 5.8. The brew is now protected from aerial infection, and we can remove the cover from the FV. (Alternatively, we conduct the entire fermentation in a closed, but vented, FV.) The temperature continues to rise slowly through *medium Krausen* to about 9–12°C, producing the typical cauli-flower heads of yeast, and the pH falls to around 5.2. Any hop fragments and oxi-dized nitrogenous brown scum should be skimmed off to prevent contamination.

Over the next 48 to 72 hours, the tem-perature of 10–12°C is maintained, and yeast metabolism is so energetic that the natural warmth produced will push the temperature of the wort above 12°C; cool-ing is necessary to prevent it rising above this figure. This is the period of *high Krausen*, at which the attenuation is at its greatest. The pH now falls to around 4.6, steadily increasing the wort acidity, stimulating yeast activity. This results in copious amounts of CO_2, dramatically changing the yeast head and forming typ-ical rocky peaks.

By day seven, the yeast has depleted most of the wort sugars and so its metab-olism slows down and the high Krausen starts to collapse. During the *post Krausen* period, the wort temperature cools a little and the pH falls slightly, to about 4.6. This acidity starts to inhibit any bacteria that might have invaded the brew. Just as in ale brewing, the temperature is main-tained for another 24 hours, and then cooled to effect the cleansing phase.

The cooling and cleansing phase is ini-tiated by slowly dropping the temperature by 1–3°C every 24 hours to about 5°C. Over the next 3 to 5 days, yeast activity is greatly retarded, but not halted alto-gether, and the beer sediments the bulk of its yeast and fine nitrogenous matter. The yeast crop is now skimmed off, with much care taken to remove the bitter-tasting scum that has adhered to the walls of the vessel, and racked into a secondary fermenter, retaining at least 4° of fer-mentable extract. Thereafter it goes through a long, ice-cold maturation period that will continue to sediment wort solids.

This is the lagering or storage period, and during this time many complex bene-ficial reactions take place. The ice-cold conditions help precipitate the protein-tannin complexes as trub and chill haze particles, so that after lagering the beer will be clear and starbright.

The yeast continues to ferment very slowly, depleting the beer of oxygen and stabilizing the brew. The evolving CO_2 purges unwanted sulphur compounds, such as dimethyl sulphide (DMS) and hydrogen sulphide (H_2S) with its 'rotten egg' smell to the atmosphere. Any excess of acetalde-hyde, with its bruised apple-like nuance, is reduced. By far the most important aspect of flavour maturation, however, is the removal of vicinal diketones (VDK).

Diacetyl (VDK 2, 3 butanedione) is a natural product of fermentation that orig-inates from pyruvic acid, which, after intracellular biosynthetic reactions, is excreted as acetohydroxy acids and fur-ther converted in the wort to vicinal dike-tones. During the long, slow lagering period, yeast reabsorbs diacetyl and enzymically converts it into alkane-2, 3 diols, which have such a high taste thresh-old and do not influence the flavour.

Diacetyl has various terms by which it can be identified, such as buttery to toffee-like butterscotch or vanilla-like. It has a low taste threshold, and levels should not exceed 2–3mg/ltr, a level that is common in some American lagers. Ideally, levels should be kept to 0.05mg/ltr to secure good flavours and keeping qualities. The higher range of diacetyl can only be tolerated in beers for quick consumption, as it is an unstable molecule that rapidly oxidizes to butyric acid and turns rancid.

Diacetyl levels in beer are related to the nitrogenous levels, and hence to amino acids in wort. Yeast requires valine, an essential amino acid to build up its proto-plasm and this is slowly absorbed by the cell throughout the period of fermenta-tion. To utilize valine, yeast absorbs aceto-lactate acid and so reduces the amount available for diacetyl formation. The excessive use of nitrogen-diluting cereals or sugars will deplete the amounts of valine, and leave too much acetolactate acid available for the development of diacetyl. Sensible use of nitrogen dilutents to achieve balanced wort should produce sound beer.

The time of lagering is dependent on the gravity and degree of bitterness. Strong, well-hopped lagers might require 8 to 12 weeks to obtain the desirable flavour and stability. Weaker brews can usually secure agreeable profiles within 6 to 8 weeks, but generally pale lagers require longer storage than dark lagers of comparable strengths. Each brew will mature at its own pace, and this will depend on the mashing regime, gravity and strain of yeast.

The strain of yeast has considerable influence on the maturation process. Just like ale yeast, some types are flocculent and separate from the wort early during the primary fermentation, and so the beer is passed to the lagering tanks with an ample supply of maltotriose to sustain it during maturation. Other strains are more powdery, remaining in suspension longer so that by the time of racking the brew is closer to its PG, and this requires the brew to be charged with some Krausen wort to help secure the desirable flavour qualities. In order to avoid such extremes, some breweries employ a mix-ture of the two types.

The foregoing represents typical histor-ical practice, but traditional lagering is actually inefficient and the process often requires yeast rousing by blowing CO_2

°C	O.G.	Low krausen	Medium krausen	High krausen	Krausen falling	Cooling/settling	pH
12	1045		A				6.0
	1040					DR	
10	1035	pH		T			5.5
	1030						
8	1025						5.0
	1020						
6	1015						4.5
	1010						
4	1005						4.0

A=attenuation. pH. T=temperature. DR=diacytel rest
(A hypothetical lager fermentation)

A profile of bottom fermentation.

163

into the fermenter. Consequently, the process has become modified and varied throughout the industry.

Many brewers have abandoned long lagering periods and prolong the primary fermentation to give the yeast adequate time to reduce the acetohydroxy acids to vicinal diketones and, eventually, innocuous diols. Others continue the primary fermentation until the brew has attenuated to the third gravity stage, and then boost the temperature to 18–20°C for 48 to 72 hours. This practice is the diacetyl rest, and the yeast activity quickly eliminates the diacetyl. The evolving gas also purges unwanted odours from the beer:

Diacetyl rest = OG–PG × 0.33

After the diacetyl rest, the brew should be chilled, and bottled or casked.

Fermentation times vary throughout the industry. The Danes typically ferment at 9–10°C for 8 days; the Germans ferment at 5–9°C for 5 to 14 days, and the Americans ferment at 10–13°C for 6 to 9 days. If craft brewers are to follow such practices, refrigeration is required, and so the problem of diacetyl is greatly diminished.

There is also a large range of true lager yeasts available for the amateur. The fermentation temperature profile for each strain is usually given, including the flocculation and attenuation characteristics. Dried yeasts are also acceptable, but beware of recommended high temperature profiles.

Yeast Cropping

The standard commercial practice for selecting yeast for repitching is to take a sample from the middle layer of sedimented yeast in the FV. The sample of yeast is either cleansed by washing it in sterile ice-cold water, or treating it in an acidic (tartaric or phosphoric acid) aqueous solution of pH 2–2.5 and, most importantly, at 5°C. A 60min rest will destroy any bacteria present. Prior to repitching, it is checked in the laboratory for a cell count and for its viability, to ensure that all the bacteria has been destroyed; top-fermenting yeasts can be treated in exactly the same way.

Whilst acid washing destroys bacteria, it can lead to the preferential survival of wild yeasts. Such yeasts can cause turbidity, sulphurous flavours, diacetyl, fusel alcohol and acetic acid, and become resistant to finings. After such treatment the amateur brewer should check the pH of the beer after fermentation: if it is below pH 3.7, then this might indicate that the yeast has been infected, particularly if it tastes a little 'tart'. A small, un-primed sample bottle of the brew with a large airspace, kept at 25°C, should quickly show up any defects.

A good alternative for the home brewer is to draw off a sample of wort during the high Krausen phase, which would eventually form the middle layer, and chill it in the fridge to sediment the cells. This can be done in a trial jar: after the yeast has sedimented, the excess beer is poured off. If the yeast is going to be re-pitched within a week, it can be kept under 100ml of sterile, ice-cold water in the fridge. Re-propagate as a starter before use. If it has good brewing characteristics and you want to preserve it, freeze it as previously explained, or use an agar slope.

Yeast in sound condition should have a fresh bready/malty aroma, and should not give off any obnoxious smells in the starter medium. Fermentations should be sound, with regular attenuation and clean yeast heads. If ever in doubt, discard the yeast immediately!

CHAPTER 17

BY-PRODUCTS
AND INFECTIONS

FERMENTATION BY-PRODUCTS

The intoxicating and flavouring compounds produced during top or bottom fermentation have a profound influence on the flavour of beer. In a sound fermentation the by-products should be present within satisfactory parameters and can contribute up to 75 per cent of beer flavour, and the overall quality of palate should be harmonious.

Ethanol

This is the principle alcohol produced during fermentation, and when consumed in moderation it produces a feeling of well-being. Ethanol contributes to the sweetness of beer, and along with dextrins adds to the flavoursome palate. It also helps prolong the shelf life of the brew, as long as the ingress of oxygen is prevented. Beer that picks up oxygen in the post-fermentation processes of racking, finings, bottling and casking, will result in ethanol being oxidized by melanoidin into aldehydes, which produce cardboard notes.

Higher Alcohols

These have a higher boiling point than ethanol, and consequently they remain after ethanol has been distilled off.

Traditionally they are called *fusel* alcohols and oils, the name coming from the German *Fusel*, meaning 'rough liquor'. They were thought to induce nausea and blinding headaches, but despite the legend, they have little physiological effects in the quantities present and are much less effective in this respect than ethanol.

Higher alcohols are powerful flavouring and aromatic compounds produced by the metabolism of amino acids by yeast. *Amyl alcohol*, an active-amyl alcohol (2 methyl-1-butanol), and isopentyl alcohol (3-methyl-1-butanol) contribute flavours with solvent-like after tastes and aromas similar to over-ripe bananas. *Phenol alcohols*, tyrisol and tryptophol are responsible for lingering and bitter medicinal-like aftertastes. Their effects are more evident in light gravity beers, and lager yeasts produce more phenol alcohols than ale yeasts. Phenylethanol is more floral, resembling roses. Propanol and butanol taste similar to ethanol, but they have a high taste threshold and are fairly innocuous.

In general, high nitrogen malts or high gravity all-malt worts will increase the likelihood of an excess of amino acids and the possibility of excessive fusel alcohol formation. Careless sparging and inefficient straining of the wort after coppering will result in an excessive carry-over of trub into the FV, with the consequential increase in fusel alcohol. High fermentation temperatures with excessive yeast growth often lead to higher levels of fusel alcohol. Fusel alcohols are also oxidized by melanoidins during storage, and produce staling aldehydes. Wort that is not adequately oxygenated prior to pitching the yeast can also produce fusel alcohol.

Aldehydes

These are potent flavouring compounds that are formed from two sources, or pathways, during fermentation. *Acetaldehyde* is the penultimate product in the fermentation of ethanol, and is noted for its green apple smell. Most of it is formed during the logarithmic, or high Krausen phase, and transformed into ethanol, but small amounts also remain unconverted. Aldehydes produced by oxygenation of ethanol, or fusel alcohol, should only be present in small amounts as they are disagreeable. Also, wort infected by *O. proteus* can produce copious amounts of aldehydes.

Some aldehydes are oxidized to acetic acid on maturation, and this process is accelerated when a brew is racked clean of yeast. As yeast will scavenge the last traces of oxygen from the wort, the worst effects of staling are reduced. Any beer that is slow to clear should not necessarily be frowned upon, as the formation of aldehydes and acetic acid are restricted.

Esters

Esters are important materials that contribute to the flavour and aroma of beer, as long as amounts are not too high. They are produced by a condensation reaction between an alcohol and an acid. They are more evident in high gravity beers and brews that are fermented at high temperatures, particularly in the presence of high concentrations of glucose.

Ethyl Acetate

This by-product (ethyl alcohol and ethyl acetate) is primarily responsible for the fruity and vinous flavours and aromas found in barley wines. However, excessive amounts can impart medicinal-like aftertastes, although this can be avoided by following the correct temperature profile. *Isoamyl acetate* (Isoamyl alcohol and acetic acid) has a ripe banana-like aroma, and *ethyl hexanate* (ethyl alcohol and hexanate acid) imparts an apple-like aroma with a hint of aniseed.

Ketones

These are compounds similar to aldehydes and are produced from hydroxyethyl thiamine pyrophosphate (TPP), an intermediate product in the formation of acetaldehyde from pyruvic acid. Further metabolism of hydroxyethyl TPP produces the acetohydroxy acids (acetohydroxybutyric acid and acetolactate acid) that are excreted and oxidized into the vicinal diketones, pentanedione and diacetyl respectively.

Pentanedione

This by-product has a fairly high taste threshold, and so its honey-like characteristics are harmless. As previously discussed, the main villain is diacetyl. Another ketone produced from hydroxyethyl TPP and acetaldehyde is acetoin: it has a high taste threshold and is innocuous.

Lipids (Fatty Acids)

Lipids are long-chain carboxylic acids such as triacylglycerols (esters of glycerol); when found in plants they are called oils, and in animals they are known as fats. Phospholipids are similar, but only contain two fatty acids. Lipids are principally derived from malt with small amounts coming from hops, particularly if oxidized due to poor storage.

Yeast utilizes lipids for cell-membrane function, and fatty acids are excreted as a by-product. The actual amount in wort will depend on the yeast strain, grist composition and the efficiency of sparging. Wort trub can contain up to 50 per cent of fatty acids, but most will be metabolized during fermentation and so little remains in the beer. If in excess, fatty acids can furnish soapy, fatty, or sweaty goat-like flavours!

Sulphur Compounds

Some sulphur is required for yeast growth, and it is primarily obtained from amino acids. For example, *Hydrogen sulphide*: most H_2S is produced during the logarithmic phase (high Krausen), and many factors influence its presence, such as nitrogen levels, fermentation profile and the strain of yeast. Bottom-fermenting yeasts produce more H_2S than top-fermenting yeasts, and it is important that amounts in lager do not exceed 10mg/ltr, otherwise the brew will become nauseating. Strong-flavoured ales and stouts can tolerate twice as much H_2S than lager, although in a sound fermentation most of it is purged to the atmosphere with the evolving CO_2. *Dimethyl sulphide* (DMS) is derived from the amino acid s-methyl methionine, but it, too, is scrubbed out during fermentation. DMS has a very low taste threshold, and can be detected at 0.03mg/ltr. It has a cooked sweetcorn- or onion-like taste, and is a feature in some lager styles when in the range 0.80–100mg/ltr.

POSSIBLE INFECTIONS

Whilst cask and brewery infections should be taken seriously, we should not get too pedantic about them, as with sensible kitchen hygiene we will be unlucky if they occur.

Gram-Positive Bacteria

Lactic acid bacteria are the most common infection with top-fermenting beers. *Lactobacillus* exists as short to long thin rods, with various amounts of single and double cells. When it infects beer it becomes opalescent, displaying a silky sheen. This haze is usually well developed and causing turbidity before sourness can be detected. In severe cases, the beer becomes slimy due to the viscosity of the cells' secretions. This mucus is thixotropic, and if an infected sample is vigorously shaken it breaks down and temporarily disappears.

Lactobacillus

Lactobacillus has an optimum growth pH of 5.5, but it can grow at pH 3.5, and so it is quite happy at the acidity of beer at racking, typically pH 3.8 to 4.2. Some strains metabolize large amounts of simple sugars, such as glucose, into lactic acid. Other strains excrete lactic and acetic acids, plus ethanol and CO_2. Little is known just how these organisms come to infect breweries, but it is most likely from atmospheric pollution and pitching yeast.

Lactobacillus is anaerobic, or at best micro-aerophilic, and will proliferate in an atmosphere rich in CO_2. Infections are more likely during racking and in the ullage of a cask after venting. A cask left standing for long periods after venting is very prone to such infections. Once the beer has become inoculated, the bacteria will metabolize the residual and priming sugars. This is much more likely if the brew has been racked at too high a specific gravity, and 3° should be quite satisfactory.

Pediococci

Pediococci will preferentially metabolize maltose and pentose sugars, and apart from ethanol and lactic acid, it is a prolific producer of diacetyl. A Pediococci infection produces the same turbidity and off-flavours as Lactobacillus, but diacetyl is very obvious due to its pungent and sickly honey/toffee-like aroma. Lactic acid bacteria survive in sedimented yeast, and Pediococci is more common in bottom-fermenting strains and seldom found in top-fermenting strains of yeast.

On a more positive theme, lactic acid infections can be kept at bay by sensible cleanliness and good brewing practice. Lactic acid bacteria are also sensitive to isohumulone, and this valuable antiseptic does much to combat growth in the early stages of infection. However, the bacteria can become acclimatized to hop antiseptics, and survive in well hopped beers. It does seem that we have no escape! However, when isohumulone is considered with the low pH and nitrogen level at casking, plus the inhibiting effects of around 5 per cent alcohol, these conditions are not considered ideal for rampant growth. Lactic acid bacteria are also sensitive to sulphites, and the addition of 50–70mg/ltr should help suppress such microbes.

Gram Negative

Acetobactor will oxidize ethanol to acetic acid, whilst the by-products of *Acetomonas* are acetic and gluconic acids. Both types require free oxygen in order to respire, and beer is at risk during racking and to a slightly lesser extent at casking. The latter is afforded some protection by the evolution of CO_2 from the cask conditioning, although they might infect a half-empty cask left standing for some time, particularly if the beer has stopped gassing.

Such microbes can tolerate the whole spectrum of acidity in brewing, and are not restricted by ethanol or hop antiseptics. They also have simple nutrient requirements, and are to be found virtually everywhere in a brewery.

Drosophila, the Fruit Fly

Another possible source of infection is by the fruit or vinegar fly, *Drosophila*, that is usually infected with the bacteria. Should this fly make an inquisitive flight over the FV, it will be subdued by the CO_2 and become buried in the head of yeast, possibly unnoticed. It can also gain access to empty casks, and unwashed casks are particularly inviting!

Once acetic acid bacteria infect brewing apparatus, they are extremely difficult to eradicate. The first signs of an infected cask are the pungent smell of vinegar, plus the cloudy mucus similar to lactic acid bacteria. Should an infected cask be left standing for some time, particularly half full, the majority of the cells will accumulate on the surface, forming a greasy pellicle. The beer drawn from the cask in the initial stages will still look relatively clear, but it will taste and smell somewhat disproportionately in relation to the actual number of cells in suspension.

The aerobic nature of acetic acid bacteria makes them common pollutants of cask taps, particularly wooden ones, beer engines, beer lines and couplings and drip trays. Such infections can be completely avoided by scrupulous cleaning.

ALCOHOL AND HEALTH 'Beer is good for us!'

Beer taken in moderation reduces one's inhibitions and induces a feeling of relaxation and well-being. It is also nutritious, containing proteins, carbohydrates and a range of important minerals and vitamins essential for good health. Beer goes well with food, and a ploughman's lunch, consisting of bread, cheese and beer, is a nutritionally balanced meal. Beer has a calorific value similar to milk, but is fat free.

Beer might also reduce the risk of heart disease, kidney stones, gallstones and stomach infections. Blood clots, too, might be prevented, as various pigmented antioxidants in dark beers and stouts help the blood platelets glide over each other.

The present guidelines for safe drinking are measured in 'units', and men are advised to restrict themselves to three to four units per day. Women may also be protected from the onset of osteoporosis, but should have no more than two to three units per day. In general, the recommended units are quite sensible. One unit equals 25ml of spirits, a small glass of wine, or a half pint of pub beer at 3.5 per cent ABV.

You can use the following formula to calculate how many units of alcohol your home brew contains:

$$\frac{\text{Volume in millilitres} \times \% \text{ ABV}}{1000}$$

$$\text{e.g.} \quad \frac{1 \text{ pint } (568\text{ml}) \times 4.5\% \text{ ABV}}{1000}$$

$$= 2.5 \text{ units of alcohol}$$

$$\frac{1/2 \text{ litre } (500\text{ml}) \times 3.0\% \text{ ABV}}{1000}$$

$$= 1.5 \text{ units of alcohol}$$

Zymomonas

This microbe thrives on amino acids, glucose and fructose, and occasionally it will metabolize sucrose, but not maltose and the higher dextrins. It is prevalent in cask-conditioned ales and is little affected by pH, hop antiseptics or alcohol, and rapidly reduces a sound brew to an unpalatable, foul-smelling mess within a few hours! The by-products are acetaldehyde and hydrogen sulphide, hence the nauseating rotten egg smell. Thankfully such infections are uncommon, and outbreaks of contamination are restricted at cellar temperatures. Prevention is by strict hygiene, and if possible, keeping the beer at 13–14°C throughout its shelf life. Priming the beer with maltose, rather than glucose, sucrose or invert sugar, will also help.

Pectinatus: is a similar organism, but it is anaerobic and thrives in fresh beer. It is capable of producing vast amounts of hydrogen sulphide and acetic acids, and prevention is by good sanitation of all utensils.

Wild Yeasts

While there is a multitude of wild yeast flora waiting to compete with the pitching yeast, not all are serious rivals, and these do not cause spoilage. The undomesticated yeasts, such as wild *S. -cerevisiae* and var *Carlsbergensis*, very closely resemble true brewing strains. *S. -cerevisiae* and var. *turbidans*, plus var. *ellipsoideus*, have the ability to resist finings because they have an opposite electrical charge and therefore sediment very slowly. They will also continue to ferment wort sugars, causing turbidity and off flavours. *S. -pastorianus* is similar in its activity, but it is uncommon in top fermenting beers.

S. -diastaticus

This will ferment maltotetraose and dextrins, and will continue to ferment after residual maltotriose has been metabolized. This leads to beer with undesirable high phenolics and aromatic alcohols. An infected beer will clear as normal with isinglass, but will slowly become cloudy again as the wild yeast starts to attack the stable dextrins. This is apparent when the beer undergoes a violent 'fret', resulting in vast amounts of CO_2 being produced over many days. After the body-building dextrins are depleted, the beer is over-attenuated, dry and thin, and also excessively flat.

Other Infections

Pitchia membranaefaciens and *Candida* can oxidize ethanol to acetic acid in a vented cask, and this usually occurs after the cessation of CO_2 evolution. *Torulopsis* will produce a dry, acidic flavour, but such infections are not common in draught beer.

Brettanomyces is less sensitive to a low pH and ethanol than true brewing strains, and can respire when other yeasts are inhibited. It is an acid-producing yeast that was isolated from mature bottled beers by Professor Claussen in 1904. Claussen was French, and named the yeast after his beloved Brittany. He discovered that when the yeast was pitched into actively fermenting wort it produced an unpleasant taste, but when it was pitched into fully matured beer it created the much-prized, piquant flavour of the original stock beers.

GLOSSARY

Acetaldehyde   The simplest member of a group of chemicals known as *Aldehydes*. A compound containing a carboxyl group with at least one H atom attached. Acetaldehyde is reduced to alcohol. If wort becomes oxidized, acetaldehyde is reduced to acetic acid, or vinegar! Stale flavours in bottled beer are caused by the oxidation of aldehydes by melanoidins.

Acetate, ethyl   The ester of acetaldehyde linked to acetic acid. It has a peardrop, or solvent-like aroma, and concentration in beer is typically 9–19mg/ltr in browns and milds; 11–69 in stouts; 14–23mg/ltr in pale ales, and 8–14mg/ltr in lagers.

Acid   A substance that releases hydrogen ions (H^+) when it dissociates in water. This activity increases the concentration of H^+ ions and hence acidity. When acids react to alkalis they form salts of the acid and alkali, *ie* Hydrochloric acid + sodium hydroxide $\rightarrow$ sodium chloride + water.

Aliphatic esters   Long-chain esters.

Amino acids   The building blocks of life. Molecules containing a protonated amino group (NH_3^+) and an oxidized carboxyl group (COO^-). When linked they form peptides, polypeptides and eventually proteins. Yeast metabolizes the nitrogen from amino acids for growth.

Amphoteric   A substance that has both acidic and base properties.

Anion   A negatively charged ion.

Asexual reproduction   The production of an identical offspring (clone) from a single cell.

ATP   A nucleotide consisting of adenine triphosphate and ribose sugar.

Attenuation   The thinning out of the wort's density due to the removal of the weight of sugar by yeast. The alcohol produced has little influence on the terminal gravity.

Autolysis   The process of self-destruction of the yeast cell after death by the release of the contents of lysosomes, aptly called suicide bags! The release of amino acids produces the bitter yeast bite, and head retention suffers due to the release of fatty acids into the beer.

Base   Any substance that increases the concentration of hydroxide ions (OH^-) when dissolved in water.

Bicarbonate   More correctly, *hydrogen carbonate* (HCO_3), but for convenience throughout this book we refer to them as bicarbonates. Water Authorities usually refer to alkalinity as HCO_3, and brewers as calcium carbonate, $CaCO_3$. Both are equivalent in their effects, but to convert HCO_3 to $CaCO_3$, multiply HCO_3 by 1.22.

Capillary action   The movement of a liquid along a surface due to the effects of combined cohesion and adhesion.

Carbohydrate   (CH_2O) Organic compounds of carbon, hydrogen and oxygen. Sugar, starch, glycogen and cellulose are all carbohydrates.

Catalyst   A substance (such as enzymes) that facilitates a chemical reaction by lowering the activation energy, and is not consumed during the reaction.

Co-enzyme   A non-protein organic molecule that plays an accessory role in enzyme activity by acting as carriers of ions from the substrate being acted on, to the appropriate acceptor.

Co-factor   Non-protein components required for enzyme activity as above. Many co-factors are metallic ions, rather than organic molecules.

Decoction   To extract or prepare by boiling. Boiling gelatinizes insoluble starch, making it readily available for simplification by the amylase enzymes.

Denaturation   The loss of the original configuration of protein as a result of boiling, (also extremes of pH, acids and chemicals) that disrupts the hydrophobic interactions, and which often results in a loss of biological activity: *ie* isinglass over 25°C is denatured to gelatine.

Digestion   The breaking down of insoluble organic molecules into simpler products to be absorbed into the cell for further metabolism to yield energy for synthetic processes.

Diols   Compounds with two hydroxyl groups (OH).

DNA   Deoxyribonucleic acid, the hereditary constituent of cells.

EBC   European Brewing Convention.

FAN   Free amino nitrogen. FAN is essential for yeast growth.

Fatty acids   (lipids) Long-chain hydrocarbons, components of fats, oils, phospholipids and waxes.

Fusel oil   From the German, meaning 'rough liquor'. They are produced by the metabolism of amino acids by yeast.

FV   The fermentation vessel.

Gibberelins   A group of plant growth hormones.

GFM   Gram formula mass. Previously the atomic weight, molar mass.

Glucose   ($C_6H_2O_6$) The most common monosaccharide.

Glycerol   A three-carbon molecule with three hydroxyl groups attached. It is formed early during glycolysis, and acts as a hydrogen acceptor for co-enzymes prior to the formation of acetaldehyde.

Glycolysis   The aerobic enzymic controlled breakdown of glucose.

Glycoprotein   A protein containing a polysaccharide unit.

Glycopolypeptides   Peptides reduced from glyco-protein, still linked to the polysaccharide.

Goods, The   The hydrated grist in the mash tun.

Gram staining   To differentiate between the structural properties of bacteria, they undergo washing in ethanol or acetone. Gram-positive bacteria retain a crystal violet-iodine complex after washing, whilst gram-negative bacteria do not.

Gyle, The   A batch of beer, or the volume of wort collected prior to pitching the yeast.

Gyle-worting   The practice of priming beer with actively fermenting wort taken during high Krausen. Old Scots; Wort. Gyle-vat, the FV Gyle-house, the brew house.

Hydrolysis   The resolution of a compound into two products by the insertion of a molecule of water (oxygen and hydrogen) by an enzyme. Protein and starch are broken down in this way during mashing. Hydrolysis can also be achieved with acids.

Hygroscope   The instrument used to measure atmospheric moisture.

Hygroscopic   Materials that absorb moisture from the atmosphere.

Hydrophilic   Water-loving.

Hydrophobic   Water-repelling.

Initial, The   The initial temperature of the goods after the mash is mixed.

Ion   An atom, or molecule, containing an unequal number of electrons and protons carrying a net positive, or net negative charge.

Krausen   Pro 'Kroysen'. From the German 'krause', meaning frizzy, or wrinkled, hence its use to describe the head of yeast on fermenting beer.

Krausen wort   Actively fermenting wort taken from the FV to prime flat beer.

Lauter   From the German, meaning 'to clear'.

Lauter tun   The clarifying vessel.

Lintner degrees   (°L) A scale to determine the degree of diastatic (amolytic) activity in malt. First tabled by the German scientist, Carl Joseph Lintner (1855–1923).

Lipids   See fatty acids.

Lysis   The break-up of a cell structure due to the rupture of its cell membrane.

Mercaptans   Materials similar to alcohol, but with a molecule of sulphur rather than oxygen.

Molecule   A collection of two or more atoms held together by chemical bonds.

Osmosis   The phenomenon of solvent flow through a semi-permeable membrane to equalize the concentrations on both sides of the membrane.

PG   The present gravity. Originally the stop gravity or final gravity. The true gravity of the brew after the metabolism of the priming sugars.

Polymer   A macromolecule such as starch, composed of similar, or identical, sub units.

Starch   An insoluble polymer of glucose typically composed of 1,000 or more glucose units. The main food storage in plants and seeds.

Stein   The German for 'stone'. A *Bierstein* is a stone drinking vessel.

Surface tension   The surface tautness of a liquid due to the cohesion of the molecules.

Thermophilic   Tolerant to heat.

Thermophobic   Intolerant to heat.

BIBLIOGRAPHY

Alexander, John, *Amateur Winemaker*. 'An Automatic Brewery' March 1983; 'Beer from the Wood' July, Aug. and Sept. 1983; 'Mixtures of Beer' Nov. 1983; 'Formulating Beer Recipes' Jan. 1984; 'Altering Beer Kits' March 1984; 'The Campaign for Real Ale' April 1984; 'Extra Strong Ales' Aug. 1984; 'Beginning With Beer' Sept. 1984; 'Party Beers' Dec. 1984; 'Storing and Serving Your Beer' Jan. 1985; 'Taking the Pils' Feb. 1985; 'History of Brewing' Apr. 1985; 'Hops are Tops' May 1985; 'Water for Beer' June 1985; 'Building a Brewery' July 1985; 'Boiling and Cooling Wort' Aug. 1985; 'Scottish Beer Styles' Sept. 1985; 'Christmas Revels' Dec. 1985; 'Mash Tun Adjuncts' Jan. 1986; 'Smashing Mashing' Feb. 1986; 'Bubbling Beer' March 1986; 'The Cask Breather' May 1986; 'Servicing Beer Equipment' June 1986; 'Beer from the Wood' Aug. 1986; 'Hiccups' Sept. 1986; 'Designing a Beer' Oct. 1986; 'India Pale Ale' Nov. 1986; 'Hopping Days' Dec. 1986; 'An Amaizing Adjunct' Jan. 1987; 'How Beer is Brewed'; 'A Guide to Water Treatments' Mar. 1987; 'Brewing with the Bruheat/Electric Bin' Apr. 1987; 'The British Pub' March 1987; 'Real Rewards' June 1987.

Alexander, John, *Beer in the Wood*, Zymurgy, 1984.

Alexander, John, *Brewing Lager* (AW), Argus Specialist Publications, London, 1986.

A Manual of Good Practice for the Production of Cask Conditioned Ale, Report of an Industrial Working Party, March 1985. Published by the Brewers' Society and the Brewing Research Foundation.

American Homebrewers Association, *Beer Styles and Beer Category Descriptions.*

Bamforth, Prof. C., *Journal of the Institute of Brewing*, Prof. C. Bamforth, Nov./Dec. 1985.

Barry-Smith, *Brewing Sugars*, Albion Sugar Co. (The New Brewer), 1977.

Bemment, D. W., *Coloured Malts*, Pauls & Saunders Ltd.

Biological Science, vols 1 and 2, Cambridge University Press, 1994.

Birch, Byron, *Brewing Quality Beers*, Joby Books, Fulton, CA 95439, USA.

Brewlab Services Ltd, University of Sunderland, 2004.

Briggs, D. E. *et al.*, *Malting & Brewing Science*, vols 1 and 2, Chapman & Hall, 1982.

Capper, W., *Bentley Licensed Houses and Their Management*, vols 1, 2 and 3, The Caxton Publishing Company Ltd, London, 1949.

Carlsberg, *Carlsberg Bryggerierne, 1981*, Boarding Grafik A.S. Copenhagen, 1981.

A Century of Brewing Clones, Carlsberg/Tuberg United Breweries, 1983.

Comrie, A. A. D., *Journal of the Institute of Brewing*, 'Brewing Liquor – A Review', 1967.

Dallas, John and McMaster, Charles, *The Beer Drinkers' Companion*, The Edinburgh Publishing Company, 1993.

Dallas, G. B., 'Cask Conditioning', *Amateur Winemaker*, December 1985.

Dallas, G. B., 'Clarification of Beer', *Amateur Winemaker*, January 1986.

Donnachie, Ian, *A History of Brewing in Scotland*, John Donald Publishers, 1979.

Duddington, C. L., *Plain Man's Guide to Beer*, Pelham Books, London, 1974.

Ebbing, Darrel D. and Wrighton, Mark S. *General Chemistry*, Houghton Mifflin Co., Boston and Toronto, 1991.

English Hops, The Journal of, 1984 and 1985.

Fix, George, *Principles of Brewing Science*, Brewer's Publications, Colorado, 1989.

Harrison, Dr John and members of the Durden Park Beer Circle, *Old British Beers and How to Make Them*, 2nd and 3rd editions.

Haugh, Prof. J. S., *Water* (undated, possibly a Cass lecture).

Hop Guide, The National Hop Association of England, undated.

Hornsey, Ian, *A History of Beer and Brewing*, RSC Paperbacks, 2003.

Hornsey, Ian, *Brewing*, The Royal Society of Chemistry, Cambridge, 1999.

Hudson, Dr J. F., *Adjuncts, Their Use in Brewing*, 1984.

Jeffery, E. J. BSc., FRIC *Brewing, Theory and Practice* Nicholas & Kay, London, 1956.

Keir, David, *The Younger Centuries* McLagan & Cumming Ltd, Edinburgh, 1951.

King, Frank A., *Beer has a History*, Hutchinson's Scientific & Technical Publications, 1947.

Laing, David, and Hendra, John, *Beer and Brewing*, McDonald Publications, 1977.

Line, Dave, *The Big Book of Brewing*, Amateur Winemaker Publications, 1974.

Lloyd Hind, H. BSc, FIC, FRMS, *Brewing Science & Practice*, vols 1 and 2, Second Impression, Chapman & Hall, London, 1943.

Lloyd, W. J. W. *Adjuncts*, Paul's & Whites, Ipswich, 1986.

Malting is Big Business,. Institute of Brewing, 33 Clarges Street, London.

Micronising Company U.K. Ltd, 1986.

Owen, Colin C., *Greatest Brewery in the World*, Derbyshire Record Society, 1992.

Pauls & Whites, *Brewing Room Book*, 1982.

Pauls & Whites, *Brewing Room Book*, 1984/85.

Plzen, N. P., *Pilsner Urquell*, Plzensky Prazdroj N. P. Plzen, 1842–1982.

Pritchard, Bob, *All About Beer*, Amateur Winemaker Publications, 1983.

Restall, J. and Hebbs D., *How to Make Wines with a Sparkle*, AW, 1973.

Solomon's Organic Chemistry, T.W. Solomon's. John Wiley & Sons, Inc., 1986.

Story of Yeast, The United Yeast Company Ltd.

The Principles and Practice of Brewing, W. J. Sykes Charles Griffin & Co. Ltd, London, 1897.

Role of Yeast in Modern Bakery Practice, H. G. Sykes BSc, ARIC, Inst. BB.

German Wheat Beer, Eric Warner, Brewer's Publications 1991, Boulder, USA.

Zymurgy Special Issue, *Traditional Beer Styles*, 1991.

INDEX